Baltic Sea

PRUSSIA

Danzig

Stettin

RUSSIA

Breslau
Liegnitz

AUSTRIA

Vienna

0 ——————————————— 150 mi.

0 ——————————————— 160 km.

▬▬▬▬	Boundary of German Empire, 1871
▬ ▬ ▬	Boundary of German Confederation, 1815-1866
▬▬ ▬▬	Southern boundary of North German Confederation, 1866-1871
⦚⦚⦚⦚	Prussian Territory before 1866

N

Droysen
and
The Prussian School
of History

Droysen

and

The Prussian School of History

Robert Southard

THE UNIVERSITY PRESS OF KENTUCKY

Copyright © 1995 by The University Press of Kentucky

Scholarly publisher for the Commonwealth,
serving Bellarmine College, Berea College, Centre
College of Kentucky, Eastern Kentucky University,
The Filson Club, Georgetown College, Kentucky
Historical Society, Kentucky State University,
Morehead State University, Murray State University,
Northern Kentucky University, Transylvania University,
University of Kentucky, University of Louisville,
and Western Kentucky University.

Editorial and Sales Offices: Lexington, Kentucky 40508-4008

Library of Congress Cataloging-in-Publication Data

Southard, Robert.
    Droysen and the Prussian school of history / Robert Southard.
        p.   cm.
    Includes bibliographical references and index.
    ISBN 0-8131-1884-0 (alk. paper)
    1. Droysen, Johann Gustav, 1808–1884.   2. Historiography—Germany—
Prussia.   3. History—Philosophy.   4. Historians, German.
    5. History (Theology)—History of doctrines—19th century.
    I. Title
    D16.8.D755S68   1994
    943'.007202—dc20   94-16878

Contents

Preface

This is a book about how the Prussian School of History came to be. Because that process occurred bit by bit and over time, I have been old-fashioned enough to resort to historical narration. Because these historians were men of ideas with a lot to say, I have explained their ideas as fully and fairly as I could. That kind of intellectual history is also a bit old-fashioned, but some ideas deserve close scrutiny. Their ideas do, because, though sometimes wrong, they are always interesting. More to the point for a historian, their ideas were strongly influential. Granted, that influence was exercised within an elite, but Imperial Germany was an authoritarian state, and, by definition, authoritarian states are ruled by elites. I was attracted to the study of this subject, in the first place, because I thought it would help in understanding the Germany that was partially created in the first unification of 1866 and 1870–71. I was, and remain, attracted for another reason. The formation of this school is a striking case in point of both the indeliberately self-serving quality of ideology for intellectuals in politics and of the essentially religious nature of some modern nationalism.

I have some intellectual debts that I especially want to acknowledge. I learned from the late Leonard Krieger to ask about the politics of history in Germany. Emile Karafiol taught me a great deal about how to read theoretical discourse. William H. McNeill taught me the need for an architectonic perspective and, always, the importance of writing punctually and clearly. My colleagues Peter Cline and Gordon Thompson read and critiqued this manuscript. I have tried to follow their advice. The late Marian Shelby, a teacher and friend for many years, also read it and offered judicious suggestions. My wife, Edna Southard, repeatedly took time away from her own demanding schedule of research and publication to read and critique what I wrote. Art history's loss was, I hope, intellectual history's gain. My gratitude and appreciation are surpassing, and I dedicate the book to her and to David and Jared. I am grateful to Earlham College's Professional Development Fund for its support and for the confidence it showed in my work. I especially want to thank the library staffs at the Frankfort Universitätsbibliothek, the Marburg Universitätsbibliothek, the Newberry Library of Chicago, the Regenstein Library of the University of Chicago, Lilly Library of Indiana University, and, of course, Earlham College's own Lilly Library. To Cheri Gaddis of Earlham's Social Science Division special thanks are due for friendliness and computer expertise in manuscript preparation.

Introduction

The Prussian or "Little German" (*kleindeutsch*) School of history is normally defined in terms of the political program that its adherents advanced: the unification of Germany, without Austria's German provinces, as a constitutional monarchy under the Hohenzollern. This definition by political program is understandable. Their major political outlook is more recognizable than the theories that underlie it, and in their mature works, historians such as Johann Gustav Droysen (1808–86), Heinrich von Sybel (1817–95), and Heinrich von Treitschke (1834–96) were stridently pro-Prussian in their German nationalism. Moreover, they enjoyed the celebrity that comes from being on the winning side. Along with other colleagues, they had predicted and, afterward, justified the national unification that Bismarck actually accomplished in 1866 and 1870–71. Finally, they were politically important. As educators at elite universities and writers of histories for an educated national readership, they helped give intellectual respectability to the nationalism of Wilhelminian Germany. Those are persuasive reasons for grouping them in terms of the political content in their histories, but this definition comes at some cost. It partly overlooks what they thought they were doing. As they viewed matters, their expectant demand for unification under Prussia's dynasty was only one of several major political goals that rested less on their personal wishes than on what they thought was a durable structure of historical theory. In any case, to define them chiefly in terms of the role they anticipated for Prussia stresses what their political program became while ignoring what it originally was until well into the revolutionary year 1848. To reduce their careers to that single, though very important, political demand is like reviewing a book after reading only its conclusion.

Droysen and his colleagues were undeniably political advocates, but they rationalized their advocacy with a conception of history that, to their minds, kept them from being what their opponents often accused them of being, propagandists disguised as professional historians. That is, they were political historians in a peculiarly intense sense of the term. In principle, as in practice, they eliminated any firm distinction between scholarship and partisanship by thinking of history as progressive, of progress as inevitable, and of inevitability as good. In consequence, present and future politics seemed merely the necessary continuation of previous history and their advocacy merely the logical extension of their interpretation of bygone events. To state the case differently, past and present were points on a continuum of progress such that their understanding of the past and their engagement in the present were functions each of the other. They did not believe that this quality made their histories tendentious, though it often did, and in fact some of their works were genial enough still to be read with profit. In the spectrum of German politics, they were constitutional moderates, always a bit to the right of center, but in one important respect they resembled the Marxists (who took some of their key ideas from the same sources as these historians did). They denied that a politically neutral history was either possible or desirable, because sound scholarship could find where history was moving and thus chart the right political course to follow. By the same token, the observable movement of history in the present told them what questions to pose of the past.

To see why they believed that, it is necessary to look at their view of the historical process. They imagined it to be unitary and progressive: unitary in the sense that it possessed a single meaning or purpose and progressive in the sense that what was implicit at the beginning of history became continually more explicit, that is, more fully and adequately realized, as age succeeded age. They were quite aware of suffering in history and they did not suppose that people in later ages were always happier than those born earlier, but they did think that history was a record of eventual betterment. In other words, history for them had an agenda, and, strange though it seems at first to those studying their ideas from the outside, they generally expected history to complete its main tasks in their own time and country. The outcome of their politics was, really, an "end of history"—not a cessation of historical occurrences, but a cessation of onward historical movement because the historical process had already achieved its long-term, beneficent purposes.[1] That was why their scholarship and their partisanship were inseparable. Their political program was not a list of things that they, personally, wanted to make happen. On the contrary, their expectations for the future were an extrapolation of tendencies that they, as historians, found at work in the past, predictions supported by historical expertise. They even concluded that the flowering of historical studies in their Germany was itself a historical necessity required to give contemporaries the insight needed for further advance. This meant that as long as they still had unification to look forward to, and before they had too many painful collisions with a stubborn reality, their ideas had a millenarian flavor so that they sometimes described the future of Germany almost as if it would be God's kingdom on the earth. No doubt that helps explain their complaints about Germany *after* unification; the reality could not possibly have lived up to their dreams.

Their vision of history had a content as well as a form. They not only believed that history had a grand purpose but also thought they knew what that purpose was and, at least in general terms, how it would be achieved. World history—and like many in the nineteenth-century West they confounded Europe with the world—began with the appearance of political freedom in ancient Hellas and would culminate in the creation of a German nation-state in which freedom would be genuine and enduring. A free people, the Germans, would freely impose binding authority on itself without, however, curtailing the freedom of individuals within the community. With the partial exception of the United States, which they admired but only dimly understood, no society and no age had achieved these things before. Antiquity had failed in this because, in the absence of Christianity, private freedom was corrosive and undermined the common good. Medieval Christianity had marked an advance insofar as it showed the way to a more responsible enjoyment of freedom, but it left this potential unrealized because, in its distrust of the world, it turned away from the state. Stable freedom would be the crowning achievement of modern history, which they dated from the German Reformation of the sixteenth century.

They saw the Reformation as simultaneously and interrelatedly a political and religious event. By purifying Christian doctrine and practice, it cleansed Christianity of the antiworldliness that allegedly barred the way to statehood, and by drawing on the civic tradition found in classical literature, it offered a vision of the state that would make it possible to institutionalize Christian teachings. Faced with the obvious fact that the two qualities in German politics they most detested, absolutism and particularism, had increased rather than abated after the sixteenth century, they argued that the Reformation foreshadowed but could not create the modern state and concluded, therefore, that the later consolidation of royal authority in the various German territorial states was as beneficial in the long run as it was relentless and hateful in the short. The princes, as agents of historical purpose, had cleared away the feudal rubble that prevented internal unity and, once this necessary task was completed in the eighteenth century, had unwittingly invited fundamental reform through the manifest illegitimacy of their rule. The revolutions of the late eighteenth century, though often misguided, were so many promising signs of ultimate freedom. More important, Prussia's performance in the last years of

Napoleon's rule showed that she was destined to resume and complete the political work of the Reformation. Their analysis of their own age, therefore, was often a matter of hopeful hunting for signs of this resumed movement forward.

They were, of course, open to the charge of wishful thinking, of making history tell them what they wanted to know. The irritability and insistence of some of their remarks on historical method suggest that they occasionally felt defensive. Nonetheless, they believed that their predictions were conclusively grounded in historical evidence, and they defended that belief by paying close attention to questions about the nature of historical knowledge. Despite considerable variety in matters of detail, their ideas on method were highly congruent in two respects. First, they thought of the historical process as a progressive development or unfolding of the "spirit" (or *Geist*). That meant that history was intellectual at the core and intelligible to the inquiring minds of historians. In consequence, the tendencies that they found at work in history were, to them, its real content. The chief, though not the only, source of this idea was G.W.F. Hegel (1770–1831), whose philosophy they had studied with varying degrees of comprehension and thoroughness. Second, they insisted, at times heatedly, that the discovery of historical tendencies had to proceed through the studious examination of empirical evidence. This insistence was in part an effort to dissociate themselves from Hegel, who increasingly struck them as the philosopher of the Restoration. It was also a matter of professional pride. By underscoring the historian's special ability to infer major conclusions about present and future from the detailed evidence of the past, they gained a welcome feeling of superior authority and a ready-made answer when someone questioned the soundness of their political pronouncements.

Because they really were trying to find the truth, their avowed empiricism had the additional function of insuring them against reading into the past whatever they wanted to find there. They needed that insurance, because their line of questioning was so present-minded. That is, discontent with their own age and hopes for the future suggested the queries they made of the past, whereas their deliberate empiricism assured them that evidence would govern their conclusions. At a minimum, then, present-mindedness would not lead to subjectivity and arbitrariness. At best, it would direct them to the right questions, and their high regard for data would lead them to valid answers. It is important to note two further qualities of their view of history. Although they thought of history as culminating in the establishment of a unified German nation-state, their ideas were both cosmopolitan and religious. They were cosmopolitan because, although they never tired of arguing that unification would be good for both Prussia and Germany, they were being more than polite in claiming that it would also benefit the rest of humanity. After all, German unification as a constitutional monarchy under the Hohenzollern was a solution to the problem of freedom posed by world history. Germany would provide a helpful model for others and would make the world a more peaceful place. Their ideas were religious in several ways. In essence, they searched history for the partly hidden workings of Providence, and their interpretation of the past was really exegesis. Further, they expected their findings to improve their contemporaries and to make them morally ready for a life of freedom. To that extent, their lectures and publications were homiletic. Their outlook, however, was religious in more than the loose, analogical sense in which any ultimate commitment can be termed religious. They believed, and Droysen believed very strongly, that the historical sequence was a continual unfolding of God's plan. They thought of history as a theodicy and of themselves as God's agents.

This gave them a self-confidence and sense of mission that is hard to imagine. To an extent given to few academics in any time or place, they thought that they had something really important to say: they were the men with the map that showed humanity where it had been and where it was going. By doing so, of course, they helped it get there. Because they really wanted to make things better, their attitude was undoubtedly unselfish. It was also self-serving. They had special knowledge, and for them, knowledge was power. They needed a sense of power. They were members of a small, urban, and highly educated elite in a still overwhelmingly agrarian and traditional society. Moreover, they belonged to an elite of attainment in a society still largely dominated by an elite of birth. In other words, they were nationalists who were divided by education and occupation from most of the nation and who had little say about the conduct of affairs. By claiming an authoritative interpretation of modern Germany's role in world history, they reunited themselves with their fellow nationals. By maintaining that this interpretation would actually help bring the future about, they enjoyed the illusion of directing events. Finally, the path they foresaw Prussia and Germany taking precluded mob rule and revolutionary violence, though not violence itself, and so avoided a challenge to elites as such. Their illusion of power was not disturbed by their own potent social fears.

They were therefore able, more or less contentedly, to engage in a "politics of expectation"—a term for their choice of political tactics during *Vormärz*, the useful German word for the period preceding the outbreak of revolution in March 1848—until, in 1848, they found themselves called on actually to do something. In that period they looked forward to the great reversal, when weak, divided, seemingly tyrannized Germany would accomplish its historical mission and become a colossus among the European powers as well as the first truly free political society in Europe. They inevitably faced the difficult question of what to do while they waited for this necessary change to occur. Because they believed that they had all history on their side, they could have chosen to do nothing, to simply let events take their predetermined course. That possibility never occurred to them. They were too impatient, too eager for the sensation of making things happen. Besides, their theories offered clear guidance for suitable political activity.

Their chief task, insofar as censorship in the German states permitted, was to reveal the future to contemporaries through an examination of past and present. This task had two advantages. It helped assure that Germans would know their parts when the curtain went up on liberation and unification and, further, that they would be morally ready for the heavy demands that statehood was bound to make. Unification and true political freedom required prior consciousness of their nature and necessity. This suggests an attitude on their part that needs underscoring. They did not think of politics in terms of setting goals and then working to achieve them. On the contrary, prior history had already set the goals, and it was simple duty to accept them as self-evidently good and to work for their attainment. That belief induced moral complacency when the future seemed secure, outright exhilaration when inevitable change seemed at last to be occurring, and a readiness for accommodation when, as in 1848, matters did not turn out as expected. In short, they lacked an independent standard by which to judge events, and in the end, events governed them. (This is not to say that their disappointment in 1848 led them to betray former liberal ideals. Their liberalism was always a bit tenuous, and what there was of it merely became more commonsensical.)

It is also important to understand that their ideas were neither idiosyncratic nor eccentric. They were as clear and forceful as possible in making their ideas known, and usually their literate contemporaries either agreed with, or at least were not contemptuous of, what they had to say. They were successful, sometimes brilliantly successful, in their professional careers. They were popular lecturers, and major publishers printed their works. Of the four historians most closely studied in the following chapters, three were elected in 1848 to the National Assembly at Frankfort, and one to the Hessian parliament at Cassell. Clearly, their views did not seem strange or exceptional, nor should they have. The originality of the Prussian School lay not in the novelty of its individual ideas but in its synthesis of them. Its adherents used familiar ideas to argue a reassuring case in a novel way. This again raises the problem of what to call this group.

The term Prussian School is enough of a historiographic convention to be unavoidable, but it is a misnomer for several reasons. Its members admired Prussia, though at times critically, but not all of them were Prussian patriots. They valued Prussia as the future unifier of Germany, as a means rather than as an end in itself. This is simply to repeat the initial point that it is a mistake to reduce a complex of theories to a single political demand. For that reason, this study is an examination of the origins of that complex before 1848, its modification in several important respects during 1848 and 1849, and, more extensively, its application by historians in subsequent decades. Chapters 1, 2, and 3 treat the period before 1848 with special attention to Droysen, who played the central role in articulating the ideas of the school. Chapters 4, 5, and 6 show what happened to these historians in 1848 and 1849, and how political exigencies forced them to revise their ideas. Chapter 7 shows the uses to which these revised ideas were put.

Admittedly, this outline excludes some material that one might expect to find in such a study. For example, it pays less attention to Droysen's *History of Prussian Politics* (1855–86), Sybel's *Foundation of the German Empire* (1889–94), and Treitschke's *History of Germany in the Nineteenth Century* (1874–94) than to less well known works from the 1830s and 1840s. The reason is that this a study of origins, and, in any case, their famous later works make more sense when their prehistory is known. By the same token, a number of historians who were in the school, or least closely associated with it, receive only general treatment in favor of close study of its actual founders. Treitschke is a case in point. He was an engaging speaker and writer who was singularly influential in popularizing many of its ideas and commonplaces. That does not change the fact that he was only fourteen in 1848 and took over these ideas from others. The same consideration applies, though less strikingly, to Hermann Baumgarten (1825–93). Other historians are excluded from detailed treatment for other reasons. Friedrich Christoph Dahlmann (1785–1860) agreed with many of the school's ideas, but he took a very different view of historical progress, largely because he reached intellectual maturity before Hegel's ascendancy. Ludwig Häusser (1818–67) and Georg Gottfried Gervinus (1805–71) shared the school's view of progress and linked politics to history but, in very different ways, did not share its ideas on the nature of the future Prusso-German state.

Having had an active role in creating the school was the standard for inclusion, and the first six chapters therefore deal with four individuals who in *Vormärz* had parallel, sometimes interconnected, careers: Droysen, Max Duncker (1811–86), Duncker's younger protégé Rudolf Haym (1821–1901), and Sybel. They differed from one another in temperament, in theoretical detail, and, more rarely, in immediate responses to events, but by 1848 they had arrived at substantially the same ideas about the relationship between history and politics and had projected essentially the same future for Germany. Moreover, they drew the same lessons from their failed hopes in 1848 and revised their theories and interpretations of history accordingly. They and other historians then incorporated those revisions into the mature works of the Prussian School, which, with the unification of Germany in 1866 and 1870–71, became the official historiography of a Prussian-oriented, nationalist, right-of-center liberalism. The study of the origins of this school, then, is a gateway to understanding how many educated, respectable Germans in Imperial Germany saw their national history.

That is reason enough to study the history of the school, but there are two other reasons. First, the careers, especially the prerevolutionary careers, of Droysen and his colleagues have some bearing on our judgments about the typicality or atypicality of German intellectual and political development. As the bibliographic essay at the end of this study shows, there is an interesting division of opinion as to whether nineteenth–century Germany developed along the same track as other modernizing, industrializing European countries (Britain, in particular) or whether Germany followed its own special path (*Sonderweg*) into modernity. The *Sonderweg* thesis arose from wartime and postwar needs to take a long-term view of Hitlerism, though it had important precedents in certain prewar German celebrations and lamentations over German distinctiveness. The stimulating challenges to the notion of German "peculiarity" is essentially Marxist in inspiration and social historical in information.[2] It is always questionable whether one can explain, in any detail, the ideas of individuals through reference to social context, suggestive though such attempts may be, and it is certainly irresponsible to try to characterize a whole society by discussing analytically the rarefied musings of prominent members of its intellectual elite. When all that has been said, however, it also remains to say that there is no western European equivalent of the historical ideas in the school's works. Purposive historical progress toward human freedom in national states was a liberal vision throughout Europe. More peculiarly German, however, was the Augustinian Christian equation of progress with theodicy and, as its corollary, the eventually worshipful acceptance of whatever history dished out. We are much in the late Leonard Krieger's debt for coining the phrase "the German idea of freedom."[3] The historians studied here represented a German idea of progress that shaped, one might say deformed, German liberalism.

Second, this study of the Prussian School affords a look into one of the final chapters in the story of an ancient, and anciently influential, idea—namely, the ideal of directional, providential history, divinely governed and working largely through unseen process toward ultimate good. The idea has multiple and complex origins in the Hellenistic intellectual mix of the ancient Mediterranean, though its medieval and modern European forms were mediated by Augustine of Hippo and Boethius in the fifth and sixth centuries C.E. The providential view of history, once so pervasive, has been banished, in part by secularization but more by the horrors of twentieth–century history, which have made the idea of beneficent purpose in history seem too widely improbable to be taken seriously by many people. Theologians can decide whether that is a sensible conclusion or not. Suffice it here to say that, in recent times, some once very familiar intellectual furniture has been removed from historical space, and now we have become accustomed to the bareness of the room. This study of the historical-political thought of Droysen and of others in the school lets us recall how the room looked until very recently and, so, lets us measure the distance from the last century to what some call the postmodern age.

1

Droysen and the Problem of Freedom

The Prussian School took form because of the severe disappointments of the revolutionary years 1848–49, but those disappointments are intelligible only after studying the expectations that, after seeming triumph, failed badly. For the most part, that is, the mature ideas of the Prussian School were transmutations and recombinations of prerevolutionary ideas made when successive defeats and failures at last forced Droysen, Duncker, and Haym—along with, of course, many other liberal nationalists—to reexamine and, then, to reformulate beliefs that until recently had seemed unquestionable and irrefutable. These men went through a crisis that few others experienced, even those who subscribed to their political program, because they based their political outlook on an interpretation of history and they thought of Germany's unification as a culminating act of world history. Therefore, their increasingly obvious inability during the revolution of 1848 to turn their expectations into reality was more than just a political failure. It was a calamity because it called into question the meaning they attributed to history. After this crisis, as before, they remained ideologues, devotees of a secular religion, but they became chastened ideologues, no longer bent on chasing the best at the expense of the good or even the relatively good. Sybel's experience was somewhat different. Even before 1848, he was less certain about what the future held, less confident that the historical process was unstoppably beneficent. In consequence, he seems to have been less surprised and less shocked by events. To a certain degree, Droysen, Haym, and Duncker ended up where Sybel had always been—except that they did so with the intellectual assertiveness of the belatedly wise. They never quite overcame their prehistory.

That prehistory began in 1831, with Droysen's first plans for open political advocacy. He had two projects in mind, although he failed to bring either to completion. First, and almost certainly with Ranke's conservative *Historical-Political Journal* in mind, he proposed creating a "journal of political-historical content" that, in effect, would have been an ideological counter to Ranke's publication. Because he wanted national unification and constitutional government of a sort, however, he did not have the backing of the Prussian government for his journal, as Ranke did for his. Second, Droysen considered publishing a political correspondence to make the same points. His model here was Paul Achatius Pfizer's *Correspondence of Two Germans* (1831), the first work to propose, if only in a letter among letters, Germany's unification by Prussia.[1] Droysen's letters about these projects are useful as evidence for his already distinctive political views, but the fact that he considered becoming a publicist is unremarkable; his doing so is just one of many examples of the political excitement that briefly filled Germany after the 1830 July Revolution in France. Along with many other young, well-educated Germans, he hoped that the Restoration might end in the Germanies as well, though he also feared renewed invasion from revolutionary France. His projects are important for another reason. They were the first instances of the close linkage between his political advocacy in the present and his philological and historical research into the past.

They make sense only against the background of the research into ancient history and literature with which Droysen was then occupied. Droysen was an intellectual prodigy from the remote districts of the Hohenzollern monarchy. The son of a Prussian army chaplain in a small town in Pomerania, he studied on scholarships (and later on fees earned by tutoring the young Felix Mendelssohn, for whom he later wrote lyrics for some *Lieder*) at a local gymnasium and, later, the new but flourishing University of Berlin.[2] In his essay of application to the university, he wrote that "nothing is more wholesome or needful for the German spirit than fertilization with the Hellenic."[3] This was more than an ingratiating piety. He exerted himself in the study of classical philology, and in 1831, when he was considering active publicism, he was deeply engrossed in major research into ancient Greek history. He was twenty-three years old and had just finished his doctoral dissertation, "On the Kingdom of the Lagids under Ptolemaus VI Philometor." He was already at work on his translations of Aeschylus's tragedies, a beautiful rendering that long remained a standard German version, which he published along with historical commentaries the next year. This work was also a preliminary to his still famous *History of Alexander the Great* (1833), which, in turn, led to the first volume of *History of Hellenism* (1836). These works fundamentally altered the way in which historians viewed late Greek history: Droysen was the first to demonstrate persuasively that Greek history after the Macedonian conquest was more a record of new, constructive beginnings than of decay and decline.[4] In these and other, less important works, Droysen offered an interpretation of ancient history in which he portrayed

Hellenistic history as the poser of a problem of freedom still current in his own time and due for solution in his own country.

Droysen's advocacy and inquiries were already functions one of the other. Considered by themselves, neither his studies of ancient Greece nor his planned ventures in publicism are fully understandable. Considered together, however, they show the outlines of the theoretical system that he applied, with some additions but no major deletions, in the first months of his activities in Frankfort in 1848. He acquired the main elements of this system during his formal studies at Berlin. Although Droysen spent most of his adult career as a historian, he began as a student of philology and, to a lesser extent, philosophy. There were, of course, no history students in Germany when he enrolled at Berlin in 1826. (Interestingly, Max Duncker, who finished his Berlin degree in 1834, was the first.) Nonetheless, history courses were a prominent part of the curriculum and were supposed to make moral citizens out of callow students. Droysen avoided all of them, whether taught by Friedrich Wilken (1777–1840), Friedrich von Raumer (1781–1873), or the already celebrated, but not yet ennobled, Leopold Ranke (1795–1886).[5] Given his strong interest in ancient Greece, he did much of his work with the classical philologist August Boeckh (1785–1867). As Boeckh's student, he not only perfected his knowledge of the corpus of Greek literature but also learned what was, in fact, a special approach to history.

Boeckh's own teacher, Friedrich August Wolf (1759–1824), had pioneered this approach when, in the course of studying Homer's epics, he became interested in Homer's milieu and used philological techniques to reconstruct the past in order that he might read texts in context. What Wolf did for Homer and his age, Boeckh did for fifth-century Athenian literature in his book, *The Political Economy of Athens*.[6] Boeckh taught Droysen that texts should suggest the questions to ask of history and that the answers should reveal the true significance of the texts. Text and context should illuminate each other. Droysen must have been impressed favorably with this approach, because he worked with Boeckh longer and more closely than did most of the latter's students in the 1820s.[7] The evidence for Boeckh's influence is clear: Droysen's *History of Alexander the Great* and *History of Hellenism* are philological in the enriched sense that Wolf and Boeckh gave the term.

Droysen acquired at Berlin a second, complementary but distinct, approach to history, namely, an insistent desire to relate age to age and to view history as a single process. Because Boeckh's use of history was primarily contextual, a means to the greater end of reading texts correctly, he paid little attention to long-term change, which was, strictly speaking, irrelevant for his purposes. Later, in 1843, Droysen (who was then leaving ancient for modern history in any case) would fault philologists for doing as his teacher had done, for failing to note what distinguished one historical epoch from another.[8] His interest in periodization and interconnection derived from, or at least was greatly strengthened by, his work under G.W.F. Hegel (1770–1831). Hegel was an immensely popular and influential lecturer when Droysen was a student, and Droysen showed more than the typical interest in his series of lectures. He heard Hegel's lectures during every term of his studies and followed "Logic and Metaphysics," "Aesthetics," "History of Philosophy," "History of the Spirit," and "Philosophy of History" with enough attentiveness that Kuno Fischer used Droysen's class notes in compiling the definitive edition of Hegel's works at the turn of the century.[9]

The question of Hegel's actual influence on Droysen, and Droysen's generation, is vexed. On the one hand, the exact extent of Droysen's indebtedness is impossible to establish because, though Droysen made occasional philosophical outbursts and had a wonderfully theoretical mind, he wrote history rather than systematic philosophy. He just did not comment in detail on the writings of Hegel or any other philosopher. Such commentary was not his metier. On the other hand, the importance of Hegel's general influence on Droysen is obviously immense, because so much of Droysen's conceptual vocabulary is Hegelian or, to coin a term, *Hegelianoid*—it resembles, but is not identical with, Hegel's. There are two compelling reasons for offering this caution. First, bright, energetic minds like Droysen's do not, normally, simply take over others' ideas without amendment or, at least, creative misinterpretation. There no doubt are people who simply parrot metaphysical systems, but such monodimensional minds are unlikely to have achieved enough to attract historical attention. Second, Droysen himself, like many other Hegelian enthusiasts in that time and place, self-consciously parted philosophical and, more particularly, political company with Hegel.

Thus, within weeks of Hegel's death in 1831, Droysen began to criticize Hegel, and German idealists in general, for close association with the hated Restoration and for insufficient attention to empirical fact.[10] Interestingly, neither of these charges is justified: Hegel was extraordinarily well read in history and was no friend of political reaction. Granted, his public comments about Prussia were respectful, but professors were civil servants who could not be expected to savage their employer in public, and, anyway, the Prussia for which Hegel left Heidelberg in 1818 was still the Prussia of the Great Reforms of Stein, Hardenberg, and Humboldt. He came to Prussia, in part, because of its liberal reputation, and was privately critical when reaction gathered in the 1820s. It is true that Hegel defended suppression of the German nationalist fraternities, the *Burschenschaften*, after the 1819 Wartburgfest, but those fraternities were rabidly nationalist and anti-Semitic, and they enjoyed burning books.[11] To oppose them was to defend order and decency, not simple-mindedly to support the Restoration. Droysen is more likely to have picked up these criticisms by listening to other young intellectuals than through serious consideration of what Hegel was actually saying. By 1836, however, Droysen offered a more original and more penetrating criticism of Hegel for contradicting basic Christian dogmas.[12] Those criticisms will receive extended discussion a little later; right now, it is important to establish what, of a general nature, Droysen and his fellows did find attractive in Hegel's philosophy.

First, there was Hegel's insistence on the rationality, that is the necessity, of the state. Hegel advanced this point in his misleading aphorism, "What is rational is real and what is real is rational" (*Was vernünftig ist, das ist wirklich; und was wirklich ist, das ist vernünftig*).[13] In so saying, Hegel meant to differ with Kant on the essential unobservability of the rational rather than to place whatever existed beyond moral challenge. For Kant, that is, the real thing, the *Ding an sich,* could be posited but not observed. Hegel, by contrast, believed that the rational was "actual" in the sense of the German adjective *wirklich:* active, present, observable. As early as 1821, however, a contemporary took him to mean whatever was rational actually existed, and, conversely, that whatever existed was rational, that is, had to exist.[14] This is an example of creative misinterpretation, and on it rests both conservative and radical readings of Hegel. For conservatives, it seemed to mean that whatever existed was legitimate simply by virtue of existing, whereas for radicals it meant that violent change, if successful, was its own justification. Droysen would elaborate and specify this general notion into a theory of ongoing, purposive change.

To do so, he had only to borrow concepts from Hegel's updating of the much older providential view of history, implicit in many of Hegel's lectures but stated with greatest rhetorical force and vividness in his *Philosophy of History.* Hegel was quite explicit in insisting that the idea that "reason rules the world" was tightly linked to a "religious truth, namely that the world is not left to accident and external, accidental causes, but, on the contrary, a Providence (*Vorsehung*) rules the world."[15] This was real providence, for it looked to the "final goal" (*Endzweck*) of history, that is, "what God wants with the world" (*was Gott mit der Welt will*).[16] Consequently, history was a "series of stages" (*Stufengang*) moving purposively toward the "consciousness of freedom" (*Bewußtsein der Freiheit*). Hegel acknowledged that this movement came at a cost, and—in a famous comparison—he described history as a "slaughterbench . . . upon which the happiness of peoples, the wisdom of states, and virtue of individuals are brought for sacrifice."[17] It is this vision of history—as providential, dynamic, and purposive—that Droysen found strongly attractive, even though philosophical technicalities did not always command his full attention and even though his view of Hegel was in part a matter of impression and misimpression.

It was attractive because, although Droysen disagreed, or thought he disagreed, with Hegel on politics, Hegel's historical and political theory reassured Droysen that he was on the right and the winning side. Not only was historical life the theater in which God's purposes were achieved, but this achievement was predictable, at least to some degree. That statement seems odd, because Hegel is notorious for believing that philosophy always arrived too late to affect action. Thus, in a famous statement in *The Philosophy of Right*, Hegel averred: "When philosophy paints her gray upon gray, the form of life has already grown old, and the gray in the gray cannot be rejuvenated but only recognized; the owl of Minerva takes flight only as dusk begins to fall."[18] This meant that philosophy can comprehend what is and what has been, not what will come to be. The fact that Hegel comprehended his own age, the age of the aftermath of the French Revolution of 1789, meant, however, that his own age was about to pass away. By implication, therefore, Hegel himself was not entirely conservative.[19] Droysen, like others in his generation, would go further and claim an ability to predict at least the near future in some detail. Here one sees the importance of Droysen's essentially exaggerated charge that Hegel scanted empirical knowledge: supposedly, historical empiricism allowed Droysen to see into the future as the philosophical Hegel had been unable to do.

Finally, it is also fair to say that Hegel offered to Droysen and his generation a sort of emotional satisfaction that was essentially religious in character. Ronald Knox used the term *enthusiasm* to describe "a clique, and elite . . . who are trying to live a less worldly life than their neighbours" and who, therefore, set themselves apart.[20] There is a lot of that enthusiastic quality in the young people who, first, used the designedly difficult, almost secret language of Hegel to put a seal on their special understanding of affairs and, second, broke with Hegel, while retaining a Hegelian vocabulary, because the great philosopher did not, in their view, carry his ideas far enough: they became a spiritual elite within a spiritual elite, and Droysen was no exception to this rule. Here a second religious term comes to mind, namely, *gnosis*, the attainment of direct, personal knowledge of essential truth. This claim is more than intuitive: Hegel, along with Schelling, directly incorporated gnostic ideas into his philosophy, notably into his insistence on self-consciousness as the ultimate goal of the spirit, and the Hegelian F.C. Baur (1792–1860), who founded the Tübingen school of theology and in 1835 published the first modern work on gnosticism, expressly viewed gnosticism as the start of the Christian philosophy that led to Hegelianism.[21] There can be no precise measurement of the sort of satisfaction that comes from feeling especially close to God (or, at least, to divine purpose) and possessed of a special knowledge, but that satisfaction sustained Droysen and his colleagues during years of otherwise depressing quiet and doubtless reassured them in drawing conclusions about history's course that no ordinary review of empirical evidence could supply. So, the philological training he learned from Boeckh helped Droysen in reaching synchronic meaning, and his philosophical initiation under Hegel aided him in discovering diachronic meaning in the historical process.

He pointed to both sorts of meaning in the planned and actual publications with which he busied himself in and after 1831. He did not get beyond planning. There was trouble with the Prussian censors, and Droysen had a lot of other work to do as he began his publishing career in classical philology. In any case, the flurry of German political excitement following the French July Revolution was short lived. Nevertheless, his analysis of Prussian and German politics is reasonably clear, because in letters to friends he included synopses of the items he wanted to write and publish.[22] Droysen plainly thought that Germany was due for major political reconstruction that would issue in a higher degree of unification. He also thought Germans were due to enjoy a qualititatively new kind of political freedom in which government would be responsible to the governed without weakening its power yet also without impinging on individual liberties. Here, too, Droysen followed the pattern of employing a broadly Hegelian concept, namely, of representation that would retain divisions within the state even while serving to create state unity, but using it to raise his own political demands.[23] To this end, Droysen advocated a new type of representative government that would increase the unity and cohesion of the state without completely eliminating the existing stratification of society or, equally important in Germany, suppressing regional peculiarities: "The essential distinctions within civil society," he contended, "are those of estate and locality."[24] He meant that a lot had to change and a lot had to remain the same. Social hierarchy and regional variety stood in the way of unity and constitutional government, so they had to change. Conversely, they existed in fact and, so, to some extent by right; therefore, they could not simply be swept away. In Droysen's view, the horrors of the French Revolution of 1789 showed the error of the second approach. His proposed system of representation was supposed to combine the needed elements of change and continuity.

He drew on his understanding of Hegel to make this case by demanding that differences of estate and locality "be abolished (*aufgehoben*) in the nation (*Volk*) as in the national representation."[25] This term, *aufgehoben*, deserves a brief discussion. *Aufgehoben* is the past participle of the infinitive *aufheben*, a significantly ambiguous term in Hegel's lexicon. It means, literally, to "lift up" or, depending on context, to "abolish." In a major conflation of meanings, Hegel gave it a third definition: to "continue" in the sense that whatever was abolished still existed by dint of being lifted to a higher level. Droysen had this third meaning in mind. Social and geographic distinctions would be abolished insofar as they retarded unity and freedom. To the degree that they reflected valid individual preferences and provided "elements of movement and formation," however, they would continue to exist, though at a higher level, as positive contributions to the new state. In somewhat more concrete terms, and with the French centralism that he detested as a counterexample, he demanded that "the monarchy . . . not send down thunderbolts from the topmost heights into the immediate sphere of private life" and that "the legislative . . . not proceed only and directly from the primary assemblies to the vanishing heights of the nation's representative." Despite the stilted tone of German academic idealism, the terms originally derived from Montesquieu's critique of French absolutism, and Droysen called instead for "intermediate stages" (*Mittelstufen*) in public life.[26] Social and regional differences would define these "stages."

Droysen left only a précis for his article on this subject, not the article itself, so it is impossible to be sure just what he had in mind. He did demand that the "cities" represent "bourgeois endeavor," the "rural communes" speak for "peasant interests," and the "regional districts" (*Landerbezirken*) express the wishes of the "land-holding nobility." Predictably, he wanted to integrate as well as preserve these separate interests, so he also proposed that they elect deputies to a "provincial assembly" that would "unite into a common provincial legislature these local and estate interests that comprise society."[27] Droysen left some major points unexplained. He did not actually describe the relevant institutions or define their powers. Although he elsewhere made it clear that he wanted national unification, he did not explain what would happen above the provincial level, or whether he was discussing provinces within German states or the provinces of the future Germany. It was clear, however, that he wanted to accommodate past and present by reconciling potentially opposed interests in the state. This shows a characteristic desire for revolutionary change without revolution.

Droysen tried to identify the principle of this change with another significantly ambiguous German word, *Volksthümlichkeit*. Like its prefix, *Volk*, *Volksthümlichkeit* can refer to either "people" or "nation" or both, with the added difficulty that in its former sense, it can mean "popularity" either in the sense of having to do with the people or in the sense of being familiar and widely approved of. His fear of censorship led him to be guarded in his discussion of this term, but he meant it to have simultaneous, noncontradictory, yet distinct meanings.[28] His use of the term had major bearing on his idea of representative government and, more particularly, the motives behind Prussian policy and the future tendency of Prussian actions. He discussed both in the abstracts of two projected articles that he included in a letter to his friend Ludwig Moser on 28 May 1831.

In a play on the words usually used to describe the program of the July monarchy in France, he planned to entitle the first *le juste milieu*. Droysen did not mean this as a compliment. Rather than signifying the "right mixture" or "happy medium," *le juste milieu* stood for the drift and spinelessness that he found sadly current in Prussian politics. Prussia had abandoned the policies of Frederick the Great and the Baron vom Stein and become "*le juste mileu* of Europe, . . . the middle point between the magnetic poles of the European axis, admittedly and unfortunately also . . . the contemptible locus of the indifferentism of the *Staatszeitung* [Prussia's often officially inspired newspaper]: neither too much nor too little, which means nothing at all, never to have a principle."[29] Droysen meant to be both witty and vehement and succeeded only in being vehement. He was not an adventurist, but, in his eyes, to be without a principle was to be despicable. Prussia needed to embrace the principle of *Volksthümlichkeit* by being both national and popular.

In his description of the second projected article, "Forward" (*Vorwärts*), he had something to say about when this infusion of principle would occur and what its beneficent effects would be. He explained that the "life force of Prussia" was the "mighty forwards" (*heftige Vorwärts*). It was in Prussia's interest and nature to act with dynamism, and in the present this meant "expressing and preaching *Volksthümlichkeit*."[30] Because he elsewhere used the term in connection with representative government, this meant that Prussia had to align itself with popularity in the sense of popular government.[31] It also entailed pursuing a form of national unification, as Droysen suggested in an interesting passage of a letter to Wilhelm Arendt on 31 July 1831: "I, at all events, insist [that] Brunswick, Cassell, etc. at least make themselves worthy through their constitutions of being members of the Prussian Empire (*Preussischen Reiches*). I think that history demands that. Granted, the path is long, difficult, perhaps bloody and filled with shame; still, hope is greater than fear and faith brighter than the night in which we now . . . dream and despair."[32]

This statement is interesting in several respects. First, it was the clearest statement to date of the central position that he ascribed to Prussia in his vision of Germany's future, though as early as 1829 he remarked in connection with German music that Prussia was "a genuine center and hinge of history (*eine wahrhafte Angel und Heerd der Geschichte*)."[33] Prussia was to unify Germany, and by "Prussian Empire" he surely meant a Germany rebuilt by Prussia rather than a Prussia enlarged by incorporating neighboring states. Second, it showed that constitutionalism and unification were functions of each other. The lesser states had to make themselves "worthy" by introducing constitutions, and presumably Prussia, too, had to become a constitutional state. This suggests that he consciously thought of *Volksthümlichkeit* in both national and popular terms and clarifies his harsh criticism of current Prussian policies: the Hohenzollern monarchy had to recover its dynamism by working for unity and constitutional government of the sort that Droysen elsewhere recommended. He believed that Prussia would eventually do so, and elsewhere in the letter asserted that "we in Germany have still to await our history."[34] In later writings, Droysen greatly elaborated this vision of the future without changing it in any essential way until late 1848.

Droysen's analysis of the German present and his sketching of the German future drew heavily on his concurrent research into ancient Greek history. Now, as at all times in his subsequent career, he thought of his political recommendations as historical necessities and, at the same time, let his present political engagement direct his inquiries into the past. The first major result of this dual approach was the lengthy historical commentaries (*Didaskalien*) he included in the translation of Aeschylus's tragedies in 1832. Their ostensible purpose was to give, Boeckh-like, the context necessary for a responsible reading of the plays. In a more Hegelian fashion, however, they were also meant to explain the origin of the political problem that Germany currently faced and would eventually, Droysen believed, definitively solve. Like Hegel, too, Droysen thought in terms of stages (*Stufen*) in world history. Hegel divided history into an oriental, a Greek, a Roman, and a German stage. Like Hegel, Droysen traced freedom back to the Greek and viewed the last, the German, age of history as the time for fully realizing freedom. There the similarity ends. Lacking Hegel's cosmopolitan erudition, he had little interest in asiatic history and, as will appear, he discussed Hellenism rather than a Roman phase in history. In the 1830s, indeed, Droysen's attention was riveted to the (in his view) related, but essentially distinct, matters of classical Greek drama and the effects and significance of Alexander the Great's conquests. For this reason, Droysen's historical overview of Hellenic history deserves close study.

Droysen's point of departure was Solon's legislation, especially his law on parties, in the sixth century B.C.E. By dint of Solon's efforts and their eventual effects, the historical process began, and Greek history had bearing on all later history. "Athens," he argued, "was the first *political* state." By this, Droysen meant that Solon's laws set the Attic people upon a "series of developments" that shaped the Greek "national spirit" (*Volksgeist*) through all its succeeding struggles.[35] That was Athens' historical "deed" (*That*), by which Droysen meant a historical accomplishment with lasting effects on the historical process. More specifically, it was Athens' "deed" to bring the "consciousness of freedom" (*Bewusstsein der Freiheit*) into world history. He equated history with politics and politics with freedom, or at least the "consciousness" of it. By writing in terms of "consciousness," he was not simply using Hegelian terms to point to the essentially mental quality of history. He meant also to emphasize the intrinsically problematic quality of human freedom, a quality that, in his account, was painfully evident in Hellenic history and posed questions not fully answered even in Droysen's own day.

From his point of view, the Athenian achievement was not pure gain. As Droysen's early remarks about the German future show, he was already a historical optimist, but his optimism, then and later, referred to the long term, to ultimate outcomes. He was keenly aware of human suffering and of the destruction of hope in the shorter run. Drawing on his sense of what had happened to modern Europe because of the Enlightenment and the French Revolution, he discussed the painful and destructive effects of the Athenian discovery of freedom:

It is the *natural* relationship in collective human existence that . . . ordering and obeying be determined according to difference of birth, that the existing favorability or unfavorability of external circumstances be viewed as essential and upheld as holy, that the nobility and the people stand opposed as castes . . . But in *historical* life, the spirit that takes form within the people (*Volk*) is hostile to the natural and the given; and as soon as doubts appear about that natural distinction and the conditions rooted in the traditions of the centuries, the awakened spirit will not weary of raising its "terrible why" (*furchtbare Warum*) against every custom, against all that exists. It shakes and buries and destroys until it has finally annihilated everything that exists . . . to the level of ochlocratic atomism. From this equality, this barren, medusa-like caricature of freedom, [the spirit] itself dies and the despiritualized mass sinks back in slow decay to the old, vegetative condition of nature.[36]

The whole passage, of course, is built on an assumed antinomy between "natural" and "historical" existence, the latter consisting in the precarious and inherently unstable enjoyment of freedom. By drawing on what he took to be the experience of eighteenth–century Europe, Droysen meant to show that the evolution of *isonomia* (equality of law) from Solon's ideal of *eunomia* (goodness of law) had a necessarily destructive logic. That idea, differently expressed, was already a commonplace in the ancient world, but Droysen put it to two novel uses. First, it allowed him to categorize the Greek tragedians according to their places on the rising and falling trajectory of Hellenic freedom. Second, and by virtue of the first, it permitted him to identify the main features of the problem of freedom bequeathed by the Greeks to history, a problem that he expected Germans to solve in the fairly near future.

His discussion of Hellenic history, therefore, was present-minded in two ways. In his strongly implied comparison between ancient Greece and modern Europe, he engaged in the familiar practice of scouting the past for parallels to the present.[37] His discussion was also present-minded in a way that is less familiar but more characteristic of Droysen's vision of history. Seen in one way, the Athenian march from "natural" to "historical" life and, tragically but inevitably, back to the "old, vegetative condition of nature" looks like a cycle of a sort through which any natural history might run, but Droysen did not think in cyclical terms. The Athenian experience was unique. Seen from that perspective, Hellenic history had irreversible consequences such that the failure of Athenian freedom itself actually contributed to the eventual achievement of a stable and enduring freedom. To show how that was so required a consistent interpretation of the intervening history, between then and his own day, and Droysen did not complete this interpretation before 1843. His discussion of what went wrong in Athens, however, shows that by 1832 he was already well on his way to such an interpretation.

Because he had to account for literary as well as political history, it was natural for him to periodize fifth–century Athenian history in terms of the careers of Aeschylus, Sophocles, and Euripides, but he claimed a more intrinsic justification for this approach. These dramatists were the spokesmen for history, because they, unlike visual artists, were specially gifted in "personifying the spirit of the people (*Volk*) and their century."[38] Because he wanted to fathom the meaning of history as well as make Aeschylus's plays intelligible to contemporaries, Droysen wanted to use texts to establish context, not just context to explain texts. He believed that their surviving dramas showed three phases in the Athenian experience of freedom: an initial phase termed the "guilt of freedom" (*Schuld der Freiheit*), a second, more or less culminatory, phase labeled the "right of freedom (*Recht der Freiheit*)," and a final, unnamed period of dissolution associated with Euripides and, also, Aristophanes and the Sophists.

Droysen's discussion of these dramatists is dialectical, though this term has to be used cautiously because, here again, he worked with a Hegelian idea easily misunderstood in studying Hegel's own writings and rather loosely used by Droysen. Hegel himself did not often write about a neat sequence of thesis, antithesis, and synthesis—that was Johann Gottlieb Fichte's doing, and Hegel rather disapproved. He did, however, see both knowledge and the reality that was known as a dialectical inasmuch as entities implied or produced their opposites before somehow combining into a more concrete reality. For this reason, he often analyzed matters through triads.[39] Droysen owed to Hegel both the practice of interrelating opposites and of thinking in triads. Both practices inform his political history of Greek tragedy. Thus in the first, Aeschylean, period, the sense of freedom that resulted from breaking the nobility's command of wealth and office allowed Athens twice to prevail over Persia and explained the beauty of Aeschylus's tragedies. It also, less happily, led to the "free man's first consciousness of his own finitude (*Endlichkeit*)."[40] Droysen meant more than that they learned that they had limitations and would one day die. He drew on the Christian conception of sin to reach this insight. Freedom, the defining quality of "historical" life, implied a moral responsibility, and human beings were too weak and inadequate always to meet their obligations. As a result, freedom showed them their "finitude" and left them with a keen sense of "guilt." The resulting anxiety receded in the second, Sophoclean, period, during which Athenians came as close as they could to enjoying freedom. Sophocles' dramas, Droysen argued, reveal the essential qualities of Periclean Athens, which possessed "undeniably the most complete political character in Greece, which in a wonderfully harmonious fashion abolished and continued (*aufgehoben*) all the particularities of private life and had only the state and its affairs for its essence."[41] Athens, that is, briefly enjoyed the reconciliation between the particular and the general that he proposed for his own scheme of representative government for Germany. Under those happy circumstances, freedom implied "right" rather than "guilt." In German, of course, "right" or *Recht* can mean either "law" or "right." Droysen had the second meaning in mind. He wanted to signal the self-evident justification of freedom in the short-lived period of harmony in Athenian politics. It soon ended, and dissolution began almost at once.

This was the period of Euripides, Aristophanes, and the Sophists. Droysen revealed his own Aristotelian convictions in aesthetics by complaining that Athenian art ceased to be something "necessary and closed" and became instead a mere "form" with the "capacity for taking up any content." Arbitrariness, preciosity, and subjectivity—for these were what Droysen was thinking of—now entered literature and the other arts because, as a result of corrosive effects of untrammelled freedom, the harmony of Periclean Athens had given way to a leveled society of atomized and self-ish individuals that reminded him of modern-day France! The effects of this change also entered philosophy in the form of Sophism, which, Droysen alleged, taught that the "consciousness of freedom was nothing more than a tyrant over men and an imposition." The arguments of the Sophists further weakened the social bond by encouraging what is now called moral relativism, and "the opinion of any single individual" acquired the status of "the eternally true." In Droysen's view, this showed that the cycle of Athenian freedom had moved almost full circle, with the result that "the state dissolved itself like a rotting corpse."[42] Droysen was usually more delicate in his use of images, but his choice of analogy underscores the mixed feelings that he had about freedom. He understood that it was a noble and desirable attainment that led Athens to political and cultural greatness, but he was also certain that its beginnings were painful and that it ended, more or less like a disease, in disablement and destruction.

Moreover, when he turned to the third period of Hellenic history, his present-mindedness reinforced his distress. What had happened once could happen again, and Droysen feared revolution and its effects as much as he loathed unreformed absolutism. There was more to his attitude, however, than disgust and regret. Hegel's lectures had helped him judge history in terms of ultimate outcomes. Furthermore, he had recently translated Aeschylus's *Oresteia*; he, too, could believe that suffering brought wisdom and that good won out in end. Finally, he was intensely Christian and, as somewhat later writings show, believed that God worked beneficently through history. He therefore accepted the dissolution of Athenian freedom as not only necessary but also desirable. It was desirable because it was in the long-term interest of progress toward an enduring enjoyment of freedom. Droysen reached this conclusion on the basis of his interpretation of fourth–century Greek history in the commentaries and developed it further in 1836 in the first volume of the *History of Hellenism* and other writings. If, he reasoned, history began in Solon's time with the first steps toward freedom in Athens, then *world* history began only with its demise there because of the philosophic form that the Athenian spirit assumed in this final period. To drive this point home, Droysen used a further analogy with the present by implicitly comparing Sophism to the destructive criticism of the Enlightenment and the work of Isocrates, Plato, and Aristotle to the synthetic philosophies of German Idealism, above all to Hegel's. He saw a two-sided quality in the mature works of Greek philosophy. They were a summing up, a completion, an end, but they were also a beginning because they were universal in scope and, consequently, universally accessible. That meant that the Greek trial of freedom would inform and, hence, change subsequent experiences of freedom. This advance grew directly out of the period of dissolution. Sophism, for example, had turned the "cutting weapon of the dialectic" against all remaining "positivities." In itself, that was a destructive development, but it had a constructive side because it freed "the spirit from all limitation by that which is given or believed."[43] Greek philosophy thus became a philosophy for all interested humanity.

Droysen meant more than just the potential diffusion of Greek ideas into the non-Greek world. In 1833, the year after the appearance of *The Works of Aeschylus*, he published his *History of Alexander the Great*. This was not just a biography but a history that he subsequently used in the first volume of his later *History of Hellenism* (1836). Droysen does not describe Alexander specifically in terms of Hegel's "world historical individuals," but it is evident that he had that concept firmly in mind. World historical individuals, Hegel maintained, worked for their own, local purposes but achieved results of long-term historical effect.[44] That was also the case for Droysen's Alexander. In these books, Droysen traced the passage of Greek ideas to non-Greek peoples in the wake of Alexander's armies, and from the first, Droysen was attracted to the study of Hellenism as a partly maligned, partly ignored topic that he thought was of the highest importance in world history.

In the foreword to the *History of Hellenism*, he argued that a phenomenon of such magnitude that lasted so long could not simply be a product of weakness and decay.[45] In its early pages, Droysen applied a generally Hegelian terminology by claiming that Alexander's conquests were not a "caprice of destiny" (*Laune des Schicksals*) but an instance of the "rule of providence" (*Waltung der Vorsehung*).[46] He had been nearly as insistent at the beginning of his book on Alexander when he termed him an "instrument of history" (*Werkzeug der Geschichte*) and used a biblical paraphrase to capture his real greatness: "All are called," he explained, but only a few "chosen" to carry out history's tasks.[47] The providentialism in both passages was genuine. God had called Alexander and his armies to the task of spreading Greek ideas, uniting the previously antagonistic East and West, and preparing the way for the advent of Christianity. In different but related ways, all these actions were necessary for finding an eventual solution to the problem of freedom.

Hellenism's bearing on subsequent world history was a result of its essential universalism. It was, Droysen argued, the "first world unity" (*Welteinheit*). Achæmenid Persia, by contrast, was a mere "external aggregation of peoples and countries."[48] This unitary and universalist quality was itself a historical necessity, and to show that Droysen invoked his characteristic (and unquestioned) assumption that, in history, success is its own justification. The fact that Alexander conquered with so small an army proved that he had to conquer because "the time had come to transform the essential relationships [among] the then existing historical peoples (*Völker*), simultaneously the aggregate condition of humanity had to change." The result was a cosmopolitan "west-eastern life" (*westostliches Leben*).[49] These claims throw a premonitory light on quality of Droysen's prerevolutionary nationalism. In the tradition of Herder, he valued German nationhood only as one among others, and was a nationalist and cosmopolitan at the same time. That, too, changed in 1848. In his books on Alexander and Hellenism, however, his insistence on the cosmopolitan character of Alexander's achievements had a more specific relevance. The unification of East and West made it possible for non-Greeks to read Greek philosophy and, as a result of the defects that he found in post-Aristotelian Greek philosophy, made religious change necessary with world-historical effects.

Droysen believed that only Christianity, rightly understood and practiced, could avert recurrences of the Athenian misadventure with freedom, and he saw Hellenism as a precondition for Christianity. He did not say it was the cause, presumably because he did not want to deny the miraculousness of the incarnation, but he did see Hellenism as an essential condition for its appearance. The Greek and Macedonian conquerors brought with them a Greek culture that, because of the decay that freedom had brought to Athens, was "light-minded to the point of feverishness, without deportment and will, without virtue and religion." This irreligiosity actually fostered religion, and Droysen maintained that "this Enlightenment, contrary and levelling though it appears in particulars, broke the power of paganism and made possible a more spiritual (*geistigere*) religion."[50] In an instance of dialectical irony, that is, Athens' malady called forth its own cure. Hellenistic theocracies and ruler cults were the first and preliminary, Christianity the final and definitive, effects of this development.[51] Although Droysen studiously ignored the possibility of Hebrew origins in explaining the rise of Christianity, he did not base his explanation entirely on Greek frivolity.[52] He pointed also to the conquerors' destruction of "old-national" (*alt-nationalen*) ways as a heavy blow to paganism that created a situation in which "a religion had to develop that rose above the sad here-and-now."[53] This is a further instance of his willingness to subordinate national particularities to world demands and is an early example of a characteristic and dialectical tendency to find immense gain in apparent loss. A transcendent religion was obviously preferable to the maintenance of old folkways.

At first inspection, none of this seems to have much to do with solving the problem of freedom, except in the diffuse sense that Hellenism created an "invisible yet all-controlling power of the spirit (*Macht des Geistes*)" that was still "seizing new ground" and, so, would surely be somehow involved in any solution.[54] One reason for this difficulty is that Droysen's remarks on the rise of Christianity and its effects were necessarily brief because he was appropriately more intent on tracing the careers of Alexander and his successors than on discussing their long-term effects. His references to religious history serve mainly to point out the larger importance of his findings and to indicate his preoccupations, without being the subject directly under discussion. Furthermore, Droysen did not yet know much about post-Hellenistic history. How could he, given his training and immersion in classical philology and given the fact that while producing these major works, he was supporting himself and, after a time, a family on the proceeds from private lessons? He detailed the political effects of Christianity only after he took a position at the University of Kiel in 1840, where he had to teach medieval and modern as well as ancient history. Nevertheless, the outlines of his thinking, which he later filled in, were already discernible. They show why he thought Christianity could prevent continual repetitions of the vicious cycle first displayed at Athens.

Basic to his explanation was his distinction between "natural" or "vegetative" existence, which was the lot of most people at most times, and "historical" life lived in the "consciousness of freedom."[55] Under the terms of this distinction, freedom was ennobling but foredoomed because, in its spiritual quality, it cut humanity off from nature without providing an alternate source of discipline. The Greek philosophers, some of them, had tried to reconcile people to this condition, but had done so only with "austerity and coldness."[56] Christianity provided what they could not. As early as 1829, Droysen wrote to his close friend Albert Heydemann that it offered a much-needed "confession . . . of the need for reconciliation" (Versöhnung) and would ultimately provide it.[57] By 1831, if not already in 1829, he thought of this "reconciliation" in political terms, for he planned to devote a quarter of his planned political correspondence to the world-historical significance of Christianity.[58] He surely had this notion of the present political importance in mind when he conjoined statements about the rise of Christianity to his discussion of late Greek politics, for he was already translating Aeschylus, and his work on Alexander was at least in a preliminary stage.

Christianity, in its first appearance and latter-day realization, somehow promised to reconcile historical humanity with its world and, so, make stable freedom possible. Like every advance in history, Droysen acknowledged that Christianity also came at some cost. In his commentaries on Aeschylus he remarked on the beauty and vigor of Athenian culture in the fifth century B.C.E. and commented:

That youthful age of the human race with its enthusiasm for the beautiful and its bubbling freshness of creaturely strength and youthful freedom is gone forever; for the greater seriousness of historical life, the religion of conciliation has formed itself, and in the long and painful centuries the stern cultivation of the Church has broken the natural strength of the new western peoples; at last ripened to the freedom of inquiry and conscience, they see themselves sunken into a terrible confusion of rights and duties, a chaos of unnatural conditions and needs run wild—the fanaticism of industry, the labyrinthine secrecy of public life, the feverish unnaturalness of a narrowly watched historical existence.[59]

Despite his piety, Droysen evidently felt some genuine regret at the loss of paganism and at the loss of "natural strength" of his and other peoples. It is also clear that, for the moment at least, Christianity and its effects actually compounded the pain that modernity caused. He was also quite certain that both loss and pain were the price of a greater and ultimate good.

Apart from his necessarily brief and imprecise statements in some letters in 1831, he said nothing in the 1830s (but a great deal in the 1840s) about the exact nature of that good. This much, however, is clear. Germany, under Prussian leadership, would unify itself and, aided by a Christianity called into existence in part by the effects of failed Athenian freedom, would succeed where the Greeks had failed in establishing an enduring freedom under a distinctive constitutional form. These achievements, collectively, would amount to the institutionalization of *Volksthümlichkeit*. Droysen left this forecast vague, in part because he had no occasion to be specific and in part because he was not a utopian who spelled out details in advance. Really, he had no need to do so, because he was deeply (or at least avowedly) confident that history would provide what was necessary when it was necessary. The references to providence in his major works were not exercises in pious rhetoric but allusive references to his fundamental belief, and that belief rationalized his continual cross-referencing of past and present. He really believed that history would have, had to have, a happy ending. His altogether interesting correspondence with his Hamburg publisher, Friedrich Perthes, in 1836 and 1838 shows this with great clarity.

The correspondence makes curious reading for those accustomed to the habitual secularism of modern historical scholarship, and it can be tempting to dismiss as rhetorical flourishes Droysen's statements of his firmest convictions. That would be a great mistake, because in private but learned correspondence Droysen could and did say things that he only alluded to in his published works, in which he continually, though mutedly, referred to providence and divine purpose in history. It may also be tempting to dismiss him as serious scholar on the grounds of evident religious bias. That would also be a mistake. His faith increased rather than lessened the burden of proof that he felt, because he believed himself to be researching the record of the sacred. Certainly his belief intensified his determination to discover a meaning in the play of events, to move from particular inquiries to synthesis.

Droysen discussed the role of God in history because Perthes, probably intrigued by some of Droysen's comments in the *History of Hellenism*, which his firm had just published, solicited his views on the currents of historical thought in Germany. He must have been fascinated by the reply he received. Droysen identified three approaches to history other than his own. The first was that of Friedrich Christoph Schlosser. Droysen curtly dismissed his work as a kind of ahistorical moralizing that found "in history not much more than good and bad deeds." Droysen was also a moralist of a sort, but he objected to applying timeless standards of judgment to a constantly changing historical process. Second was the work of Leopold Ranke. Although Droysen later collaborated with some of Ranke's students, notably Duncker and Sybel, he had no better an opinion of Ranke and his students. He claimed that they "place the *certainty* of the fact above everything, indeed declare it the tendency of written history; that would make the work endless and certain of an absolutely worthless, negative result."[60] The accusation is unfair, and it is hard to believe that Droysen had read much of what Ranke had already published. It is also easy to see why he made this charge. Droysen believed in careful and critical use of evidence, but, from, his point of view, Ranke's proclaimed empiricism had prevented him from finding a single meaning in history. To Droysen the interpretation of one age seemed worthless unless it helped in understanding other ages.

Third came the Hegelians. Perhaps because people often reserve their fiercest hatred for those with whom they almost, but not quite, agree, Droysen saved his harshest criticism for the Hegelian historians, whom he personified in Heinrich Leo. Droysen himself, however, was too strongly influenced by Hegel for him simply to dismiss Leo's work in a few sentences, and he had, instead, to sort out truth from error. He admitted that Leo's approach rested on some sound insights and remarked: "I would acknowledge it myself if it were less tendentious." Hegelian history suffered from the converse of the flaw that he found in the Rankean: it was only interested in long-term development, only interested in imposing a unified meaning on history. "Insofar," Droysen wrote, "as it appears only to pursue the direction of developments, their paths and detours, I believe that it sacrifices the truth." Droysen was a philologist trained by Boeckh, and he understood that much of what mattered most in a given period was peculiar to it. Moreover, he was an empiricist. It was a commonplace in post-Hegelian Germany to insist that empiricism replace speculation, but Droysen based his empiricism on specific theological premises.

As early as 1829 he claimed in a letter that "the counterpart of empirical knowledge is not speculation but absolute knowledge, the immediate which is God's alone." Human inquirers could find "laws" in history, but not the "law of laws" which was God.[61] This was Droysen's initial statement of the key distinction that he made to Perthes in 1836 and kept in mind throughout his career, namely, that there was a divine and a human knowledge of history that were qualitatively different, even though they dealt with the same material. The former was absolute, the latter empirical in nature. By 1831 at the latest, he saw political implications in this distinction. In the letter to Moser in which he discussed founding a political journal, he faulted German philosophers for being too speculative and, so, demanded: "One must begin to live, to think, to hope, to despair more from moment to moment and empirically (*ephemer und empirice*)."[62] The empiricism that he recommended was a precondition to political reconstruction because it was the means to a predictive certainty that could accurately inform political conduct.

Now, in 1836 and with major publications to his credit, Droysen explained the bases and implications of this outlook. Droysen was a predestinarian. He described himself to Perthes as a "strict believer" who was "so permeated" by a belief in the "omnipotent governance of God" that he felt certain that "not even a hair may fall from the head without his will." Stated differently, God "sees in the present what is and what will come to be." For that reason, it was "the sublime duty of scholarship to proceed from the mortal and human standpoint to that which the teaching of Christ has revealed to us." In other words, he was called as a historian to track the workings of Providence, but, unlike the Hegelians, to do so through the careful empirical research that was suited to merely human capabilities. The historian so engaged would find repeated evidence of human "free will," which, though free, nonetheless obeyed "eternal necessity."[63] Freedom and necessity coexisted in the created world, just as they would in the political community whose establishment he anticipated. He was, in fact, looking forward to the creation in Germany of a stable freedom that would be the culmination of history in the specific sense that it would be a living emblem of the defining feature of all history properly so called: freedom working in tandem with necessity.

Droysen was, of course, asking a lot of historians. He was giving them (or, more accurately, claiming for himself) the task of discovering God's purpose in history, both as it had operated in the past and as it would operate in the future. He did not mean to be arrogant and took seriously Christian injunctions to be humble. In fact, it was the Hegelians whom he accused of the sin of pride. Only God knew everything and knew it absolutely, all at once. Human beings were left, at best, with faith and the invitation to a rigorous empirical knowledge. It was on those grounds that he attacked Hegel and his followers. In a later letter to Perthes, written in February 1837, he made this attack specific, even while admitting his lingering admiration for the philosopher's system. "Hegel," he contended, "assumed the spiritual activity of the centuries [to be] a fact and derives from it that which is the natural historical peculiarity of the human race, that the human being thinks." Hegel, he continued, considered this "thinking" to be the "in-dwelling divine spark" in humanity.[64]

Droysen had the greatest admiration for the workings of the human intellect, but he found Hegel's vision not just erroneous but irreligious and heretical:

At all events, one can see no more sublime conception of human spirituality and development than the Hegelian; but what an error! Here is that absolute that is not God, not the eternal, the unique, that revealed Christ to us, but—the hand on the clock to show at what hour the human recognition of God stands; nothing higher or even quantitatively higher than that which the pagans imagined in their ideals; because that really is pagan, that this [should be] the highest: human knowledge and intuition being form and prayed to as divinity.

In contrast to this irreligiosity, Droysen insisted: "The basis of all human knowledge is empirical." Empiricism was more than a sound research strategy suited to human minds. To Droysen, it was a condign recognition of humanity's weak, no doubt fallen, condition. Moreover, it allowed conscientious historians to see what Hegelians could not see, namely, that "the human being with his freedom of will, in his struggle and split between good and evil, is only the organ of God's eternal will (*Organ ist zu Gottes ewigen Willen*), and despite all absolute soundness of judgment formed in the struggle of necessity."[65]

Neither in this, nor in his earlier letter of 1836, did Droysen claim to be able to explain the real existence of human free will in a historical process ruled by divine necessity. His failure to do so is hardly surprising, because that problem baffled the best theological minds from the patristic age to the present, and Droysen never claimed to be a theologian. His theory of history had theological bases, but by reserving absolute knowledge to God alone and insisting that human knowledge had to be empirical, he tacitly renounced theological argument in favor of dogmatic certainty based on faith in the sense of the earlier Latin *credo*, best rendered "I trust" rather than "I believe." Accordingly, and as a continuation of his attack on the Hegelians, he confessed to Perthes that "the historian cannot understand in every detail the necessity of events" and that the historical process was, therefore, bound to be a "wonderful mystery" to those who lived and acted in it. This genuine admission bespoke an attitude that helped keep his anger and despair in bounds—no easy task for Droysen—when things did not work out as he expected. If only on religious grounds, he had to be willing to admit that he might, after all, have been wrong in his predictions. Again, he believed that there was a necessary and fundamental distinction between sequential, and hence empirical, human knowledge and immediate, and hence absolute, divine knowledge. The former could err; the latter could not.

The terms of Droysen's argument are familiar. They derive from the late writings of St. Augustine; received clear and compact, and therefore very influential, statement in books 4 and 5 of Boethius's *Consolation of Philosophy*; and were exhaustively rehearsed during the sixteenth–century Reformation that so interested Droysen.[66] The argument turned on the difficulty that the acceptance of either free will or necessity had unacceptable consequences. Free will without necessity severed the creature from the Creator, whereas necessity without free will made the Creator responsible for the sins of the creature. Therefore, both free will and necessity had to exist, and Droysen evidently accepted on faith the view that St. Augustine first propounded and that Boethius expressed nicely in his distinction between *sæculum* and *nunc stans*. *Sæculum* is the etymological root of our "secular," which is often misused as a synonym for "worldly." In fact, it is a time word, not a place word. The *Sæculum* is the order of time in which human beings live and in which they experience things one after another, that is—in Droysen's language—empirically. The *nunc stans*, by contrast, is the "eternal now" in which God lives and knows all things at once. It is eternity in the sense of a simultaneous existence of all events and things, rather than of their infinite perpetuation.[67] St. Augustine and Boethius used this distinction to demonstrate the possibility of there being both free will and necessity. In their view, human actions were free in the *sæculum*, where act follows decision, but necessary, that is determined, in the *nunc stans*, wherein God always knew, and always will know, every outcome.

For St. Augustine and Boethius, this distinction was mainly a contribution to the Christian discussion of sin and redemption, but even for them it had major historical implications. By its terms, human history, all of it, had a single meaning known fully to God. That left unanswered the question of whether it could have an intelligible meaning for human beings who lived in history. Two answers were possible. One was that human beings were trapped in the historical sequence, where they moved blindly, if freely, and could understand only as much of its meaning as was offered by divine revelation. The other answer, and this was the one that Droysen accepted, was to undertake the obviously difficult but, if successful, rewarding task of studying the history that had already occurred in order to discover, as nearly as a merely human mind could, the realization to date of the meaning that God saw in history.[68] Because this meaning came about over time and somehow involved every event in history, Droysen insisted on the empiricism that he found the Hegelians lacked. Because he trusted that there was a meaning to history, he felt confident in looking for it. Finally, his belief that such a meaning existed made him confident that history had a happy ending and, given the long-term tension between freedom and necessity, that the problem of freedom would ultimately be solved. Working with these assumptions, he turned increasingly in the 1840s to prediction, that is, to surmising not just what came next but what Providence meant to have come next.

2

Droysen: Interpretation and Prediction

In the 1840s Droysen turned to prediction. This was less a new departure than a logical extension of ideas he had long held. In the preceding decade he had linked past and present by identifying historical life with human freedom and the historical process with the search for an eventual solution to the problem that freedom posed. His critical revision of Hegel's philosophy in the light of Augustinian theology enabled him, or so he thought, to trace the continual realization of divine purpose in the historical record. The result was an extraordinary burst of political activity, especially after 1845. As scholarship was the other side of partisanship, these years were also historiographically productive: he became a modern historian, without losing his original interest in antiquity, and in the process wrote some fine history, especially his *Lectures on the Wars of Freedom* (1846–48). Prediction, when he turned to it, was simply a matter of extrapolating into the future historical tendencies identified in the past, and his comments in 1831 on representative government and Prussia's German mission were really foreshadowings of the more detailed predictions that he later made. At least, in principle it was that simple. In practice, as the pace of his political engagement quickened, he was occasionally unsettled when the history he experienced failed to conform to the history he had anticipated.

His increased and increasingly detailed interest in the German future was a single instance of the heightening of liberal and nationalist expectations that many German intellectuals experienced in the 1840s, but Droysen's shift to foretelling had specific causes as well. Again, his vision of history invited him to anticipate the future, and his personal circumstances now allowed him to accept the invitation. In 1843 he published the second and final volume of his *History of Hellenism*. At the same time, Georg Waitz joined the faculty at the University of Kiel, where for three years Droysen had been teaching ancient and medieval as well as modern history. Waitz took over the lectures in ancient and medieval history. As a result, Droysen had sufficient time to concentrate delightedly on modern history.[1] This allowed him to base his predictions on a reasonably detailed knowledge of recent events. Moreover, his earlier stint in teaching medieval history made it possible to link antiquity and modernity, so that his discussions of the future could follow from a grand interpretation of world history.

At the same time, Droysen became an energetic publicist. Far from keeping his supposed insights into the future to himself, he used both the spoken and written word to bring them to the attention of the German public. His major work from 1843 to 1848 was the *Lectures on the Wars of Freedom,* a two-volume edition of the lectures he had delivered at Kiel that offered a detailed exposition of European and American history and purported to show the historical inevitability of Germany's unification as a constitutional monarchy by a revivified Prussia.[2] During this period, politics in general and political change in particular became the chief focus of his attention in a special and peculiar way. On the one hand, he believed that his lectures and publications were themselves historically necessary as a means to needed change. That is, he was still enough of a Hegelian to assume that spiritual change had to precede institutional transformation and confident enough of his forensic and compositional abilities to suppose that he could help ready the German spirit for national unification and political freedom. On the other hand, the constitutional practice of the German states and the German Confederation meant that he had no say in and, of course, no experience of practical politics. He therefore viewed politics as an outsider, a difficulty compounded by having followed his career to the then tiny port city of Kiel in the remote northwest. He looked at German politics from a geographic as well as an intellectual distance. Probably for these reasons, before the revolution of 1848 he was often more confident than circumstances warranted and, during it, he became more disappointed than he should have been.

This is not to say that he was otherworldly or naïve. As always, his optimism referred to ultimate outcomes; Droysen was too aware of human sinfulness to feel any other way. In his discussions of the past and anticipations of the future, he therefore tried to take human self-interest carefully into account. Furthermore, though he thought that it would be possible to limit the role of violence in the coming transformation of Germany, he never doubted that a more or less forceful break with existing legalities would be necessary. In order to make that point, he called on the more or less Hegelian conceptions retained from his student years and coined and contrasted his concept of the "right of history" (*Recht der Geschichte*) with the familiar idea of "historical right" (*historisches Recht*). The concept dates from 1839 at the latest, though he appears not to have used the actual term before 1843. In a letter in 1839, his friend and frequent correspondent Justus von Gruner criticized the existing French bicameral system and argued that the future German national constitution would have to reflect German traditions by embodying "historical right."

Droysen agreed that the French system was deplorable, but took issue with the rest of Gruner's argument: "Every historical right," he countered, "is in fact a non-right that has become established or made itself current. There is no right established by history for which it cannot be shown that it has modified, covered over, or destroyed an earlier right." Droysen's meaning is quite clear. In negative terms, historical or prescriptive rights turned out to be fictions when examined in terms of origins. Because everything began as an innovation, continued existence through time alone could not make a practice or an institution legitimate. Droysen did not use this distinction solely for negation. It also had an important positive implication in certain historical circumstances because it conferred as well as denied legitimacy. Significantly, Droysen chose the eighteenth-century German territorial princes, whose system of government he detested, to illustrate this application of his argument. He claimed that their powers derived from usurpation rather than right, but then conceded that, after all, they possessed a certain kind of right because "the course of history has proven their necessity." In making this admission, he recurred to his long-held belief that everything in history was necessary and, therefore, somehow good, even the division of Germany among absolute princes and princelings. He now applied this logic to his own day and in the defense of future change: "If historical development has the right to create developments of right, then . . . the present has the very same right." Used in this way, his concept of the right of history delegitimated for his own century the German political system that it had justified for the eighteenth and legitimated radical political change in the present or near future. This was potentially a revolutionary doctrine, though in his instinctive moderation Droysen predicted that Germans would bring about change "quietly and properly."[3]

This was a potentially cynical idea because it made historical success its own justification, but equating historical necessity with God's will and supporting his theory by referring to "our Christian view of God's world governance,"[4] Droysen did not see this implication. These qualifications could be, and at times were, tenuous in practice. Droysen wanted to validate change, but he had in mind only desirable change that occurred with as little disruption as possible. Moreover, in using God's plan as a standard of judgment, he was invoking an invisible criterion. He could not, of course, know exactly what God intended. All he could do was to trace what, evidently, God had accomplished up to the present and make an educated guess about what would occur next. When events displeased him, he would feel momentary bitterness, but, by the terms of his argument, there was really no arguing with the judgment of history. That fact required him to make some major compromises and accommodations in

1848 and 1849, but before the revolution his distance from actual politics and the seemingly unchanging condition of Germany usually, but not always, saved him from having to reappraise his views. He thought about the promise that the future held, and he judged events by the contribution that they made to reaching that future. The result was a sort of principled opportunism that made it impossible for Droysen and his fellows to resist on ethical grounds whatever succeeded, however seemingly unwelcome it might be. He became adept at finding silver linings in dark clouds.

His first use in 1843 of the actual term *right of history* provides a nice case in point. It appears in a letter to a friend that Droysen had published in a limited number of copies of his *History of Hellenism*. Later, an editor entitled it the "Theology of History." There, in a sustained comparison of Hellenism with the French Revolution of 1789, Droysen noted the vast destruction of old ways that each had occasioned yet insisted that both were justified because the former had promoted, and the latter was still promoting, historical progress.[5] This was as close as Droysen could come to applying to history the external moral standards that he deplored in Schlosser's writings. His vision of history as the sequential unfolding of a plan seen all at once by the deity saved him from judging history by a universal criterion without forcing him to accept the present as simply and self-sufficiently good. His concept of the right of history perfectly met his needs. It sanctioned change, even far-reaching and sudden change, without praising change as such or subjecting history to review according to timeless principles, and it allowed him at the same time to batter the defenses of what he called the "historical" party: "If the so-called historical view has no higher criterion than that of the *fait accompli* . . . then logically it can raise no kind of appeal against the phase of development that it damns. It is thoughtlessness to appeal to historical right without at the same time being willing to recognize the right of history."[6] In other words, Droysen was a liberal not just in the sense of seeking, through reforms, greater individual freedom and state responsiveness to society, though these objectives were central to his program. He was a liberal also in the sense of relying on the progressive march of historical process, though for him the invisible hand was providential rather than economic.

Droysen had a strong sense of invidious contrast between conservative defenders of the existing order and those, himself among them, who were ready to lead the way to historically necessary change:

As long as they see in history only the right of *vis inertiae*, they can justify only with exclamations, count only on the sympathy of [those who share] common privileges, and their judgment is only arbitrariness and prejudice, confusing rather than enlightening, embittering instead of preparing for reconciliation. . . . For only a *truly historical point of view* of the present, of its tasks, its means, its limitations, will be able to remedy the sad disorder of our political and social affairs and to point out the correct route to a happier future.[7]

That is, Droysen's concept of the "right of history" allowed him to point out what he saw as the mindless and self-serving character of conservative appeals to "historical right." Of course, his own argument was also self-serving, because it was not hard to imagine where, or to whom, contemporaries would have to look for the needed "truly historical outlook." His legitimation of historical change was an assertion of the special authority and dignity of historians. It was also an appeal to thoughtful conservatives inasmuch as he suggested that the present was at an impasse such that only men like himself could be "enlightening" rather than "confusing," "preparing for reconciliation" rather than "embittering."

This approach was problematic in two ways. First, it was an instance of the natural fallacy, namely, the practice of deriving an *ought* from an *is*. Droysen had granted history an unimpeachable right to its contents and freed it from judgment by any external standards. History provided its own justification. That being the case, it might be presumptuous to demand change and difficult to explain why one change would be better than another. History, not the historian, had the last word. Second, and equally serious, the predestinarian quality of Droysen's argument also made questionable the wisdom of working for change. In practical terms, intervening in behalf of change might, at best, be redundant and, at worst, mistaken because it was obviously difficult to discover God's intentions. That is, human intervention might simply be a matter of trying to make history do what it would do in any case, and it might also mean unintentionally trying to force it out of its proper channel. In psychological terms, the call to action was contrary to the historical complacency that Droysen's theory logically implied. If everything would ultimately work out for the best because of historical necessity, then, in a sense, everything already was working out for the best at any moment in history.

Droysen's efforts to master and remove these difficulties were not completely consistent. That is not surprising. Simultaneous insistence on the reality of free will and necessity creates enormous, probably insoluble, problems. Droysen admired order and system, but not oversimplification. At times, he seemed to counsel either confident expectation or, failing that, resigned acceptance of whatever God might send. Thus, in 1843 in his "Theology of History" he wrote: "The highest task of our scholarship is really theodicy."[8] Similarly, in 1846 in his *Lectures on the Wars of Freedom* he wrote that "faith offers us the consolation that a hand of God bears us" and then remarked that "the discipline of history" consequently had "no higher task than to justify this faith."[9] By claiming that the proper task of the historian was to demonstrate divine benevolence in history, he was by implication advising people to reconcile themselves with history rather than to change it. As Droysen's remarks about the "right of history" show, however, he really wanted change and he also wanted to take a hand in bringing it about. He had arguments to justify this more characteristic position.

These arguments rested on the theology that Droysen had expounded to Perthes in and after 1836. At that time Droysen distinguished radically between the divine and human experience of history. God knew all things at once, so that everything appeared meaningful and necessary. Human beings, however, saw events only in sequence, so that actions seemed free and contingent. In short, they lived and acted in history. Standing aside expectantly, therefore, was nonsense because there would be no history unless human beings acted. Their actions would succeed or fail to the extent that they realized God's plans. That meant that it was really a question of knowing what actions to take and when to take them. Only historians could supply that knowledge, and that was why Droysen thought of history as a calling. Without claiming infallibility, he thought that he was well placed to tell people what to do and when to do it. His predictions were just a matter of supplying as clear and reliable a map as possible. Before 1848 he was generally confident that his map was of high quality, though he never actually proved that valid prediction was possible. He seems to have been aware of this fact, because in the "Theology of History," he admitted that no adequate philosophy of history yet existed and that no "Kant" had yet demonstrated a "categorical imperative of history."[10] In the absence of such a systematic philosophy, Droysen chose the next best thing and reasoned from analogy by employing an image first used in 1838 in his article "On Greek Literature," in which he referred to history as a "stream" and a "linear directedness."[11] Between 1843 and 1848, these and their equivalents were Droysen's standard metaphors for historical progress. They served not only to suggest ineluctable, onward flow but also to indicate how he inferred the future from what had gone before.

His fullest and most revealing use of the stream analogy occurred in a passage from the "Theology of History," possibly because he wrote the piece for selected readers and, so, could be franker than when writing for the general public:

Only by collectively regarding history as the development of humanity can individual formations (*Gestaltungen*)—nations, cultures, states, individuals—acquire their true significance; even that which is true, beautiful, right, noble does not transcend time and place but, on the contrary, possesses its mass and energy as a result of the fact that it is, as it were, projected upon a here-and-now. And, again, this collective life of humanity is an uninterrupted stream—in the thousandfold eddies and whirlpools [there is] a direction that all the water follows, whether quickly or slowly—there is a restless movement onwards, whose goal we may intimate from the direction. Not a stream of the sort where stagnant pools and puddles may not form on the shore, but the next flood drags them along downstream; nor is it a progression such that every kind of spiritual existence, every form of human activity *simultaneously* develops more highly in equal pulses.[12]

In this dense passage, Droysen presents a series of his major ideas that explain both his confidence in the future and his confidence in discerning it. First, human history was a unified and single process with a collective meaning. That was why he felt justified in discussing German politics in world-historical terms. Second, events could be judged only in historical terms, only in terms of a "here-and-now" (by which he really meant a "there-and-then"). That was why he avoided conscious use of external standards and tried to make history reveal its own meaning. Third, history's unity did not mean that progress occurred with uniform rapidity at all times and places.

This explained away potentially embarrassing cases of stagnation and partly accounts for his repeated insistence that historians be empirical in order that evidence might govern their conclusions. Finally, and most important, prediction was possible, at least in general terms. To the degree that his riverine analogy was apt, he could foretell the future because it is obviously possible to learn a lot about where a river is headed by noting the direction of its flow. By the same token, and without inconsistency, he spared himself the impossible task of trying to describe the future in detail. From a vantage point upstream, after all, it is not possible to anticipate every twist and turn ahead. With those points established, or at least asserted, to his own satisfaction, Droysen undertook to instruct his public so as it prepare it for its future. Again, his vision of history had both a conservative and a revolutionary aspect, and his belief that history was predestined could imply that one should either wait for history to happen or actively help it achieve its necessary results. Despite continual ambivalence in both areas, Droysen generally wanted to help change occur as quickly as possible, though without resort to revolution. His sense of his own role in forwarding change is a further, and an important, part of his resolution of the difficulties that his theories raised, but his understanding of this role makes sense only in light of his reading of the tendency of modern history as the latest and, as far as solving the problem of freedom was concerned, the final stage of world history. The year 1843 was a benchmark not only for his articulation of historical theory but also for his interpretation of the historical process. In the latter, as in the former, area he elaborated more fully ideas that he had already entertained in the 1830s. Now, as in those earlier statements, he employed Hegel's conception of a final, Germanic age completing and perfecting a freedom only limitedly achieved by the Greeks. Now, as then, he filled those Hegelian forms with a content based on his own reading of the classics and increasingly, because of his teaching load at Kiel, data from medieval and modern history.

His basic claim was that his own age and country would soon complete in political and social terms the agenda set by the sixteenth-century Reformation, which he deeply admired and which, at least since 1829, he had closely associated with Prussia.[13] History, he thought, was about to complete its tasks. That is, he saw in sixteenth-century Germany the preliminary, and in nineteenth-century Germany the final and definitive, solution to the world-historical problem of freedom. For this reason, his interpretation of the Reformation turned on his understanding of the periods preceding it. His discussion of antiquity drew on the ideas that he had already published in the 1830s, whereas his more schematic discussion of the Middle Ages was the result of what he had learned in preparing his lectures at Kiel before 1843. He was therefore able, not altogether convincingly, to portray the classical and medieval periods as dialectical opposites that the Reformation mediated on a spiritual level and that his own age would reconcile in actual political practice.

Droysen sweepingly characterized antiquity in terms of a tendency to remove God, and the supernatural in general, from the world, a tendency that he labeled *Weltentgötterung* ("de-godizing the world").[14] This was a highly abstract way of describing the combined effects of Greek irreligion and the Macedonian conquest on paganism. He had discussed these effects in the first volume of *The History of Hellenism*, where he had claimed that they invited religious innovation and, more specifically, the advent of Christianity.[15] Given the circumstances of its appearance, Christianity (and, interestingly, medieval Islam) before the Reformation displayed the countervailing tendency of detaching God from the world. This he termed *Gottentweltlichung* ("de-worldizing God").[16] These characterizations, which are hardly fair to either the ancient or the medieval world, received fuller treatment later in 1843 in his public lecture "On the Millenial Celebration of the Treaty of Verdun," which he delivered to students and townspeople at Kiel.

A speech on the occasion of the thousandth anniversary of the treaty that divided the Carolingian Empire into three parts obviously encouraged the speaker to take a long view of events. Given his preoccupation with the past and the future, Droysen really needed no encouragement to take this view of affairs. He explained to his possibly baffled listeners that pagan antiquity had treasured an ideal of freedom limited only to this world. That ideal could briefly support a vigorous political life, as it had in fifth-century Athens, but it was flawed because it was a form of "acosmism." Droysen meant that when it did not ignore divinity altogether, it recognized merely a "dualism" in which nature and supernature coexisted but did not interact. That was why Athenian freedom destroyed itself and why paganism did not endure. The ancients divorced God from the world and thus cut themselves off from the restraints of divine guidance. The converse Christian doctrine of the word made flesh, Droysen continued, promised to remedy this defect but was unable for centuries to keep that promise because medieval Christianity replied to the excessive secularism of "declining antiquity" with "an equally blind hatred and rejection of the secular."[17] Here, too, the effect was to separate God and the world.

Droysen's sweeping generalizations may seem oddly out of place in an attempt to explain why humanity had not yet achieved a lasting political freedom, but to Droysen they seemed very much to the point. Though he did not explicitly identify it, his underlying assumption is clear enough: life in the state had to embody the central principle of the historical process where contingent human actions fulfilled God's immanent purpose and where freedom and necessity were simultaneously present. On that premise, it was clearly necessary to link God and the world. That was why Droysen admired the Reformation so deeply and saw it as both the start of modern history and the beginning of history's completion. Modernity, in this view, eliminated the dross and combined what was best in the two preceding periods. It combined a profound "enthusiasm for classical antiquity" with a deep and purified religiosity and thus summoned Christianity to its true historical mission "in the ever vital and present interpenetration of the mortal and the eternal (*Durchdringung des Endlichen mit dem Ewigen*), in the priesthood of all believers, in the most intimate and personal participation of each individual in his justification." Christianity could at last overcome the "complete dualism" of antiquity that had destroyed the original "intermeshing of God and world" (*Verschlungenheit Gottes und der Welt*) while also escaping the "equally unfruitful extraworldliness, the equally blind despisal and rejection of the secular" characteristic of the Middle Ages.[18]

It would be a mistake to make these ideas seem clearer than they are, though it is possible that Droysen buried a reasonably straightforward argument under the murky abstractions he used to state his major points. This much is clear: He thought of history as beginning and ending with a close association between God and the world, and he did not see the intervening periods as wasted time because the reunion between the worldly and the divine that the Reformation began would be at a higher level than that which preceded the discovery of freedom in ancient Athens. It would be higher because, at last, political freedom would exist under the seal of divinity. Droysen left no doubt that his excursus on religious history was laden with political implications. Thus, in another and nearly contemporary work, he followed Hegel fairly closely in blaming ancient worldliness both for the decline of ancient Athens and, a novel claim, for the low esteem in which the ancients held "private life."[19] Moreover, he accused the undue elevation of the divine during the Middle Ages of lowering the power and prestige of the state to such an extent that political authority "consisted of nothing but rights and freedoms, private legalities."[20] Political practice, in other words, was a direct result of the Christian religious outlook.

That was why the Reformation seemed so filled with political promise. In Droysen's view, it laid the spiritual foundations for modern statehood and, moreover, foreshadowed the future harmony between public and private, between community and individual. That is, it sought to restore the embracing public demands of ancient statehood without damaging "the entire plenitude of the Christian development of the personality." As in 1831, so now more than a decade later, Droysen wanted two things that were hard to combine: both protection of the private and individual and the creation of a strong state that could draw on the energies and loyalties of its citizens. Because of the Reformation, he believed, the private and the public would not merely coexist; they would complement and draw strength from each other. Individual freedom, the political extension of Luther's "priesthood of all believers," would flourish because the state was powerful, and that freedom would, in turn, greatly strengthen this state, which would be "absolutely immoral" (*absolut unsittlich*) without it: "Only through freedom and for the sake of freedom can the state possess that unlimited power; the state must, like the Reformation before it, recognize, establish, and activate in reality a priesthood of all believers."[21]

The freedom that Droysen had in mind was a perfect case in point of what Leonard Krieger called the "German idea of freedom." On the one hand, it gave scope to individual preference and idiosyncracy only in matters in which the state, by any definition, was uninterested. On the other hand, and insofar as properly public matters were concerned, it was a freedom of each to agree with all, really a freely willed acceptance of authority.[22] In order fully to understand Droysen's conception of freedom, however, it is necessary to review his descriptions of the future state in view of his discussions of post-Reformation history. He discussed these matters in compact form in the "Verdun Speech" and in scattered comments and asides in various pamphlets and articles. He gave them extended and systematic treatment in the two sizable volumes of his *Lectures on the Wars of Freedom*. Although the first volume did not appear until 1846 and the second only in 1848, the work is good evidence for Droysen's views at least after 1843. His extended arguments in these volumes are congruent with what he had been saying since 1843, and, in any case, his chapters are just polished versions of the lecture series in modern history that he gave at Kiel from 1843 to 1848. His point of departure was the growth of absolutism, despite the Reformation's invitation to freedom under authority, and his argument rests on a crucial distinction between "powers" (*Mächte*) and "states" (*Staaten*).

By "powers" he meant the absolutist states that began to appear in the sixteenth and flourished in the seventeenth and eighteenth centuries. Although he acknowledged them to be historically necessary and therefore good, he termed them "powers" in order to signal that their authority was a matter of fact rather than of right. In doing so, he did not mean simply to delegitimate them. He had no absolute standards of moral reference by which to do so. By the "right of history," they were legitimate for the time and place in which they existed, but, in his view, they were no longer necessary in his own century. He therefore felt entitled to point out their flaws through an invidious comparison with the "states" that would soon supplant them. Droysen, therefore, discussed their appearance with a measure of ambivalence. He thought that he knew what political life ought to be like, so he praised the "powers" for contributing to its eventual appearance while damning them for not conforming to its standards. On the one hand, their advent was welcome because they had a major historical task to perform inasmuch as there could be "no mention of statehood and the common good" as long as political power, which was properly unitary, remained divided between princes and estates.[23]

This was basically a utilitarian argument in which he justified the "powers" in terms of the eventual (and unintended) effects of their construction, though he of course also meant that God had foreseen and willed both cause and effect. On the other hand, because he was fighting the continued existence of "powers" in the German Confederation, he found much to object to in them. When the princes defeated the estates, they also defeated the principle of representation, and the principle of acquisition by conquest and inheritance meant that frontiers were drawn without reference to the wishes of the affected populations. In the *Lectures*, therefore, Droysen described this as a "political system . . . that . . . was sick, unwholesome, monstrous through and through." At another point in the same work he asked rhetorically who owned a "power" and answered: "Not this land, not this people, but a monarch who possessed land and people as property, as a domain that his avarice counselled him to exploit as well as possible;—what was the state? Not the immanent generality of the historical and legal life of this naturally united population but the triumph of the landlordly over every other historical right, an abstraction of enormous power, of infinite pretension, and this left to the arbitrariness of a mortal who, by his power, was like a god on earth."[24]

In so arguing, Droysen was well within the European tradition, feudal in origin, of regarding patrimonial government with horror. He was more original in expressing a further ambivalence. The "powers" were detestable, but their very wrongness was really a hidden blessing because it assured an eventual moral reaction against them. Not only did their external expansion and internal integration make it possible to realize the political potential of the Reformation, but their essential arbitrariness was also good, because once their historical tasks were accomplished, it called forth the resistance that would finally produce the state as "the highest moral order (*sittliche Ordnung*) in which a man can live."[25] This was a logical consequence of viewing history as theodicy. Seeming bad, including despotism, was really hidden good, in this case because it would, in fact had to, destroy itself. Self-destruction was the last of its necessary historical tasks.

The manifest illegitimacy of the "powers" required their replacement with "states." Droysen's use of this key term is clearest in his discussions of the first, partial attempts at statehood in late-eighteenth and early-nineteenth-century Prussian history. In keeping with the demands of his historical theory, he preferred to discuss principles through specific historical instances rather than in general terms. He had, nonetheless, a working definition for the state. The state, he argued, "lives and is indestructible in its people (*Volk*)" because it "awakens life, strength, dedication in all its members and they, again, certain of finding in it their noblest good, spare no trouble to raise it, no danger to advance it, no sacrifice to preserve it." The state, in other words, was an intense community whose strength derived from the voluntary exertions of its citizens. This was in marked contrast to the powers' need to compel their passive subjects to act in their behalf. Droysen saw statehood as so self-sufficiently attractive that he believed that the "poverty of special dynastic interests, the pretension of caste privileges, the rottenness of ecclesiastical inheritance should vanish before so elevated a task." Again, he thought of the state as the "highest moral order."[26]

Before reviewing Droysen's analysis of the inevitable approach of statehood in Germany, it is important to note two major assumptions on which it rested. First, the essential morality of statehood did not mean that amoral, or even immoral, motivations were unnecessary for its establishment. Droysen's vision of the historical process required this to be the case. Historical outcomes were not simply the will of God; they were also the products of human decisions, frequently made out of self-interest and frequently having major unintended effects. This belief was theological in origin, and it placed Droysen in the liberal tradition, broadly defined: the common good was a result of individual pursuits. Second, Droysen's evident nationalism coexisted with a marked cosmopolitanism. He was, of course, mainly interested in freedom and unity for Germany, and he saw Prussia as the chief actor in the approaching drama that would lead to those results, but he also insisted that Germany's task had been set by world history and that Germany's accomplishment would benefit the rest of the world. Only after the disappointments of 1848–49 would he write of peculiarly German virtues and think of German gains as coming at the expense of other nations.

He did, however, think that history had selected Germany, and especially Prussia, for the unique historical role of solving the problem of freedom through the introduction of statehood. Admittedly, the replacement of powers with states was an event in world history, and Germany was not alone in moving toward political reconstruction. Germany was, however, the only nation situated to do the job well and in such a way that her example would set the standard for other nations. In so doing, Germany would continue and perfect a process already begun in the Protestant North, for example, in British North America. His admiration for the American Revolution and for the United States was very real, though his discussions of American politics were poorly informed and probably had more to do with an affinity for American Protestantism than a critical understanding of American history.[27] In any case, American events had a mainly indicative significance for Droysen. They showed which way history was heading without speeding history's progress: America was too unlike Europe to teach political lessons to the old Continent.[28] He saw in the French Revolution of 1789 another indication of coming change, though he distinguished sharply between what it promised and what it delivered. Its outbreak was a welcome sign of the approach of statehood, but its actual course seemed to him a terrible example of how not to go about building a state. He deplored French centralism and believed that the revolution created only an inverted power in which political property was in the hands of an atomized populace rather than a hereditary monarch.[29] Only Germany or, more precisely, the Hohenzollern monarchy was historically placed to bring true statehood to the Old World.

At first glance, this conclusion seems strange, because under Droysen's terms of analysis, disunited Germany was very far removed from statehood. Droysen's view of history, however, provided for the last becoming first. In Germany, the contradictions that the powers presented were so glaring and so hateful that they provided the needed impetus for change. Moreover, Germany was the land of the Reformation and therefore possessed the moral and intellectual prerequisites for statehood. Statehood required both a harmony between government and governed and the possession of a territory and population large enough for the state to make its wishes felt beyond its borders. Neither was possible in Germany without major constitutional changes and a redrawing of the German political map. In the pursuit of statehood, that is, Germany had, in dialectical irony, the advantage of singularly pressing need. Because of the peculiar nature and situation of Prussia since the Reformation, she also had the advantage of opportunity. Droysen searched the Prussian past and present for indications that history had prepared her for the inevitable task of unifying Germany as a state, and he thought that he found the evidence that he needed. He did not yet argue, as he would after 1848, that Prussia had always acted in the general German interest. Instead, his argument turned on a reading of the supposedly objective requirements of Prussian self-interest: Prussia would unify Germany into a state in the full sense of the term because it was in Prussia's interest to do so and because the legacy of the Reformation provided Prussia with the moral equipment necessary for this task. Despite his obvious (and often disappointed) Prussian patriotism, Droysen tried to be as unblinkered and unsentimental as possible in presenting this case. Prussia had been, and currently was, a power among the powers of Europe, though with the important distinction that her devastation during the Thirty Years' War forced her rulers to be especially ruthless and unbending in asserting and consolidating royal power at the expense of all competitors. Once that historically necessary, and therefore justifiable, assertion and consolidation was complete in the reign of Frederick William I, an opposing tendency toward statehood appeared under Frederick the Great that moved the monarchy well, if only temporarily, on the way to "state citizenship" (*Staatsbürgerthum*).[30]

Droysen had in mind two accomplishments, both occasioned by Frederick's perception of Prussia's political interests and both filled with promise for the Prussian and German future. The first was Frederick's embracing of the German national cause in the not very successful League of Princes (*Fürstenbund*). In his article "The Political Position of Prussia" (1845), he attributed to this early effort the "development of nations" (*Entwicklung der Völker*) in the nineteenth century and the maintenance of peace among the German states.[31] The second, and more important, accomplishment was Frederick's attempt to raise political life in Prussia to a "higher formation" by conceiving of the polity as "the common property of everyone." Droysen expressly acknowledged the limited and partial nature of these achievements. Frederick's subjects, he claimed, were "on the way to state citizenship," but "only just on the way." In addition, he believed that Frederick resolved the contradiction between public and private "only in an extremely superficial fashion." These limitations did not bother him because he was convinced that Frederick had done all that could be done without undercutting his position as a hereditary monarch.[32] Again, Droysen believed that history moved through specific decisions undertaken out of self-interest, which both caused and constricted Frederick's reforms. It was inevitable, and therefore good, that after Frederick's death Prussia became again a mere "power." Observable political interests would assure that the relapse was only momentary and, he found, lasted only until Prussia's crushing defeat in the battles of Jena and Äuerstedt in 1806, after which Prussia made a second, and more nearly successful, approach to statehood. In discussing the effects and significance of the Prussian reforms, he singled out the Baron vom Stein for special praise, but he really had the objective situation of Prussia in mind, and, to the extent that his history could have heroes, the real hero was the Prussian monarchy itself. In his treatment of vom Stein (or of Frederick the Great or, for that matter, Alexander the Great) Droysen, following Hegel, thought of great men as agents chosen to perform, often indeliberately, tasks that history had set and that they identified in terms of immediate exigencies and opportunities.[33] Droysen nonetheless saw Stein's brief tenure in office as a major foreshadowing of subsequent Prussian, German, and world history.

He believed that under Stein's leadership, Prussia had achieved something "qualitatively different" in history. The "reborn Prussia," he urged, was "a state of the new age, the first that began to mediate in a *positive* way the great contradiction into which the Revolution had polarized Europe."[34] The choice of terms is significant. "Positive mediation" is the same term that Droysen used to characterize the sixteenth-century Reformation. He now used it to suggest that Stein's reforms prefigured the second, social and political, reformation that was yet to come. This mediation would be institutional and practical. The "contradiction" to be mediated was between the older kind of "power" in which the monarch owned land and people and the newer kind, created in revolutionary France, in which ownership was vested in the populace. That is, Droysen wrote in the nearly obsequious language that he reserved for feats of Prussian statesmanship, the "firm, keenly perceptive, powerful" Stein "for the first time raised Prussia's vision far beyond and above the old dynastic politics to [one that was] German-national; annihilated as a power, it began to establish itself as a state." In explaining this development, Droysen again made significant use of the dual meaning of the German noun *Volk:* Under Stein, he claimed, "the *Volk* of Prussia began to see itself to be a *Volk* and to be German." In other words, the Prussian "people" became aware of itself both as a community and as a part of the German "nation." The Prussian reforms, then, were a step on the way to both statehood for Prussia and unification for Germany as a whole. In both aspects, the reforms led both to the empowerment of the citizenry and to a major increase in state power by virtue of the newly forged union of rulers and ruled. Droysen made this point when he argued that Stein began "that massive transformation . . . of all the internal political relationships (*Staatsverhältnisse*) that one describes as the first attempt to combine civil liberty (*bürgerliche Freiheit*), as England preserved it, with political energy (*staatliche Energie*), which the Revolution created, or more correctly to augment the full power of the throne through the citizenship of the nation (*Staatsbürgerlichkeit des Volkes*), to comprehend and form the state in the truth of its moral calling, to establish it in this its historical position."[35]

This analysis bore in two ways on creating a stable freedom by resolving the contradiction between the old monarchic and the new revolutionary practice. First, a prince could not own a self-conscious nation in the way that, in a "power," he owned a population. Second, and conversely, a nation that saw itself as such would possess a degree of internal unity that would prevent it from owning the governmental apparatus in the way that the atomized population of revolutionary France supposedly had done. In fact, and for Droysen this was the defining essence of statehood, there could no longer be a contradiction between the interests and wishes of the government and the governed. He consequently reserved an area of "civil liberty," of purely personal freedom, that stood apart from the state, but he could not accept the idea of rights held against the state or popular control over it. This outlook had powerful effects on his attitude toward constitutional projects during the meeting of the first Prussian United Diet in 1847 and during his membership in the National Assembly in 1848–49.

Droysen stated these ideas in synthetic form in a very important passage in which he tried to sum up the historical meaning of Stein's work. His language is almost rapturous, and his successive abstractions show how the state was the solution to the problem of freedom that was central in his theological reading of world history. The excitement that the passage shows is both a function of the religious conviction that underlies it and of Droysen's belief, of course untested by experience of his own in German politics, that freedom in the state would be incomparably satisfying to its future citizens. "The many and the one, the people and the state," he reflected, "that is the old contradiction." In Stein's Prussia, however, for the first but not the last time in history the units of those pairs were

no longer externally along side of one another, nor against each other, nor the one instead of the other, but the state is the nation's, the nation the state's (*der Staat ist des Volkes, das Volk des Staates*) in essential reciprocity, like the body and soul of a man, only incomparably richer than a merely organic life. For the nation is not merely the sum of its statistical strengths, not a barren monotony of political voices; the state is not the patrimony or . . . a common denominator of innumerable arbitrary privileges and traditions. Its basis and objective is the "will of free men," is the "royal emancipation of the moral man"; therein it desires its existence in law and history, just as it desires its final certainty in religion, its recognition in scholarship, its achievement in property . . . for it is that in man which is godly.[36]

The state, that is, would give freedom a durability that it had lacked in ancient Athens by suiting it to the requirements of human nature and, in so doing, would complete the work of the sixteenth-century Reformation in constitutional terms. To underscore that implication he included the brief quotations from Fichte and made the state into a kind of community of believers by identifying it with "that in man which is godly." He had made the same point, more briefly but in more explicit language, in 1843 when he described the state as the social and political version of Luther's "priesthood of all believers."[37]

Droysen's characterization of Stein's accomplishments was, of course, highly idealized and was as much the product of wishful thinking as of empirical research. In any case, the moral qualities to which he pointed would not be revealed by data in the normal sense of the term. The important point is that he was subjectively certain that he had discovered a historical truth of the first magnitude, one that explained the real significance of early-nineteenth-century Prussia and that also foretold what the completed Prusso-German state would be like. In this certitude, Droysen parted company with most European, though not most German, liberalism. In explaining the rise of the powers and, further, people's subsequent rejection of them in favor of statehood, he invoked what can be called market forces, namely the progressive role of the competing play of individual interests and preferences. In the state proper, however, this competition ceased or, more accurately, became confined to the limited and secondary zone of private interests. Now, as in earlier years, Droysen valued these interests and wanted them freed from unnecessary controls, but they had no direct bearing on the state, which, again, he identified with "that in man which is godly."[38] Under statehood, self-interested competition ceased, and freely willed acts in the common interest replaced it.

This is not to suggest that Droysen was an early totalitarian. After all, he not only took care to reserve an area for private rights but also insisted that the unity of the state could exist only because its citizens really would be in free agreement with each other, and, perhaps naïvely, he never suggested that this agreement would have to be compelled. Moreover, it was only common sense to acknowledge that private interests are often parochial and selfish. Droysen the Christian no doubt wanted to see humanity redeemed, and he imagined the state as the agent of redemption. Redemption in the form of public-mindedness must have seemed especially attractive in a Germany divided among competing sovereignties, sharply defined social orders and classes, East and West, North and South, and still distrustful confessions. It is also true that he thought of statehood, as anticipated under Stein and as it would be in the future, as a qualitative change in the human experience of history: the people, the nation, would at last really be one.

In view of the vast importance that Droysen attached to Stein's work, it is at first surprising to note the lack of rancor with which Droysen noted Stein's dismissal at Napoleon's command and his replacement with Hardenberg, who, in Droysen's opinion, made Prussia a "power" once more. His calm could be explained by piety, because his concept of the "right of history" logically required him to accept whatever happened as necessary and therefore good, but that cannot be the whole answer, because Droysen was not always psychologically capable of such acceptance. He could be accepting in this case for several reasons. First, he was dealing with events three decades in the past, so he did not have to deal with disappointed hopes. Second, he could take comfort in the belief that Stein had planted the "seeds" of a future and irreversible shift to statehood.[39] That was why he wanted to instruct his listeners and readers in Stein's accomplishments.

Finally, and most important, he could again use his consistent talent for finding the real good in seeming evil. Just as Prussia's defeat had made Stein's work possible, so Stein's defeat and, more generally, the inadequacies of the 1815 settlement made the ultimate triumph of statehood in Germany all the more certain. As long—but only as long—as eventual victory seemed inevitable, Droysen did not worry about a delay of a few decades in the solution of the problem that had haunted humanity, by his reckoning, since the sixth century B.C.E. His belief in the inevitability of victory rested on two factors in the 1815 settlement that he singled out as especially important: (1) the constitutional inadequacies and the arbitrary frontiers of the German Confederation and (2) Prussia's internal composition and disadvantageous position among the other great powers. These factors were specific instances of how the powers, once they had accomplished their necessary historical tasks, invited their own destruction and replacement with states. This specification, however, had the added advantage of allowing Droysen to point to current politics to show why Prussia, prodded by self-interest but acting for Germany, would perform the central task of world history by politically completing the Reformation.

Although Droysen detested the German Confederation, he took pleasure in its establishment and constitution for several reasons. First, its construction made unification easier to accomplish. Its founders had not tried to restore the Holy Roman Empire. On the contrary, and in a way that reproduced the constructive work of absolutizing monarchs two centuries earlier, its authors had cleared away the rubble of tiny sovereignties and quasi-sovereignties to create a smaller number of more or less enlarged monarchies and independent cities. In this respect alone, he thought their work "endlessly valuable to Germany."[40] Now there were fewer German polities to unify. "It was," he argued, "a great necessity that divided Germany and then decimated its countless little principalities and then so wonderfully . . . united so loose and irrational a compound of sovereign princes and free cities." This was not the founders' intention, but it was also not mere accident. The negotiators at Vienna in 1815 acted either with "cleverness or blindness, good or ill will, weakness of character or strength of will." The important point was that they were "only the means or instruments with which the necessity of our historical developments were realized." Not only had they made unification easier by simplifying Germany's internal frontiers; they had undertaken that simplification without the consent of the German populations and in defiance of historical tradition, so that their creation was entirely lacking in popularity and legitimacy. The confederation, he contended, marked "a deep cleavage between Germany and its great past with its thousand-year-old legal continuity."[41] This meant that the "new Germany of 1815" came into existence by the "right of history," with the further implication that "this most legitimate of all rights is just as applicable against this new creation, is just as empowered . . . to criticize its tendencies and principles."[42]

He believed that this criticism would lead to action and that Prussia would be the actor because, for historical reasons and especially because of the terms of the Vienna settlement of 1815, Prussia "was not a great power that, acting by itself and standing for itself, could make its interests and development of strength current against the other great powers."[43] That is, Prussia as reconstituted in 1815 could satisfy her own political interests only by acting in behalf of Germany as a whole, by merging her own identity with that of the larger German nation. In advancing this argument, Droysen seriously underrated the power and durability of Prussian particularism, although he was perceptive enough to note in 1847 that a Prussian constitution might divert Prussia from her national mission.[44] He did not, however, simply ignore the fact of Prussian self-esteem and self-interest. On the contrary, he emphasized the unsatisfactory nature of Prussia's position after 1815 in order to show that Prussia's rulers, when they finally took an unblinkered look at her situation, would work for national unification and statehood as a means of redress.

Droysen recurred to this argument frequently before and during the revolution of 1848, but he first and most fully presented it in 1844 in the article "The Political Position of Prussia," which he wrote for the political and historical section that Max Duncker edited for the *Halle'sche Allgemeine Literatur-Zeitung*. His central, and easily demonstrable, contention was that "size and geographical position" made Prussia the weakest of the five great powers (the others were England, France, Austria, and Russia). Within her 1815 frontiers, Prussia was the smallest of the five, and, equally damaging, her Rhineland province was cut off from her other provinces by intervening German states. The only remedy was to "identify fully with Germany." This meant, of course, unifying Germany, in which, at this point, Droysen almost certainly included Austria's German-speaking provinces. The benefits for Prussia were obvious: she would gain in territory and population and, so, equal or exceed the other great powers in strength. Droysen did not, however, recommend a Prussian hegemony over Germany. To have done so would have been to renounce his belief in the inevitability of true statehood in Germany, for the state properly so called could not be a result of conquest and compulsion. To achieve unification, Prussia needed the active consent of non-Prussian Germany, and, to gain that, Prussia had to transform herself, had, in a sense, to cease to be Prussia. Prussia had to become resolutely and consistently German; otherwise, "the small states' fear of Prussian hegemony" would contain her within her existing frontiers.[45] This meant more than advancing German interests, even when these differed from or conflicted with those of Prussia. Droysen also maintained that Prussia would "merge into" (*aufgehen*) Germany and, during unification, would cease to exist as a political unit. While the Hohenzollern became the national dynasty, Prussia's provinces would severally join the once-sovereign German states as component units of the German federal state.[46] This was asking a lot of the Hohenzollern monarchy, but Droysen felt confident in predicting this outcome.

Droysen had two historical reasons for thinking Prussia capable of dissolving herself in the national (and, rightly considered, her own) interest. First, there was the internal variety of Prussia that made her, he thought, a Germany in miniature. Droysen admitted that "the progressing inner development of the Prussian state," notable during the reign of Frederick the Great and under Stein, *would* have been a threat to national unification *if* it had led to "Prussianism" (*Preußenthum*). That is, Droysen also acknowledged the dangerous possibility that Prussia, like, France, might give a common political identity to originally diverse territories and populations, but he dismissed the danger because Prussia's populations were too diverse to be united on a subnational level, though he thought that they could be welded together through a common German nationality: "The East Germans and the Rhinelanders and the Saxons will be bound to each other only as German." Second, statehood was the coming thing and history showed that Prussia possessed "incomparable bases for state citizenship." It followed, Droysen believed, that Prussia would become a "state" in his sense of the term. Statehood, however, now entailed being a *Volk* in his rich sense of "nation" as well as "people." Germany was a nation, and Prussia was not; therefore, Prussia would fulfill her destiny by merging into Germany and thus creating a German "state."[47]

This demonstration, by itself, left unanswered the question of whether other German states would welcome the advances even of a transformed and self-annihilating Prussia. Despite his immense optimism, Droysen could not ignore this matter. He had, in fact, addressed it slightly earlier in his "German Letters" (1844). There he made his familiar point that in the present, it was necessary "to be a state" in order to possess "genuine sovereignty." "The German peoples (*Völker*) feel that," and, he continued, "they have the right to demand from the state to which they belong and for which they are supposed to be ready to sacrifice life and property . . . the kind of protection and power that would give them a claim to a noble, strong, proven nationality." Just as Prussia needed them, so they needed Prussia, for they would be content with nothing less than a unified Germany of the sort that only Prussia could create.[48] Prussia would transform herself in order to unify Germany, and the rest of Germany would welcome and follow her lead. Droysen was quite certain that all this would happen.

He could not be sure when it would happen, however, and in the meantime, he faced the difficult question of what to do while he waited for the inevitable to occur. He was not in a position to influence the day-to-day conduct of events because the political institutions of the German Confederation and its member states were inaccessible to him. Even if he had been interested in elective office, and there is no evidence to suggest that he was, the sorts of decisions that his predictions called for would have been taken by princes and governments that were not responsible to legislative bodies even where these existed. Nor, for the most part, were they interested in out-of-doors opinions, even when the expression of such opinions was legal. Of course, political opposition is possible under conditions more unfavorable than those faced by Droysen, and he could have carried the struggle underground, but that would have been unimaginable to him. He was unrevolutionary both by temperament and conviction. He feared and disliked disorder, and, in any case, his image of the future called for collaboration with the princes. He wanted to reconstruct, not destroy and replace. In practical terms, then, he could be active in one or both of two ways. When circumstances seemed favorable, as they did in the crises of 1844 and 1846 over Schleswig-Holstein or in 1847 during the sessions of the first Prussian United Diet, he tried to influence Prussian policy by writing to old acquaintances then rising in the Prussian bureaucracy. At all times, he did what he did best and most easily, namely, write and teach history in such a way as to prepare the present for its future tasks.

This latter tactic, which accounted for the greatest share of his energies, was more than just a grudging concession to reality. It was a logical conclusion of his interpretation of history, especially recent history, and rested on his often repeated claim that the state was an expression of morality and therefore required moral preparation. Admittedly, it was convenient to have theory require him to do the only thing he could do, something that he did well and liked doing, but that merely made the theory all the more convincing, because theories are persuasive to the degree that they correspond to practice. Droysen consequently sought both to tell Germans what their future held and to make them ready for that future through persuasive prediction. His clearest description of this task appeared in the opening issue of Adolf Schmidt's *Zeitschrift für Geschichtswissenschaft*. This was an appropriate forum for such a discussion, because Schmidt's journal in its four years of existence—it permanently suspended publication during the revolution of 1848—was the forerunner of the *Historische Zeitschrift*, founded in 1859 under Sybel's editorship, both in the sense of being a learned journal devoted entirely to history and in the sense of being outspokenly liberal and nationalist. Droysen used it to publish an open letter to the Hamburg publisher of Friedrich Bülau's *History of Germany from 1806 to 1830* (1842), in which he faulted Bülau for being too uncritical of confederation politics.

That topic was well suited to allow Droysen to expand on his sense of the historian's duties to the public or, to put it differently, to explain what he thought he was doing. Predictably, he laid heavy emphasis on the moral and, hence, political improvement that should result from the right kind of historical instruction. It was, he claimed,

a serious and sacred office to hold before princes and peoples the mirror of self-observation, to be the translator of history for them. There they shall perceive where they have erred and incurred guilt and how the beneficent hand of Providence has turned their error and guilt to the good. There they shall discover what they have irretrievably lost and to what they have a right, a claim, a hope. There they shall observe both their strength and their weakness in order to raise themselves with more serious purpose to the acknowledged calling of their historical position.[49]

Droysen's meaning is clear enough. By helping people understand the past, the historian helped them master the present and anticipate the future, for example, by making them see why the age of the "powers" was past and why Germany would be the first European nation to achieve true statehood. He also meant to show that the historian's task was basically a moral one because historical knowledge was a form of self-knowledge that suited the knower for moral action by both making the past intelligible and making the future visible and attractive. The historian hastened travel by providing the map.

The latter notion is by now quite familiar. Droysen had to show people where they were headed if they were to get there. His depiction of history as self-knowledge, which is conceptually distinct from his assertion of predictive certainty, also deserves some attention. It was a thesis that he would later develop in great and often compelling detail in his lectures on historical methodology. In this early form, however, it showed very clearly a quality that it never completely lost, namely, a strongly implied identification of historical study with the sacrament of confession. Along with pointing out the interventions of Providence, historians had to identify errors and other instances of guilt. In the passage just quoted, Droysen said nothing about cases in which individuals earned merit by doing the right thing at the right time. This is not surprising, because, first, in his accounts, great men usually did not really know what they were doing and, second, and more generally, because Droysen took sinfulness as the usual human condition. He therefore needed to discuss what historians typically could do for typical people.

Typical people, he believed, needed redemption, and redemption required confession and sincere penitence; he surely understood the commonplace Christian doctrine that unrepentant confession was no better than a failure to confess in the first place. Of course, this is not to say that he thought that a review of collective error and guilt was by itself sufficient for national redemption. There was no contradiction in supposing that although penitence does not always lead to redemption, there can be no redemption without penitence. This is also not to say that he was imposing spiritual exercises suited to individual believers on the whole German nation. In Droysen's scheme of things, to redeem Germany meant redeeming Germans. Otherwise, the German "state" could not be the political realization of the "priesthood of all believers."[50] Its citizens had to (and, with proper instruction, would learn how to) will the state before it came into existence and, thereafter, had willingly to subordinate themselves to it. Both acts of will required moral energy and, in order that this energy be expended properly, considerable moral preparation.

He did not limit this work of preparation to historians, indispensable though he thought their work to be. In 1846 he wrote a little known, though interesting, pamphlet entitled "On our Secondary School System" in an effort to occasion basic reforms in the gymnasia of Schleswig-Holstein, a subject of obvious interest to him as a professor at Kiel, which was mainly attended by their graduates. He recognized that these institutions, with

their heavy emphasis on Greek and Latin classics, existed mainly to prepare students for university study, but he denied that this should be their
sole, or even their chief, purpose. Education, he insisted, should prepare
future citizens.[51] That meant building character by teaching self-control
and methodical application. Droysen took these virtues so seriously that,
evidently in the belief that many adults in Schleswig-Holstein were unre-
deemed, he called for legislation to make parents responsible, under
penalty of law, for promoting "stern order, ruliness, legality in their children's lives."[52] In the same spirit, he called for a great reduction in teaching loads so that instructors could spend more time with individual
students.[53] Admittedly, much of his case reads like the understandable
self-pleading of a harried college teacher who does not altogether approve
of many of his students, but, as usual, Droysen was thinking in terms of a
larger moral objective. He wanted the educational system to make it possible for students "to attain, through instruction and cultivation, a particular intellectual and moral education, specifically that which may hold as
the general prerequisite for all who belong to the cultural estate (*Stand der
Gebildeten*)."[54]

- On the face of it, this recommendation seems apolitical enough. Droysen believed that there was and should be a cultural elite, and he advised
educational reforms that would improve the means by which students became members of it. In fact, his proposals were highly political because he
was trying to use educational reform to meet the moral and intellectual demands of statehood. The state needed highly educated citizens, at least a
leavening of them, and Droysen wanted its cultural elite to be recruited on
the basis of promise and talent, not just wealth or inherited social standing. This meant that the government should pay the tuition of deserving
students who could otherwise not afford gymnasial study.[55] In making
that recommendation, Droysen conjoined a liberal belief in careers open to
talent with autobiographical memory. His own career, for instance, would
have been impossible had he not been able to study on a scholarship. Relatedly, he wanted urban and rural schools to be merged so that students
would grow up thinking of themselves as members of a single community.[56] Apart from making the community solidary, this measure was in
principle egalitarian inasmuch as it was designed to eliminate, at least for
the educated, inherited social distinctions. His suggestions, then, were political at least in the general sense of creating a basic precondition for political life as he envisioned it, namely, the existence of an educated elite
recruited solely on the grounds of merit.

They were also political in a more specific sense. Droysen was an ed-
ucator who took education very seriously. Combined with his conception
of political life, that basic attitude made him think of simply going to

school as a political act. A child's entrance into school, he explained, opened "for him a kind of public life (*öffentliches Leben*)," with the result that school was "for youth what the state is for adults, only more directly intervening, more specifically leading, working up cultivation and freedom that shall eventually benefit the state."[57] Given this assumption, it was entirely logical for him to insist that the moral experience of schooling was more important than the acquisition of ideas and information, though he did not propose a relaxing of academic standards. If one can trust the memory of one of his former students at Kiel, Droysen tried to pattern his own university teaching according to these standards.[58]

Droysen's uninterrupted seriousness should not lead one to suppose that he was opposed on principle to human happiness, though it is a measure of his seriousness that he actually tried to use historical instruction to demonstrate the need for human enjoyment or "eudaemonism." He saw this quality as central to life in the state and based this claim on his larger interpretation of modern history as a progressive reconciliation between Christian religiosity and life in this world. In his "Theology of History" (1843), for example, he argued that historical understanding had to inform faith in order that both might "collaborate as much as may be in the great work of the [human] race, 'leading creation back to the creator,' as the old mystical saying has it." To be sure, this task was part antiworldly: "Between God and us is the world. It is a matter of overcoming the world." But overcoming meant taming and appropriating, not despising and rejecting. Asceticism, he claimed, had not worked in the Middle Ages and would not work now. Droysen therefore called for "searching and shaping, comprehending and using," and he acknowledged that what he delicately termed "eudaemonistic necessities" would and should come into play. "Not now, not ever," he insisted, "will a moral system of ethics appear or Christian morals transcend the Law if eudaemonism does not acquire its right and position; heed the word of the Apostle to give the flesh its due."[59] The fleeting reference to St. Paul, admittedly, suggests that Droysen made this concession with some reluctance.

Droysen did not limit his political use of historical instruction to general sketches of the future or to moral education of the sorts just discussed. His appointment as professor at Kiel gave him the opportunity, because Kiel in the 1840s was the chief theater for contention between Danish and German nationalism and the problems of Danish constitutional reform and laws of succession created crises over the duchies in 1844, 1846, and 1848. Droysen held pronounced opinions about the prevalence of German nationality in the duchies, and these crises seemed to him promising opportunities for Prussian leadership in Germany. In order to make sense of his thoughts and actions, however, it is first necessary to review the situation in the duchies.

The Duchies Schleswig-Holstein

DENMARK

Kongeaa River

Flensburg

SCHLESWIG

Baltic

Sea

North

Sea

Eider   *River*

Kiel

Rendsburg

HOLSTEIN

Elbe River

Hamburg

N

| 0 | | 50 km. |
| 0 | | 30 mi. |

jmh

From the perspective of ethnography, the conflict in Schleswig-Holstein is just one of many continual conflicts caused by failure of historic and linguistic frontiers to correspond. The population of Holstein, situated between the Elbe and Eider Rivers, was almost wholly German speaking, but there were also Danish speakers, the so-called Eider Danes, as far south as the Eider River. The duchies' leading city, Kiel, was linguistically mixed. Schleswig, extending north from the Eider to the Kongeaa River, was German speaking in majority, but with a sprinkling of Danish speakers even in the south and almost solidly Danish speaking in the north (which became part of Denmark in the Treaty of Versailles in 1919). It has seemed well to use the terms *German speaking* and *Danish speaking* rather than *German* or *Danish* because the distinction was purely linguistic until, in the nineteenth century, national consciousness intruded and many in the duchies felt the need to choose sides. Of course, national consciousness was not identical with political consciousness: Uwe Jens Lornsen (d. 1838), for example, won a following in the 1830s for a liberal constitution for a liberal Schleswig-Holstein existing in binational independence rather on the model of the one then being framed for newly independent and linguistically divided Belgium. Within ten years of Lorensen's death, however, such a dream seemed inconceivable because of the growing clash of rival nationalisms. The first notes were sounded on the Danish side by the Kiel publicists Christian Flor and Christian Paulsen (who, interestingly, came from a German-speaking home in Flensburg and studied at Göttingen in Germany before going to Norway and becoming passionately Scandinavian in outlook).[60] In accepting a position in Kiel in order to support his young family, then, Droysen coincidentally chose to work in a place in which teaching German history was a profoundly political act and in which his audiences, largely local, were really interested in politics.

There was a lot to interest them. Not only did political and linguistic frontiers not correspond; that was a common situation even in western Europe. The constitutional status of the duchies was also confused, notoriously so, in consequence of dynastic inheritance and traditional legalities. This confusion had four aspects. First, the duchies were under the rule of the king of Denmark, at this time Christian VIII, who was by personal union the duke of each duchy. Second, and peculiar to Schleswig-Holstein, the duchies were legally inseparable—*op ewig ungedeelt* in the local German dialect—but occupied quite different positions in public law. Holstein was a member state in the German Confederation, whereas Schleswig was simply a duchy that happened to have a German majority and which, in the nature of things, was a possible candidate for integration into the Danish monarchy. Relatedly, Danish nationalists thought of both duchies as part of the *Helstat*, the Danish term for the polity of Denmark proper, its colonies, and Iceland.[61] Thinking of the problem in terms of the *Helstat* had the advantage of preserving the link of the duchies to Denmark without tinkering with their constitutional peculiarities. Third, Christian VIII was old and had no sons. He had a designated heir, who became Frederick VII in 1848, but Frederick inherited through a female. That was not a difficulty for Denmark proper, but in German states, including the duchies, the Salic Law prevailed, and this law forbade female succession. Germans argued, in terms that of course did not persuade the Danish authorities or the Danish nationalists, that on Christian's death the duchies should pass to his nearest male heir in the German Augustenberg family. German nationalists, however dim their private views of dynastic inheritance, liked this solution because it would keep the territories German. A fourth aspect must also be mentioned. These legal niceties were not only a subject for dispute between Germans and Danes. Denmark was on the southern shore of the strategic straits of Skagerrak and Kategat between the North Sea and the Baltic. This meant that Great Britain and Russia were deeply interested in Denmark's fate and, by extension, the fortunes of its monarch.

By 1844 tempers had risen on both sides, thanks in part to Droysen's growing influence among young German intellectuals in the duchies.[62] The first of several crises occurred in October 1844 as a result of a book, *The State Inheritance of Schleswig-Holstein and connected Lands,* ably written by the young lawyer Karl Samwer, a student and friend of Droysen's. Samwer used detailed constitutional history to strengthen the succession claims of the Duke of Augustenberg. This promised an alliance between traditional German princes and the newer German nationalism and, therefore, thoroughly alarmed the Danes. In response, Algreen Ussing, the Mayor of Copenhagen, moved in the Schleswig Estates at Roskilde that King Christian issue a declaration that the *Helstat* was indivisible and the duchies subject to the same law of succession as the rest of the monarchy. The failure of the royal official A.S. Orsted to decry the motion made many observers, Droysen among them, wrongly conclude that the monarchy was colluding with the Roskilde Estates to absorb the duchies into Denmark. Droysen was prominently active in the public outcry that followed.

Droysen's immediate response was to draft and publish a piece entitled "Kiel Address," in which, surely insincerely, he claimed to speak as a loyal subject who had his sovereign's best interests at heart and argued that King Christian should leave the duchies' traditional legal status intact.[63] He really meant that if they could not yet be detached from Denmark, they should certainly not be detached from Germany, and his real fear was a unilateral Danish change in their inheritance law that would have the former effect. Predictably, he did not rely solely on the impression that his address might make in Denmark. On 18 November he wrote to acquaintances in Prussia and enclosed copies of the address in his letters. To Johannes Schulze, now highly placed in the *Kultusministerium* (so called because it dealt with educational, religious, and cultural affairs), he offered specific suggestions for Prussian policy toward Denmark and remarked on his own good fortune in being able to "take part in such major state actions."[64] To Justus von Gruner, now a member of the Prussian delegation to the Confederate Assembly at Frankfort, he offered the same advice, namely, that Prussia should oppose any change in the duchies' status, and boasted about the deep impression that his "Kiel Address" had made on Germans in the duchies.[65]

In 1845 he explained more fully what Prussia should do in his essay "The Political Position of Prussia," in which he demonstrated why Prussian self-interest would require her unselfishly to embrace the German cause. For example, in a letter written shortly before the crisis, he had claimed that Prussia could exchange weakness for strength only by assuming the leadership of *Kleindeutschland*, a term that still referred not to Germany without Austria but to the little states of Germany such as Schleswig-Holstein, and concluded that such leadership of "the downtrodden lesser powers [was] a first and major step toward national unification."[66] His letters to Schulze and Gruner expressed the confidence that Prussia now had the chance she needed. He was puzzled and then angered when she did not seize it. He complained that nothing was happening and expected that, some time soon, decisive changes would occur. In that spirit he wrote from Kiel in 1845 to his friend Wilhelm Arendt: "Here, like everywhere else in Germany, the situation is now stagnating in intolerable fashion; or, more correctly, it is brewing under water."[67]

Although he clearly believed that it was in Prussia's interest and power to work for the duchies, he seems this time not to have been very hopeful that she would actually do so. In 1844 he had been almost ebullient, but he now wrote to Arendt: "Prussia in particular—and the decision again depends on Prussia—is far too backward in her inner development and liberation to take a step from which she retreated in 1815 when Germany was also loudly and freshly ready to join her."[68] He was, therefore, more or less resigned to the prospect of Prussian inaction and the consequent loss at least of Schleswig, though, in his characteristic celebration of the future benefits of moral education and with an embarrassing display of self-importance, he consoled himself with the thought that this loss would ultimately strengthen Germany through the example of men like himself remaining at their embattled posts until the end.[69]

By the time conditions in the duchies became settled again in early 1845, the Holstein Estates at Itzhoe had passed a declaration to counter the Ussing Motion and German nationalism in the duchies had grown both in numbers and fervor while—liberal, middle-class movement that it originally was—it formed a closer alliance with conservative German landown-ers.[70] The calm that returned in 1845 was temporary and was broken as soon as the Holstein Estates reconvened in 1846. King Christian had not originally welcomed the Ussing Motion, but, alarmed at the agitation that followed it, he now sought to subdue German nationalism by taking a firm stand against the Augustenberg succession. The Holstein Estates met on 15 July 1846, and Christian sent them his Open Letter, stating that a female succession was legitimate in Schleswig and many parts of Holstein and that the duchies would remain undivided whatever happened to the suc-cession in the rest of Holstein.[71] Droysen's response to this turn in events was twofold.

First, taking advantage of the relative leisure of studying chiefly mod-ern German history since the medievalist Georg Waitz's appointment to the Kiel faculty in 1843, Droysen had immersed himself in Schleswig-Holstein's tangled legal history. He was, therefore, able to meet the crisis of 1846 by providing most of the contents of the ponderous *Public Law and the Law of Inheritance in the Duchy of Schleswig,* though other professors at Kiel made contributions and received credit as coauthors.[72] If nothing else, the work is a monument to his erudition in a difficult area of a legal his-tory and testimony as well to his willingness to change tactics when cir-cumstances warranted. After all, by the terms of his concept of the "right of history," the mass of legal precedent that he uncovered had only anti-quarian interest. Nonetheless, he was happy to argue from precedent when precedent bolstered his case. Second, and with the dynamic "right of history" in mind, he again tried to spur Prussia to action by pointing to the vast opportunities that events in the duchies opened for her.[73] He was, of course, interested not only in the fate of the duchies but also in the national consequences of Prussian action on their behalf. He argued that Prussian intervention would not only prevent Schleswig's integration into Denmark; it would also lead Prussia to abandon her un-German foreign policy and her bureaucratic absolutism in domestic affairs.[74] In his view of modern history, those changes would be major advances toward national unification and statehood.

Despite the resignation he had felt at Prussian inaction in 1845, and de-spite Prussian inaction throughout the 1846 crisis, his underlying confi-dence in Prussia remained strong. At least, in January 1848, when the new king Frederick VII published the January Rescript, which proposed once again to change the status of the duchies, Droysen was inexplicably opti-mistic. He again urged firm action on Prussia, and his letter to Gruner, now promoted to Really Privy Legation Counsellor in the Prussian Foreign Ministry, suggests that he expected Prussia to act this time.[75] Perhaps this was because, with the Salic Law to invalidate Frederick's succession, he thought the legal grounds for intervention too compelling for Prussia to

resist. Inasmuch as domestic events in Prussia in 1847 had successively inflated and deflated his hopes, his optimism is remarkable.

His reactions to the convening of the diet provide a good index to his
political hopes and fears in 1847 and also provide a chance to see him
trying to grapple with immediate and practical politics that lacked the
geographical immediacy events in Schleswig-Holstein provided him.
Moreover, exciting events were now occurring in Prussia, and in Droysen's scheme of things, these might be foretokens that history was at last
ready to complete itself. He felt the need to show people just what parts
they would have to play when the curtain eventually went up on German
statehood. After all, it followed from his theory that true statehood was
possible only when people actively wanted it, and he made it his business
to instill in them the necessary desire. Without such preparation, which he
presumably saw as itself a historical necessity, he feared a very unhappy
outcome. Characteristically, Droysen arrived at these conclusions in reference and response to specific, current events. In February 1817, Frederick
William convened a united diet (*Landtag*), that is, a joint convention of the
individual diets of the seven Prussian provinces. The king's general purpose was to ease the growing discontent in Prussia by making a constitutional gesture without granting a constitution. More specifically, he
needed money for a railway to East Prussia and, so, sought the diet's backing in order to obtain loans at favorable rates. This tame, if interesting, gesture raised liberal hopes, which the monarchy systematically disappointed
throughout the summer and autumn of 1847. Droysen's hopes, too, went
through this boom-and-bust cycle.

Thus, in an unpublished manuscript written in the autumn of 1847
after it had become clear that Prussian United Diet would not accomplish
very much, Droysen reflected on the inevitability of "further development"
(*weitere Entwicklung*) and concluded:

Not as if it would not occur if one did not want [it]; rather, it would come unbid-
den like a thief in the night or even with the fury of elemental forces, sooner, later,
certainly irresistibly; destroying in order to create anew, for that is the nature of
the vital. To want it means nothing other than to recognize what is germinally
present, . . . than to recognize in advance where the general movement of affairs
wishes to move from the here-and-now, to follow freely and consciously the path
along which one would forcibly be dragged, not to retard or interrupt the dangerous tumult of movement, but to rule and control, to change those blind forces into
victorious powers.[76]

In this passage, Droysen did more than reiterate his central contention that
the historical process was both ineluctable and predictable. He also offered
another, more novel, idea in the form of an urgent warning. A major his-

torical transformation, he believed, was about to occur, whether or not people desired and expected it. This created two possibilities. If they were foresightful and welcomed what would in any case occur, they could control progress and make its result an altogether happy one. If, on the contrary, they ignored or, worse, resisted historical change, it would occur anyway, but with otherwise avoidable violence and destruction. His statement of these possibilities, his hope for the first and fear of the second, is yet another manifestation of his painful attempt to forward revolutionary change without revolution, without violence and upheaval. It also marks the first, at least the first recorded, instance of uncertainty when events failed to conform to his expectations. In 1844 and 1846, Prussia had already failed, in the struggle over the duchies Schleswig-Holstein, to do what he thought Prussia had to do. This did not necessarily mean that his predictions were wrong. Possibly, those in power in Berlin did not yet understand what history expected of them. Still, Droysen worried that such misunderstanding might prevent timely and peaceful change. Certainly it was hard to imagine creating the state in his sense of the term during a civil war. To understand more clearly the source of this anxiety, it is necessary to look closely at Droysen's excitement when the first Prussian United Diet met in 1847.

Although Droysen was not impressed by the February Patent that called the diet into session and, like many other Germans, he was disappointed by Frederick William's address to its opening session, at first he thought the united diet was the start of rapid progress. By April 1847 he had expressed delight at the "surprising speed" with which the delegates had acquired "bearing, purpose, method." "However little has been achieved," he commented in a letter on 22 April, "the main thing is that a moral force is gathering there and becoming conscious of itself as a result of which the Austrianized Prussia of 1819 and 1830 is no longer possible." That is, the changed consciousness that preceded major historical transformation had already formed or was now forming. This was his basic appraisal of the diet. He valued it less for its actual achievements (which, given its narrowly circumscribed powers and the king's stubbornness were bound to be few) than for the irreversible precedent it set and the further progress it promised. Once again, as briefly in 1844, he thought he was witnessing the beginning of the "most comprehensive reshapings of domestic and foreign policy for first Prussia and then all of Germany."[77]

He developed this estimation of events, along with other major ideas, in "The Prussian Constitution," a lengthy review article he wrote for the *Halle'sche Allgemeine Literatur-Zeitung* at the solicitation of Max Duncker, its political and historical editor.[78] In it Droysen repeated themes already found in his letters and remarked happily on the political maturity that the delegates had shown so far. He expanded on this idea by claiming that Germany and Europe as a whole were impressed by the "amazing spectacle of these proceedings;—amazing not only on account of the quickly acquired exercise of parliamentary skill or on account of the wealth of political sureness and insight that the speeches and votes proclaim; amazing above all in the way that the crown and the estates deal with each other, I may say [in] the political ethics that have never more happily dealt with a more difficult task."[79] Droysen made this observation as evidence of the readiness of both sides, the king and the delegates, to cooperate in the furtherance of necessary historical development.[80] In other words, he already found signs of the reciprocal trust on which statehood had to be founded.

He therefore thought that he discerned in the sessions a "silent force of affairs" (*Stille Gewalt der Dinge*) that was "more powerful than all intention, all knowledge, all humanity." That force, he continued, worked quietly "in the hearts of men" to produce major changes in history, "and where it works, there is God's hand, as in the first bloom of spring, as in the first light of dawn—Who will stop it?" In short, Providence was at work. Droysen gave a clear indication of the magnitude of the change that he thought was in prospect when he criticized his fellow historian Georg Gottfried Gervinus for stressing too strongly the need for legal continuity. Without abandoning his deep dislike of revolution, Droysen pointed out that "no flower has yet bloomed without tearing the bud; there is no becoming without abandoning the form that once enchained, and those are not the worst moments in the lives of individuals and nations when the fullness of their most particular life breaks through the shells that had value and purpose only as long as they protected the life that was coming into being."[81] Without using the term expressly, Droysen was invoking his idea of the "right of history" for, appropriately, one of those rare moments when breaks in formal legality were necessary for major historical progress.

He evidently thought that a breakthrough into true statehood was in near prospect, for he invoked the characteristic themes of his analysis of world history to claim that history, working through the diet, would soon

make all state citizens into priests and shrines of the public good and would advance law and order by making it reborn in every free individual will that fulfils it as its own genuine will. The state will no longer be because it is but because every instant the wills of free men justify and assure the fact that it exists; the state will no longer be the privilege or the property of the crown, still less the accidental burden borne by men and lands thrown together . . . Prince and people, crown and land, government and governed: all of them together are under the state, are organs and functions of the spirit that lives and works in it, that Hellenic antiquity regarded as the divinity of the state.[82]

In view of those conclusions, his excited optimism is entirely understand-able. He had in mind more than incremental progress toward a still distant goal. He thought that Prussia and Germany were on the verge of the true statehood that he had long thought to be the necessary outcome of history. He tempered his joy, however, with a fear that someone might uncom-prehendingly compromise the great work at the last moment.

Specifically, he warned against giving Prussia the wrong kind of constitution. As far back as 1843 he had inveighed against the "damned error" of using the separation of powers as a "guarantee for the constitu-tion," because he believed that "the essence of the state" lay in its "cohe-siveness" (*Einheitlichkeit*). The object was not to protect the ruled from the rulers but to have the entire citizenry join the "hereditary prince" in the determination and conduct of state policy.[83] He proceeded from these premises to a sweeping attack on all written guarantees as contradicting the essential quality of statehood: "Not the people, not the citizenry is the state, not the sovereign, nor the collectivity of state servants; but all of them in their mutual activities and reciprocal effects compose the vital ex-istence of the idea of the state in the way that body and life, will and knowledge jointly are the existence of the idea for which a man lives."[84] In 1843 these were only propositions; in 1847 Droysen used them to com-ment on current practice.

Because he thought that history conferred its own right, Droysen was not very interested in guarantees merely legal in nature. Furthermore, he was afraid that excessive legalism might result in a defective Prussian con-stitution, one that contradicted the principle of statehood. He did not, however, attack law itself, and he therefore remarked: "Let us understand ourselves correctly. Law is much, infinitely much, but not everything (*Das Recht is viel, unendlich viel, aber nicht alles*)." The wholly unsatisfactory feu-dal monarchy of the Middle Ages, he pointed out, had also been a "state of law" (*Rechtsstaat*).[85] Good laws had a place, an important place, in the new state, but they must not divide rulers from ruled. Contemporary Eu-rope, he claimed, wavered between the "monarchical principle" and "pop-ular sovereignty," both of which sought to reduce the state to "a mere legal relationship." In the former, monarchs tried to guarantee their powers and prerogatives, whereas in the latter the people sought legal assurances for their rights against, and their control over, the government. Droysen re-jected both attempts. He insisted that "Prussia's development—and, in this as in all that noblest and best, let it be Germany's leader—must [lead to] a different relationship."[86] That relationship had to be one of mutual trust rather than legal guarantees: "God willing, juristic law is not the final instance for the Prussian state and its future; in bitter days, the king and people set up another holy bond between themselves."[87]

These statements show that Droysen's contempt for legal guarantees was an integral part of his larger case for Prussian and German exceptionalism. By avoiding the opposed errors of monarchism and popular sovereignty, the Prusso-German state would be qualitatively different from any other European polity. That is, its ability to abide by a constitution without formal guarantees would show a strength of moral character to be found nowhere else. These claims show a remarkable degree of historical confidence, but their emphatic reiteration suggests anxiety. What was Droysen worried about? He may have been afraid that a constitutionalized Prussia would become a state apart from the larger Germany and would therefore turn away from the task of unification.[88] This was probably part of his motivation, because in "The Prussian Constitution" he included a strong paragraph warning about the dangers of Prussian selfishness and specifically asking Prussia not to pursue unification in a spirit of aggrandizement, though he qualified this advice by admitting that in the past God had usually worked through self-interested agents.[89] This was probably not his chief motivation, however, because his objections to constitutional guarantees were of long standing and because his surprise in the late summer of 1848 at the appearance of Prussian separatism was too great simply to be a reappearance of an old worry.

He was more likely afraid that, at least for the present, Prussia might turn out not to be exceptional. Despite his markedly favorable comments on the quality of the diet's sessions, he was surely aware that those meetings were often acrimonious and that demands for guarantees against the throne were popular. The recurrent inability of delegates and representatives of the king's government to agree might mean that Prussia was just like any other European power. In those circumstances it was only sensible for Droysen to remind Prussia of her higher calling. A decision to do so did not imply a lack of faith in the basic soundness of his predictions. He believed that Prussia would seize the opportunity to unify Germany, but he could not say when she would seize it. It was reasonable to worry that she might now be missing an opportunity. Moreover, it was, by the terms of his predictions, the task of historians like himself to make Prussians aware of their historical responsibility, in this case a responsibility not to frame a legally cluttered constitution.

That was certainly his attitude by the autumn. In an unpublished essay entitled "Prussia and Germany," he both roundly condemned constitutional guarantees as contrary to the real essence of statehood and tried to demonstrate the need to continue and complete the "historical development" begun the previous spring. To a degree, this essay is the complement to his earlier piece, "The Prussian Constitution." There he warned against obstructing progress through an overly watchful constitutionalism; here he inveighed against obstruction caused by too-jealous a defense of monarchic prerogative.[90] In both essays the message was the same: the letter of the law must not be allowed to compromise the spirit of statehood. He also offered the same inducements for trust and cooperation: just as the people would be freer without formal guarantees, so the real power of the king and his government would increase to the extent that he shared it with the people of Prussia and Germany as a whole. Progressive change, he assured his readers, was the normal content of history, and this sharing of power was the next necessary instance of that change.[91]

Droysen characteristically supported this contention with historical illustration. He pointed to the upswing in German political expectations and to the general improvement in the quality of Prussian politics that resulted from Frederick William's ascent to the Prussian throne in 1840. He claimed to be especially moved by the king's appeal to his people for support.[92] This was transparently an attempt to associate the entire reign with liberalization and to show that convening the diet was a continuation of, not a risky departure from, long-term and well-advised policies. Relatedly, Droysen argued that the king, far from having come into conflict with his people, now more than ever had them on his side. In other words, timely concessions to historical necessity strengthened rather than weakened the monarchy. These concessions, however, were not cases of surrendering a little to save a lot. Droysen insisted that they would actually improve the situation of the monarchy. He chose a telling metaphor to underscore this claim. A steamship, he urged, hoisted its sails only when the wind behind it was blowing faster than the ship could travel under its own power.[93] The ship, of course, was the monarchy, and the wind from the stern was progressive public opinion, which would actually help the monarchy navigate its set course. Droysen added a warning to this promise. If the monarchy did not accommodate itself to inevitable change, it would be overborne amid needless violence.[94]

The present tasks of the Prussian monarchy, therefore, were utterly clear to Droysen. It had to use the diet to gain the trust of the rest of Germany as a means to introducing constitutional government in his sense of the term to Germany as a whole. In its dealings with the diet, it had to remember certain fundamental facts of history, facts that he had often before included in his speeches and writings. In negative terms, it had to acknowledge the futility of simply defending outdated privileges, because no monarch, not even Louis XIV, had possessed really "unlimited" authority.[95] Furthermore, it had to bear in mind the precariousness of Prussia's position within its 1815 frontiers. Only half the population had binding "historical memories" of Hohenzollern rule, and the population as a whole lacked identical material interests and a common religious confession.[96] This situation could be improved only by bringing true state-hood to Germany.

Late in the essay he tried to identify the major advantages that would accrue to the monarchy if it followed this course:

The value of a constitution is to be recognized in the government that its brings into existence, because the strongest best fulfils the tasks assigned to it. But this strength does not consist in the arbitrary power that it exercises, in the acts of self-will that it perpetrates, even less in the monies that it can heap up in the treasury, in the masses of men that it trains for war and accustoms to blind obedience, in the omnipotence of an officialdom entrusted with everything. . . . The strength of the government is the greater, the more deeply it recognizes the true task of the state, to satisfy which is its function . . . the more surely according as the governed see that it really values and protects all strengths, energies, and interests.[97]

This was Droysen at his best and his worst, his most and least convincing. Indeed, the passage nicely shows the tenuousness of his prerevolutionary formulations. He promised to the king and his government a vast access in power if they surrendered their current position in the interest of eventual national unification. That was to ask them to join him in an imposing leap of faith. They had to believe that he had correctly interpreted all previous history and that his consequent predictions were sound. As self-3interested historical agents, they had trustingly to lay down tangible and immediate powers in exchange for a new kind of strength that, they were to believe, would be theirs after the historical Prussian state had ceased to exist. Droysen must have had some sense of the magnitude of this request. Prussia was still ruled by the men who had disappointed him over the duchies in 1844 and 1846, and there would have been no point in writing either of his 1847 essays if he had assumed that Prussia's governors were ready unreservedly to play their parts. He plainly believed, however, that they would be ready when they had to be ready, and he seemed unaware that he was submitting his most cherished notions about the national future to a pragmatic test that they were bound to fail.

3

Parallel Careers:
Duncker, Haym, Sybel

While Droysen moved from ancient into modern history and used his historical expertise to supply predictive analysis and advice in the crises over Schleswig-Holstein and in observing the abortive convening of the Prussian United Diet, his future allies and collaborators—Duncker, Haym, and Sybel—were also beginning their careers as scholars and as partisans. Their early works show neither the theoretical grasp nor the historical range of Droysen's, both because they were younger than he and, frankly, because they could not match Droysen, who possessed one of the greatest historical imaginations of all times. Their early ideas demand study, nonetheless, because of the light they shed on the mentality of prerevolutionary Protestant liberalism in Germany and because their early ideas make intelligible their actions and reactions in 1848 and 1849 and, consequently, the convergences of their careers with Droysen's in the creation of the Prussian School. Duncker and Haym at times worked together, but they also often worked alone. Sybel still worked by himself. Their careers before 1848, therefore, are best studied one by one.

Max Duncker

Max Duncker was the first, after Droysen, to effect this merger. He, too, had an excited early encounter with what he understood of Hegel's philosophy. Duncker, in fact, was personally acquainted with Hegel because of the latter's recurrent social and business visits to his publisher father's home, and, at the University of Berlin, he heard his lecture series "Philosophy of History" and "History of Philosophy" before Hegel's death in 1831.[1] The immediate effect was on Duncker's inaugural dissertation on Germanic origins, which Haym rightly described as mainly "philosophy, Hegelian philosophy."[2] Like Droysen, like many in his generation, Duncker soon persuaded himself that he had broken with Hegel, and this persuasion was an important part of his mental make-up in this period. As with Droysen, however, it is not clear that Duncker saw things quite as Hegel did, and anyone reading Duncker's works from the 1830s and 1840s would admit that he continued to view matters through more or less Hegelian concepts. The lasting effect of his encounter with Hegel's system, then, was a vision of historical progress that let Duncker interrelate past historical periods so as to make sense of history and to permit confident projection of the future.

Obviously, these tasks came easily to Duncker, whose education differed from Droysen's in several respects. Duncker also attended and enjoyed Boeckh's lectures in classical philology, but his real interest, even as a student, was in history as historians, not philologists, taught it.[3] The first person to take a degree in history from a German university, Duncker attended Friedrich Wilken's lectures and historical exercises, heard Ranke's lectures, and was a member of Ranke's Historical Seminar for one semester (the normal length of membership in those years).[4] In addition, he worked closely with the literary historian (and distant relation) Johann Loebell when, during his half year of compulsory military service in an ulan regiment, he was stationed near Bonn where Loebell taught.[5] Duncker continued, however, to view the data of history in terms of preconceived ideas that he borrowed and adapted from Hegel.

Hegel's influence is, for example, clearly evident in the preface that Duncker wrote in 1836 to the three volumes that he edited, under Loebell's guidance and for the family publishing house, of the twelve-volume *World History* by Karl Friedrich Becker. His statements there would probably have irritated Hegel himself had he read them, because they greatly oversimplified his arguments and because, naturally enough, Duncker stressed only those parts of Hegel's philosophy that served his purposes. He wanted to show history to be an orderly spiritual process that moved toward a goal, and he valued historical evidence only insofar as it helped him do that. For that reason, he in effect apologized to his readers for including so much information in the sections that he edited. An evolving "spirit" (*Geist*) was at work in and behind the details of history, and the development of this spirit was the real story the historian had to tell. Duncker insisted, however, that a historian had also to give evidence for, and examples of, its workings, even though he preferred to display "the deeper content of the facts and the essence of the reigning ideas" in place of "multifold reasonings, considerations, and evidential relationships."[6] The presentation of evidence, then, was an inconvenient yet necessary means to a more important end because it allowed historians to explicate the past in context by studying one age in relation to the periods that preceded and succeeded it.[7]

In practice, this meant that Duncker would supply information, but only in order to illustrate the onward evolution of the spirit. Rather than inferring his claims from evidence, he used evidence to define and detail his claims. To take a case in point, he excused his decision to eke out the meager information on medieval constitutional history that Becker himself provided because, despite the "difficulty bordering on the impossibility" of an inexpert reader thoroughly understanding it, constitutional history was especially suited to "permitting the inner life and drive of nations (*innere Leben und Treiben der Völker*) to emerge."[8] Those, of course, were what really interested him. In a related instance, he promised to deal at length with what he defined as "important events," for which he had a more or less technical definition. These were those "points in history at which the spirit, after it has lain in concealment and worked in silence . . . suddenly breaks forth and brings new instruments and tendencies to the light of day, or, strengthened in one and played out in another, now extinct direction, raises one nation (*Volk*) and lowers another [and] steps into the next stage of its development." Events of such magnitude, he claimed, showed so much about the course and purpose of history that it was "necessary to display the entire breadth of the phenomenon in order to bring before the eyes of the reader the spiritual content, the leading ideas, and the driving forces (*geistige Inhalt, leitende Ideen, treibende Kräfte*) not in abstract translation into thoughts but in the fullness and power of their concrete immediacy."[9] He wanted to track historical progress. This required including a lot of evidence, but it also made the evidence secondary in importance. The function of evidence was to illustrate abstractions. That changed in Duncker's later writing.

By 1845, Duncker, still intent on tracking and projecting tendencies in history, had become rather more empiricist in principle, though the change was not complete and was more evident to him than to anyone reading his statements with care. Perhaps teaching history for two years at the University of Halle made him skeptical of generalizations not induced from evidence. It is also possible that his recent intellectual friendship with the young philosophy student Rudolf Haym was a cause of this change, as their association dates from the period immediately following Haym's reading of Ludwig Feuerbach's works under the guidance of an older colleague at the Berlin gymnasium where he had taught for a year. In that year, Haym finally rejected Hegel's system in favor of a more empirical philosophy and may have persuaded Duncker of the need to adopt the new philosophical fashion that Feuerbach introduced.[10] In any case, Duncker now earnestly and energetically asserted the need for historical empiricism. The change was real: in 1836 Duncker had written about data as a regrettable necessity. Now, in 1845, he treasured information, and he described treasuring it as the promising aspect of the present age.

The earliest existing evidence of Duncker's new outlook appears in a letter that he wrote to Droysen on 11 February 1845. There he congratulated Droysen on the second and final volume of his *History of Hellenism* and professed his own deep respect for the close scrutiny of empirical detail. Only in that way, he explained, was it possible to detect and trace the movements of the "spirit" through time. Duncker developed his case with appropriate examples. Thus, he explained that he traced the evolutions of battles not because of their intrinsic interest, but because they let him show "the spirit triumphantly penetrating the combatants." Similarly, he studied "great men" closely because "they stand at the peak of events, and in their spirits appear more or less entire series of the strivings and capacities, indeed the very particularities, of nations and periods (*Völker und Perioden*)."[11] Although Duncker was no doubt too intent on finding pattern in history to notice it, his examples partly undercut his case for the primacy of historical evidence. He was still justifying it as an illustration and elucidation of history's real content. Of course, one should probably not attach too great an importance to generalized compliments of this sort, nor contrast them pointedly with Duncker's earlier effusions. It is worth noting, nonetheless, that Duncker himself thought that he had said something important.

He explained the nature of that importance in the introduction to his roughly contemporaneous *Crisis of the Reformation*, a slender volume published in 1845 that was supposedly a printed version of a lecture given in August 1844. (The introduction, however, dates from 1845, and he probably revised the central text; if he gave it in the printed version, then his audience had sat still for the best part of three hours). In this introduction he claimed that historical empiricism was the necessary outcome, in fact the culmination, of German intellectual history since the eighteenth century, and was still Hegelian enough to think of the onward progress of the spirit as the real content of history. He divided modern German history into four successive and dialectically interrelated phases in the development of the spirit. The last of these, which he termed "historical rationalism" and in which he located himself, had finally achieved an adequate theory of historical knowledge that would, he was sure, lead it to change Germany very much for the better. His exploration into the recent intellectual history of Germany deserves careful attention, specifically because it illuminates his new attitude toward historical method and, more generally, because it shows his sense of the historical significance of his own political and historical strivings.

The first period was the Enlightenment, about which Duncker, like Droysen and many other contemporaries, had major reservations—combined with real admiration for its historical accomplishments. Duncker found it shallow and judged it destructive. He accordingly cited its attacks on religion in Germany and both state and religion in France. At the same time he noted that the spirit did not make unnecessary movements. In part, this was a matter of saying that what happened had to happen and was therefore somehow good. In part, too, it was a specific argument about the Enlightenment. The Enlightenment was negative, but its negativity had positive effects. It was negative in the sense that the "enlightened gaze of the understanding (*Verstand*) . . . was unable to comprehend and conceptualize (*auffassen und begreifen*) the products of drives, of fantasy, of feeling."[12] This was not a compliment, for, in the language of German Idealism that Duncker was applying here, the "understanding" was merely the uncreative faculty of rational calculation. He meant to fault the Enlightenment for being too prosaic to appreciate the irrational and, more specifically, for lacking a sense of history. For dialectical reasons, however, this defect was actually a virtue because it provoked a very strong interest in the past in what Duncker saw as a second period.

This second period was Romanticism, which in Duncker's reading would not have existed had there been no Enlightenment. He clearly admired it, though he thought that it, too, was one-sided. He praised it for preferring "feeling" (*Gemüth*) to "understanding," for putting the "full heart in place of keen, intellectual insight, immediacy in place of reflection, poetic darkness in place of prosaic light." These compliments seem oddly misplaced in an academic's writings, but Duncker was not really an irrationalist; rather, he believed that these attitudes had allowed the romantics to perform the valuable service of restoring "their rights to traditions in church and state." That statement seemed to rank him among the conservative defenders of historical rights. In fact, though Duncker was no more a revolutionary than Droysen, he justifiably thought of himself as a partisan of progress, and he accordingly leveled some serious charges against the romantics. He accused them of distrusting critical thought, with the result that their otherwise admirable attempts at "reconstruction could occur only in a fantastic manner." More serious, in their love for the past the romantics failed to take sufficient account of historical change. That is, they did not see that the "substance" of history was "self-producing" and "both the same as in ages past yet new, purifying itself from stage to stage."[13] History was a continuum, but it moved to newer and better. If the Enlightenment erred by preferring "pragmatic" reasonings to history, Romanticism had the equally serious flaw of trying to halt historical change at some point in the past.[14]

With that criticism, Duncker was making the same point that Droysen had made by invoking the "right of history" against "historical rights."

Both men had the same motive, namely, to legitimate continued historical change without resort to revolution. Duncker evidently believed that the "spirit" took the same view of the matter because, in the third and fourth periods that he identified, he portrayed it as preserving the good and eliminating the bad features of Enlightenment and Romanticism in order to produce views of history that were decently reverent toward the past yet acceptant of change in the future. The spirit used the German "national character" (*Volscharakter*) to produce these syntheses that, generally speaking, corresponded respectively to his earlier, Hegelian, phase and to his present, more empirical, one.[15] In fact, they were much alike. The fourth period was the corrected, really the perfected, form of the third.

He labeled the third period "Philosophical Rationalism," by which he meant German Idealism in general and Hegel's philosophy in particular. He described it as an instance of "placing an illegitimate content in a legitimate form."[16] Duncker's attack on its "content" was in part a recanting of his earlier disdain for empirical knowledge, but his praise for its form was sincere because it corresponded to his own vision of historical progress. For that reason, he offered some very admiring statements: "Philosophy rejected the one-sidedness of both phases of cultivation (*Bildungsstufen*), of Romanticism and Enlightenment, of the heart and the understanding . . . [and] discovered in history the process of the spirit (*Process des Geistes*), of an unconscious drive [moving] through reflection to new formations (*Gestaltungen*)." He found this discovery to be formally correct and to be a very positive development because it made it possible to see in the state an "objective form" (*objektive Gestalt*) and to understand that "a substance reigned in ethics that lay at the bottom of naive morals."[17] These generalizations are tantalizingly abstract, but their general purport is clear enough. Philosophy had shown history to be a moral process that moved from truth to higher truth. These truths underlay human morals and, most important, affected action in the state, the highest human institution.

These gains, however, came at some cost, because they did not proceed "from practice" but "from the topmost peaks of metaphysical thought."[18] That is, they were too abstract to take adequate account of empirical evidence and to adequately inform action in the empirical world. The mediation between Enlightenment and Romanticism had been only preliminary because it was "purely metaphysical." In the fourth and final period, therefore, the spirit concretized and completed its work in "historical rationalism." This completion, he argued,

could come about in no other way than that of returning to the world from the heights of the Idea, of using historical rather than logical explication, of abandoning mystical empiricism and speculation in order more realistically to comprehend the real process of history (*um den realen Process der Geschichte realiter zu begreifen*). The concept of history as an objective development, as a spiritual process, was discovered by philosophy—it was now a matter of really carrying out this concept, of realizing it in all its real moments.[19]

This passage shows nicely the real continuity that he saw between "Philosophical" and "Historical Rationalism" and the applicability of both to the stages of his career. That is, he had himself moved from "Philosophical" to "Historical Rationalism." The latter did what the former only promised. By abandoning the former and embracing the latter, he, Duncker, was acting on history's dictates and in history's behalf. This made his work as a historian a calling performed in the interest of Germany, the nation that had, in his scheme, been chosen to discover and develop historical rationalism. This celebration of empiricism deserves some discussion. It rests on an unfair appraisal of Hegel, who was not anti-empirical, as Duncker alleged. Like Droysen, Duncker was judging Hegel more in terms of his reputation among young intellectuals than in terms of his actual argument. This undeserved criticism, however, helped Duncker and others to a sense of intellectual and moral independence. It allowed them to borrow and use Hegel's concepts while claiming a superiority to him by virtue of their chosen study of historical detail.

The national aspect of his argument deserves strong emphasis. Since 1843 Duncker had argued to his students at Halle that a nation's practices and institutions reflected the level of its spiritual development.[20] By implication, it spoke well for German brilliance (especially the brilliance of German historians) that Germans had discovered these fundamental truths, and this discovery promised well for the German future. In the introduction to *The Crisis of the Reformation*, Duncker made this implication fairly explicit. This "mediation" between the Enlightenment's ahistorical but critical understanding and Romanticism's uncritical but profound love of the past would "deepen and form reason (*Vernunft*) in substance" and thereafter lead to "shaping the world according to contemporary perception (*gegenwärtige Einsicht*)"[21] In the parlance of German Idealism, after all, "reason," as opposed to mere "understanding," was a shaping and creative faculty. Historical Rationalism, therefore, would see past and present as they really were, would discover what needed to be done, and would make sure that someone did it. Duncker wanted not only to understand history but also, by understanding, to help it along, chiefly by showing present and future needs to those who would read and listen and, more generally, by providing contemporaries with the moral preparation that he, too, saw as a precondition for effective political action.

This desire to help history was not simply a personal predisposition. At least in principle, it was a logical conclusion from Duncker's interpretation of modern history. The "Historical Rationalism" that informed this desire is obviously very similar to Droysen's view of his own role as a historian, and, like Droysen, Duncker used religious improvement as a means to political change. The few excerpts included in Haym's adoring biography record such suggestive statements by Duncker as a desire "to live virtuously . . . striving and in unconscious union with God" and to lead a "life of active love, as it is prescribed by Christianity" in order to serve "universal history" and to bring "freedom and right" to the "Fatherland."[22] Duncker, with the younger Haym in tow, was excitedly involved in the work of the theologically progressive Friends of Light (*Lichtfreunde*), a Protestant movement that established "free congregations" in many Prussian cities—Halle among them—and sought more liberal governance of the established evangelical church in order to make it more responsive to the laity, and readily moved through religious to political reform.[23] Duncker unquestionably saw in Christianity the basis for ethical and, so, political action; he even thought that Droysen, in the *History of Hellenism*, underestimated the role of "ethical process" in revolt against "demoralized practice" as a cause of Christianity.[24]

That polite criticism probably means only that Duncker either did not read carefully (or did not read at all) the first volume of *Hellenism* in which Droysen made that point. It certainly shows their agreement that Christianity, at least as a historical reality, had ethical causes, and underlies their agreement that it had ethical consequences. This fact is especially evident in Duncker's discussion of the Reformation, which he, too, saw as the beginning of modern history. In his view, the Reformation was not simply a turning point in German history. It was the necessary and promising outcome of at least all previous European history, an outcome that Germany was historically privileged to achieve. The four periods he discussed in his introduction to the *Crisis* were themselves the long-term results of sixteenth-century religious reform in Germany, and he devoted the body of the work to explaining the latter's significance and why its full effects could not be enjoyed until his own age.

Like Droysen, he believed that the Reformation began a course of development that would culminate in Germany's unification as a constitutional monarchy. That is evident from a review published in 1844 and a piece of surviving correspondence.[25] In the *Crisis* he offered, though in his own words, the same arguments that Droysen had. Just as Droysen had defined the Reformation as a revolt against a supernatural outlook that detached God from the world *Gottentweltlichung*), so Duncker described it as Germany's affirmation of "sensual health" (*sinnliche Gesundheit*) against the prevailing "Catholic annihilation of sensuality" (*Vernichtung der Sinnlichkeit*). By "sensuality" he meant less a celebration of the physical than the substitution of "natural morality" for medieval "asceticism."[26] In both pairings of opposites, he wished to contrast a religion that led out of this world with a revivified Christianity that inspired and informed action in it. Of course, he strongly approved of the latter, and, as Droysen had, explained this advance as a synthesis of the virtues of classical antiquity and Christianity. The reformers, in his opinion, were deeply pious Christians, but they were also moved by a wish to "take over into the present the virtues of antiquity" in order to achieve "national freedom from Rome, national independence and greatness, national unity as opposed to the particularism of the Middle Ages."[27]

This was, of course, a very present-minded reading of Reformation history, and one wonders just which ancient texts, in Duncker's view, showed the reformers the need for national unification. Yet this view of the Reformation no doubt seemed as convincing to Duncker as it did to Droysen. They were doing more than indulging in Protestant fantasies. They wanted Germany unified, and as historians they sought to find a pedigree for their desire. Two obvious enemies were particularism and at least the ultramontane version of Catholicism (Duncker, by the way, had considerable respect for German Catholicism, and once explained to Droysen that religious reunification might soon be possible).[28] By thinking of the Reformation as a break with the Middle Ages, it was possible to see it as a break with medieval political forms, and it undoubtedly entailed a break with Rome. The association of it with classical antiquity was also plausible, although the conclusions that they drew from this association were tenuous. Some of the reformers, after all, were classical scholars. To Duncker and Droysen, the appreciation of classical letters implied agreement with the civic ideals found in some classical literature. That conclusion seemed unquestionable to mid-nineteenth Germans who were unimpressed with constitutional government as practiced in western Europe and who had experienced political freedom only vicariously by reading ancient authors. By casting his argument in these terms, of course, Duncker also raised the embarrassing question of why the Reformation had not achieved national unity and freedom. If it had been just a foredoomed episode, national unification and constitutional government might seem to be as unattainable now as then. Droysen had tried to solve this problem by explaining the historical necessity of "powers" preceding "states," by showing that the apparent curse of intensified particularism combined with royal absolutism was really a blessing. Duncker posed a rather different solution, which, however, offered the same explanatory advantages that Droysen's had. It allowed the Reformation to set the agenda for the present century while showing that more had been gained than lost in the intervening period.

῾ He held the emperor Charles V responsible for the delay in bringing unification and freedom and maintained that if Charles had supported the Reformation's efforts at political reconstruction, "England's political development would also have been ours."[29] That is, Germany could have been a unified state with a national church under a national monarch. By refusing to play that part, Charles brought about "territorial particularism in place of unity, a victory of dynastic elements instead of democratic, the triumph of princes instead of the emperor."[30] Duncker did not, however, simply blame Charles, because the latter obviously did not consciously intend those results. In any case, Charles was less responsible for them than were the circumstances in which he operated. The key point for Duncker was that so much could have depended on the will of one man. Unification in the sixteenth century was possible only under the exceptional condition that a great national leader embraced it as a cause. It was not enough that every social order except the courtiers and ecclesiastics wished for it. They needed to be united, but they were divided instead. The Peasant Revolt and the rising of the knights under Franz von Sickingen, for example, were symptoms of a general demand for change, but both were too narrowly based to become national in scope. Similarly, many in power wanted fundamental reform, but the elective monarchy of the Holy Roman Empire was too weak to reform itself and the imperial estates too divided to work together in the national interest.[31] Germany could recognize the need for unity, but it was not yet ready to achieve it. As a result, "political reform was completely defeated, the religious not half completed."[32]

This defeat, however, was only temporary. For the next centuries, it meant that German history ran in the channel of particularism and absolutism grounded in "foreign and inaccessible law."[33] For the present century, the nineteenth, it meant a return to and completion of both the Reformation's religious and political tasks. Of this Duncker was certain. He seems not to have had—at least he did not publish—a detailed analytic scheme of how Germany's misery between the mid-sixteenth and mid-nineteenth centuries would actually assure the eventual triumph of unified statehood, but he, like Droysen, believed that this had not been a hollow period. After all, in his view the spirit did not work in vain; whatever happened was ultimately to the good. His publication of the *Crisis* with an introduction is evidence of this, inasmuch it shows that he believed that the Reformation and its partial failure, if comprehended by "Historical Rationalism," was a needed spur to unification. Moreover, in the long term it produced a Germany capable of achieving "Historical Rationalism." The German nation was now spiritually ready and morally capable, as it had not been in the sixteenth century.

Ready for and capable of what? The "national" or "popular state" (*Volksstaat*) was his answer. Like Droysen, Duncker used *Volk* to denote both "people" and "nation," and he saw as the state's proper essence a constitutional system that would overcome both the one-sidedness of royal absolutism and the "state of law" (*Rechtsstaat*) through a "continuing process of mediation." In this respect, too, his ideas were very close to Droysen's. Both, of course, belonged to the larger grouping of German constitutional moderates who wanted to institutionalize political freedom without seriously impairing royal prerogative and without violent revolution, but their fundamental similarity was closer than that. Both saw a special German constitutional state as a predestined historical imperative, and both strongly insisted that its essence was a coming together of rulers and ruled. Rather than opposing and checking each other, they were to cooperate in harmony, a cooperation made possible by the undeniable historical justification that each possessed and, more specifically, by the historically necessary spiritual transformation of the German people in which both were engaged and which was only now being completed. The new state, Duncker explained both in his university lectures and in 1844 in an article in the *Halle'sche Allgemeine Literatur-Zeitung*, whose political and historical editor he was, would embody "the spirit of the present" (*Geist der Gegenwart*), just as political institutions always reflected the present condition of the "public spirit" (*öffentlichen Geist*).[34]

That was why, in 1845 in the *Crisis*, he was so excited by the advent of "Historical Rationalism" with its promise of "shaping the world according to contemporary perception."[35] Its appearance suggested to him that the potential was about to become actual, that the transformed spirit was now ready to transform political institutions. The only questions were by what means change would come and what would be the nature of that change. Duncker was no more ready than Droysen to engage in the utopian pastime of mapping the future in great detail, but he had to say more than that the future state would be neither absolutist nor rigidly constitutional. Despite his avoidance of major publication in this period—and it was not then unusual in Germany to defer publication after assuming a professorship—his speeches and writings give a reasonably complete picture of his prerevolutionary thinking on these subjects.

He was, for example, certain that it was not enough for the governed to be willing to cooperate freely with the government. In part, no doubt, because he feared revolution from below, he expected governments, primarily the Prussian government, to take the initiative that could now succeed. In order to make people receptive to these approaches when they came, he made what he termed Prussia's "shining history" a favorite theme in the lectures he delivered to lay audiences in Halle between 1843 and 1848.[36] If the samples that survive are a fair indication of their quality, these were highly charged rhetorical exercises. When, for instance, he spoke on the occasion of the return of Frederick the Great's dagger by France in 1846, he evoked the king's memory and declared: "May his soul and his victory dagger . . . remain with us forever and lead us onward from clarity to clarity and from victory to victory!" These were not simply pompous phrases; he wanted his listeners to be mindful of what Prussian rulers had done in the past, and he wanted the Prussian government to be similarly active in the present. Thus, on another occasion he spoke of the importance of the Prussian Reforms in German history and defined his own "political standpoint" as working to "carry out the ideas" of those reforms "in their progressive aspect" as the sole means by which Germany could avoid the equally repellant extremes of continued absolutism or revolution in the French manner.[37] Obviously, this meant that Prussia was indispensable and that official Prussia would have to reach out to the nation.

Accordingly, he looked to Prussian leadership in the present, notably during the crises provoked in 1846 by Christian VIII's Open Letter and in early 1848 by Frederick VII's January Rescript with respect to Schleswig-Holstein, and in 1847 during the hopeful excitement that preceded and followed the convening of the Prussian United Diet. In the latter case, he even insisted that a necessary historical connection existed between Prussia's "state development" (*staatliche Entwicklung*) and Germany's "national development" (*nationale Entwicklung*).[38] Obviously, this was identical with Droysen's way of thinking, and, unsurprisingly, Duncker was strongly attracted by Droysen's arguments, notably by his thesis that Prussia's position as the weakest of the five great powers would compel her to unify Germany as a constitutional monarchy. He strongly and explicitly agreed with that analysis in three letters to Droysen and gladly published Droysen's fullest exposition of it, "The Political Position of Prussia" (1845) in the *Halle'sche Allgemeine Literatur-Zeitung*. He was impressed enough that in 1847 he solicited Droysen to write and publish "The Prussian Constitution," obviously with a fair idea of what Droysen was likely to say.[39] Duncker's acceptance and choice of articles is good evidence of his own views, because, as he boasted to Droysen, he used his editorship to proclaim "the tendency of constitutionalism," that is, his own political outlook.[40]

His hopes for actions by Prussia, and if possible by other states, included, but were not limited to, military action in behalf of the duchies. In the aftermaths of both Christian VIII's Open Letter and Frederick VII's January Rescript, he involved himself in the Schleswig-Holstein crises as deeply as his presence in distant Halle permitted. Duncker clearly hoped to exert some influence on events and, beyond that, to use the crises to instruct his public. As early as June 1844, while the situation in the duchies was still fairly calm, he had noted in a letter to Droysen that tensions between Germans and Danes provided a welcome opportunity for political education in Germany.[41] In 1846 he tried to put that opportunity to use by directing the citizens of Halle toward "national affairs."[42]

He began by drafting a public letter to Germans in Schleswig-Holstein, for which he collected signatures among the residents of Halle. In its central portion it read:

You are fighting for your and our rights, for your and our constitution, for your and our nationality, for your and our future: for we must be beside and upon the sea, must reunite to ourselves all the lost members of the national body. You will be the first to return to the Fatherland. Just as you have often prevailed against the sword of the Danes, so you will prevail over their perversions of the law. In this you will not stand alone. Impossible that our princes, impossible that our German-minded monarch should remain non-participants in your struggle![43]

No doubt as much for the benefit of his neighbors as to reassure the Germans in the duchies, he linked the latter's immediate situation to national strivings for constitutional government and a united Germany, providing the needed linkage by asserting Germany's need to become a naval power and citing the inspiration that the duchies could provide to the rest of Germany. He obviously sympathized with the German population of Schleswig-Holstein, but he even more obviously hoped that its plight would lead to results good for Germany as a whole. This is evident in his stated hope that the struggle would move the princes, especially the Prussian monarch, to action. Duncker in Halle and Droysen in Kiel were in complete agreement on this.

Some of the language in the letter also suggests another characteristic of Duncker's expectations for the future German state. He described the duchies as the "first" of the "lost members" to be reunited with the "national body." This language implies a program of reacquiring lost territories, a policy that would surely involve the use of force. He listed the territories that he had in mind in 1848 in an article that he first published in the local *Hallische Courier*, and then, in slightly shortened form, in the *Deutsche Zeitung*, the organ of southwest German liberalism. He wrote in response to Frederick VII's 1848 January Rescript, which stated his claim to the succession and revealed plans to incorporate the duchies into an integrated and constitutional Danish monarchy. "We have," Duncker lamented, "lost Alsace and Lorraine, Switzerland, Holland, and Flanders; we are losing Lithuania and the Courland; but more than everything that has pounded Germany in her centuries of debasement: Denmark's victory over Schleswig-Holstein would be the most shameful."[44] In logic, the two documents suggest that, after securing the duchies, Germany should regain territories currently held by Switzerland, France, Belgium, the Netherlands, and the Russian Empire. This would have required war with much of Europe, and Duncker surely did not have that in mind. He wrote the pieces at different times and probably just wanted to recall old hurts in order to prevent new injuries. It is nonetheless clear that a chief trait of the new Germany would be power, at least power to defend, and possibly a power to recover, territory. In 1849, after the revolution, Duncker recalled that the achievement of adequate power through unity had been one of its chief attractions for him in earlier years.[45] Such attraction must have been strong when all he could do about the duchies was to collect funds for the legal defense of German agitators there and wait, hopefully, for action by Prussia and other German states.[46]

His response to the meeting of the first Prussian United Diet in 1847 was cut according to the same pattern. On the one hand, he hoped and asked for decisive actions by Prussian authorities that would keep Germany on track for eventual constitutional unification. On the other hand, he tried to use present events for public instruction in order that the population would be receptive to whatever moves the authorities made. These tactics were complementary, and he employed both in his responses to the summoning and meeting of the diet. Right after Frederick William IV's issuance of the February Patent convening the diet, for example, Duncker drafted a public letter to the king for which he collected two hundred and twenty-five signatures in Halle. The letter was to embolden Frederick William to further actions in the interest of constitutionalism and unification by congratulating him warmly for acting in a manner "destined to lay the firm foundations of a new epoch in our political and national development (*staatlichen und nationalen Entwicklung*)."[47] The letter had a further and more immediate purpose, however; namely, to make the signatories, after they read what they were signing, see events in their real significance and rally to the royal government.

If his hopes were to become realities, after all, both king and people had actively to cooperate, and they could do this only if both knew what was at stake. Accordingly, on 13 February 1847, he addressed a political banquet at Halle to impress on his audience the claim that now, as in the time of the Prussian reforms, the drive for national unification and political freedom came "from the government, not the people." The government's forthcoming attitude was encouraging but insufficient; further progress depended on popular support. In order to avoid a relapse like the one in 1820, the people of Prussia and, more generally, all of Germany had to invest their energy in the present process of political reconstruction, primarily by accepting that the state was the supreme secular good. Nothing that the diet did would have a lasting effect, Duncker explained, until the people clearly and visibly realized that "the state stands above family, trade, life." In other words, and as a logical consequence of his theory of constitutional government, he was not calling on his listeners to force reform on recalcitrant authorities but to be ready to submit freely and happily to the state life that these authorities were trying to bring into existence. He also wanted them to understand the special role that history had assigned to Prussia, and therefore argued that further progress could occur only when they understood the tendency of Prussian history and desired actively to continue along its "shining" path.[48]

Duncker was still very optimistic about the course of affairs in the late spring of 1847. He was favorably impressed by the bearing and behavior of the delegates, chiefly because these qualities suggested that they were ready for responsible enjoyment of political freedom. On 1 June he wrote to Droysen: "It finally appears that air and light want to come forth for us in Germany." "God be praised," he continued, "but we will have to drive valiantly forward if we want to progress any further."[49] By "we" he likely meant Droysen and himself (and other like-minded people). Government and people needed historical instruction, and when Duncker wrote these sentences he wanted Droysen to write "The Prussian Constitution" for the *Halle'sche Allgemeine Literatur-Zeitung*. Given his premises, this was a thoroughly reasonable view to take: the future German state would be an ongoing collaboration of rulers and ruled, of government and people, and the natural task for historical publicism was to predispose both parties to this collaboration. Without this predisposition, progress would cease, and further letters to Droysen show that he shared the latter's fear that legalistic constitutionalism and royal obduracy might yet put an early end to the hopeful current developments.[50]

This persistent desire to unite government and people resulted not just from Duncker's belief that such union was the means to national unification. He also believed that it was the end to which unification led, for continuous collaboration was, for him, the essence of state life. As he explained to his students in previous years, the future German state would be "an enduring process of mediation" (*Vermittelungsprocess*) between private and public interests, between rulers and ruled, really among all groups in the state.[51] That was why he insisted on avoiding the rigidities both of constitutionalism and of absolutism, though he did want constitutional government and a strong monarchy. It was also why he applauded Droysen's "Prussian Constitution," with its attacks on the separation of powers, though it is important to note that his greatest fear was public apathy.

More than Droysen (or Haym and Sybel), Duncker worried that the German state might founder on the political indifference of its citizens. His ideal of political life, after all, placed very heavy moral demands on the citizens. Consequently, in his banquet speech in 1847, Duncker implored his audience to support the monarchy in its reforms and reminded it warningly of 1820, when, allegedly, Prussian citizens "handed over to officials the reins of the state." If citizens would keep their political energies engaged, however, two benefits would follow. The government's real power would increase as citizens subordinated everything else to the state's welfare, and the citizens would secure their own legitimate interests through what he termed the "principle of self-government" (*Selbstregierung*).[52] This emphasis on mutual advantage, of course, is essentially identical with Droysen's definition of the state.

Duncker's conception of German statehood in these terms throws an interesting light on his political tactics before 1848. They often seem timid and self-protective, not least to his biographer Haym, writing long after the event. As remarked, Duncker published very little as yet, and in political matters seemed to prefer to have others do the writing, by soliciting reviews and articles for the columns of the *Halle'sche Allgemeine Literatur-Zeitung,* for example, or by persuading Rudolf Haym to prepare *Speeches and Speakers of the First Prussian United Diet* for the Duncker family publishing house and then trying, unsuccessfully, to persuade Droysen to review it.[53] This was, incidentally, also his practice right after the revolution, when he forced a harried and thoroughly unhappy Haym to edit the *Konstitutionelle Zeitung,* showered him with uninvited instructions and criticisms, and submitted little copy of his own to its pages.[54] Those cases, of course, could be interpreted as laziness or, more favorably, a busy academic delegating tasks that he lacked time to complete. The situation is a little different with his public speaking, for he preferred to address the so-called Friends of Light at Halle. Haym clearly thought that Duncker was active in this group less out of religious interest than out of a desire to propagandize under the safe cover of religious activity.[55]

Timidity would have been understandable on Duncker's part. Though Germans could and often did write about political matters in a general way, censorship existed, and there was no guaranteed right to free expression. Professors were state employees with their careers to think about, and Duncker had gotten an early taste of state hostility. While performing military service near Bonn in 1832 he had attended a *Burschenschaft* meeting and made the mistake of referring favorably to it in a letter to his brother. The authorities distrusted these nationalistic student organizations and, in view of recent student disturbances in Germany in the wake of the French July Revolution, the Prussian authorities who read

Duncker's letter took a dim view of this reference; Duncker was sentenced to and served six months fortress arrest at Köpenick.[56] This conviction for a political crime threw his career into doubt, especially when, a decade later, he had to approach the Prussian *Kultusministerium* to receive permission to teach at Halle, and especially as the minister at that time was the very conservative K.D.F. Eichhorn, who, along with Friedrich von Savigny, was a founder of the Historical School of Law and, given his academic background, very attentive to who taught and what was taught in Prussian universities. Duncker hoped for some protection from Johannes Schulze, with whom he, like Droysen, was on friendly terms, but a great deal depended on the contents of his letter.[57]

The letter reads like an attempt to win official favor, or at least to quiet official fears, and that was certainly part of Duncker's intention. He insisted, quite accurately but possibly contrary to appearances, that he was not a revolutionary and was not subversive. As a professor, he promised, he would "seek historical progress not in destruction but in spiritual renewal and moral awakening." After he was granted permission to teach, he kept his promise by informing his students that "objective freedom is a child of the subjective" and insisting on the need for "beginning with our individual ethical, or individual intellectual liberation."[58] Neither statement, however, in any way belied Duncker's convictions or theoretical postulates. In 1848 he would serve in a revolutionary parliament, but he never was, and never would be, a revolutionary. Moreover, the terms of his political theory really did mean that private and moral must precede public and political reform. It would be a mistake, therefore, to call Duncker timid in any ordinary sense of the term. His fear was that the people would not be worthy of the authorities, not that the authorities would oppress the people or repress him. In consequence, he lived in the expectation that official Prussia would carry out its assigned tasks and that the German people, thanks to his efforts and the efforts of others, would act as they had to act. He consequently devoted his early career to preparing them for these tasks in the certainty that history's provision of "historical rationalism" gave him the needed means for their preparation. If the people were not ready when the time came, it would not be his fault. He evidently did not consider what would happen if Prussia itself were not ready.

Rudolf Haym

Rudolf Haym pursued a career in some ways similar to, but in others quite different from, either Droysen's or Duncker's. The differences were the result of age and training. Born in 1821, he was ten years younger than his friend Duncker and twelve years younger than Droysen. His father was a Protestant clergyman from Silesia and an admirer of the Enlightenment who, Haym reported, sent his son to Halle, where he had himself taken his degree, to study theology in the hope that he, too, would become a pastor. Haym's own, more secular tastes quickly asserted themselves, and after a year's study, he shifted from theology to philosophy. This meant that when, under Duncker's influence, he became deeply interested in history, he had little knowledge of history, at least of political history, and no experience in the techniques of historical research or, despite the fact that he wrote his inaugural dissertation on Aeschylus, historically oriented philology. As he reminisced fifty years later, in the 1840s he "lacked not a sense for but a knowledge of history."[59]

In 1847 he acknowledged that lack in his attempt to decline Duncker's request that he write a book on the Prussian United Diet.[60] The effect of this historical interest without historical training on his career was that he compromised by writing intellectual histories, especially intellectual biographies. In political terms, it meant that the historical aspect of his arguments, though strongly present, was always weakly informed and often ill defined. This is not to say that his ideas differed fundamentally from those of Droysen and Duncker. On the contrary, he took the same view as they of the German present and future and liked to think that, in doing so, he had the authority of history behind his views. It was just that he could not cite much history to prove his points. Similarly, he pursued the same tactics as they, namely, preparing future citizens through present instruction; but, inevitably, his instruction lacked historical depth. Insofar as he could, however, he compensated by putting his philosophy to use by trying to give a reasoned explanation of the need for moral readiness grounded in historical empiricism. That was a promising idea, but Haym was still too young to have a lot to say. Moreover, there was a difficulty in finding readers and commanding their attention. Droysen and Duncker were appointed professors with growing reputations; Haym was still just an advanced student who had not yet completed his second dissertation (*Habilitationschrift*). Consequently, he could reach the public only through incidental writings, but he did what he could once he was ready to make the attempt.

He was not ready until he first accepted and then in part rejected Hegel's ideas. He was, of course, too young to have learned Hegel's philosophy from Hegel himself. He first encountered his ideas through contacts with authors of the *Halle'sche Jahrbücher* at a time when, ironically, they were already revising Hegel's philosophy in terms of its latent revolutionary implications. Haym, by contrast, was attracted to the system in what he took to be its orthodox and unrevised form. His conversion, for such it was, can be dated fairly precisely. In 1842 he reviewed two histories for the *Halle'sche Allgemeine Literatur-Zeitung* (Duncker was not yet one of its editors), a history of English Deism and Ranke's *German History in the Age of the Reformation*. The reviews show that Haym's ideas were still unformed and contradictory. He demanded that historians pay attention to unchanging, rational values, but he also called on them to show irreversible onward change over time.[61] Haym later explained this contradiction as a result of a continued adherence to the ahistorical rationalism of the Enlightenment and an incomplete assimilation of Hegel's concept of an evolving "spirit."[62] The latter strain triumphed when, in the same year, he wrote *Gesenius: A Remembrance for his Friends*, a work of which he was subsequently understandably ashamed.

Wilhelm Gesenius (1786–1842) was an expert hebraicist who taught Haym Hebrew and who prepared the standard German-language grammar for that language. (After many editions, it is still a standard work). Haym, using personal characterizations read in the Young Hegelian *Halle'sche Jahrbücher* as models, wrote a commemorative essay on the recently deceased professor that, in essence, took him so harshly to task for not being a Hegelian that one wonders whether the phrase "for his friends" in the title was intended or unintended irony. Haym insisted that the historical process consisted in the progressive development of the "idea" that subsumed all facts and values, and then complained that Gesenius had ignored this truth and merely confined himself to the close study of a language. In Haym's view, that was a sufficient explanation for the many personal and intellectual limitations that he catalogued unmercifully in the body of the essay.[63] The work is useless for understanding Gesenius, but it shows a lot about the young Haym. It displays the characteristic intolerance of a young believer who has just acquired a new faith. More specifically, it shows what Haym had assimilated from Hegel: a vision of progress as a spiritual process and a theory of knowledge that made him contemptuous of empiricism. The latter, justified in terms of the former, was very visible in this work. In the course of denigrating Gesenius's study of Hebrew, Haym remarked contemptuously about the "mindlessness (*Gedankenlosigkeit*) of the empiricist" and dismissed as "naive" the willingness to study individual phenomena—as if there could be any other way to grammatical certainty in a language whose syntactic problems are attested only in scattered passages of Scripture.[64] This is another, though unusually extreme, example of drawing from the admittedly non-empirical system of Hegel's philosophy a lesson with which Hegel would surely not have agreed. Part of Hegel's fascination for the young may have been the seeming offer of a short-cut to important knowledge. However that may be, this anti-empiricism went well beyond that which Duncker had displayed in 1836 and was a good example of the Hegelian defects to which Droysen pointed in his letters to Perthes in 1836 and 1837.

These notions, of course, crept into Haym's other writings as working assumptions and go far to explain why, when he sent Droysen a copy of his inaugural dissertation on Aeschylus, Droysen could manage to be no more than vaguely polite.[65] Working from these premises, Haym could think in terms of inevitable historical progress, but he could not take adequate account of historical data. During the next two and a half years, he abandoned these youthful ideas, though they continued to have a certain importance for him. More clearly than was the case for Droysen and Duncker, his having once entertained these notions only to reject them later, meant that his conversion to empiricism, which he equated with moral empowerment, seemed a triumphant, because hard-won, victory. Moreover, the fact that it coincided with a larger shift away from philosophical idealism in Germany gave him the sense of experiencing in his own intellectual development a vast and inevitable historical change and the heady feeling of embodying historical progress. Both Droysen and Duncker had felt the same way at comparable stages in their careers.

Haym could feel that way because he did not revise or reject the other lesson that he learned from Hegel, the vision of history as a process of ineluctable and essentially spiritual progress. In 1843 in an essay on his goals he apostrophized: "I would like to devour whole centuries of the future and carry my tent from epoch of humanity to another—not like the eternal Jew but like the eternal man, like the developing, marching history of humanity itself."[66] If in less inflated language, he could have written that at any time before 1848. He thought of history as a progressive march of which he wanted to be an integral part, and this wish survived and informed the major intellectual change that he experienced in 1844, namely, a conscious and passionate rejection of the epistemology that he had adapted from Hegel on the grounds that it was morally disabling to individuals and to the German nation as a whole.

This change was as rapid as his initial conversion to Hegelianism, and its causes are not altogether clear. When Droysen and Duncker undertook similar revisions, they did so more gradually and were surely helped by the professional requirement for historians to work continually with empirical data. Droysen also had theological objections to, among other things, Hegel's theory of knowledge, which may have at all times prevented him from accepting the system fully. Haym was not yet engaged in detailed research, and, despite the fact that he came from a clerical home, he was not especially religious. In any case, the record shows that he rejected what he understood of Hegelian epistemology after reading Feuerbach under Wilhelm Busse's instruction in 1844, and in January 1845 he wrote to his friend Hermann Finke that no one could any longer suppose that "the empire of the little Hegelians still stands in full force and bloom."[67] This raises the question of why he changed his mind, because people do not usually reject hitherto cherished beliefs in a few months simply because someone has shown them another way of viewing matters. The letter to Finke suggests one possible motivation: Hegelianism now seemed out of fashion. Haym was following his generation. This does not mean that Haym was merely a conformist of the mind. Given his theory of progress, a change in fashion would imply a change in validity, would imply, that is, that humanity had moved beyond Hegel's philosophy to a higher truth. That claim was present in the distinction that Duncker drew between "philosophical" and "historical rationalism," a distinction that he may have developed through conversations with Haym. It is also possible, as a case of a virtue having its defect, that Haym was irritated by the very comprehensiveness of Hegel's system and began to feel it to be a sort of tyranny. The evidence for this possibility is both speculative and retrospective. In 1857 in his genial *Hegel and his Times* Haym described Hegel's as an age when all the disciplines "gathered at the well-spread table of Hegelian wisdom," when one was "either a Hegelian or an idiot and a barbarian." He concluded by remarking: "One must hark back to that time to know what the supremacy of a philosophical system really means."[68] This is an apt, if overdrawn, description of German academic life a generation earlier, but it also reads a little like a former lover trying to explain what was wrong in a failed relationship.

In his long, nearly book-length article "Philosophy," written between 1846 and 1848 for the *General Encyclopedia of the Arts and Sciences* (an early version of the famous Brockhaus encyclopedia), Haym explained what he now thought was wrong with Hegelianism. He, too, summarily accused Hegel of endorsing political reaction and accused him of fostering moral complacency:

Hegel is the philosopher of the Restoration, his philosophy a glaring reflection of the indolence and self-satisfaction, of the prostration and covering-up under which the German nation (*teutsche Nation*) lay buried after the Enlightenment had wearied and withered her, and after the Romantic upsurge had seized her so powerfully. She then covered herself in the memory of these periods that she had survived and had no more significant work to produce than this philosophy that like a dream led past her the substance of her life. . . . There is no room for character in the closed structure of Hegelianism, [for] all the points of subjectivity are broken off. . . . The absolute does not have the German nation in its foundations or elaborations.[69]

Haym used the same highly generalized, stereotypical periodization of recent German history that Duncker had: prosaic, essentially destructive Enlightenment gave way to unruly romanticism, and both gave way to an Idealism that was now itself being rejected in a fourth period concerned with moral action. Germany, he insisted, needed a philosophy that left room for the "points of subjectivity," by which he meant individual and collective moral action in the real, empirical world.

This was what really interested him. He believed that individual ethical action and commitment would find its completion in the state and, further, that a real state was unthinkable without morally adequate individuals for citizens. Haym believed that these ethical and political necessities were the cause of the German rejection of Hegel's philosophy, though with the important qualification that the philosophy's defect was actually a virtue. "The historical situation of the present," Haym explained, "has undeniably grown out of the tight confines to which absolute idealism accustomed her . . . the seams with which that idealism contained us are tearing." If this odd metaphor meant anything, it was that Germany's liberation from "absolute idealism" would not, could not, have occurred had that idealism not been present in the first place.[70] In one way, that was a truism, but in another it was a reasonable inference from a historical determinism that always celebrated the necessary as the good: if Germany learned to respect empiricism and the need for individual ethical action by rejecting "absolute idealism," then "absolute idealism" had been good for Germany.

Haym did not cast his argument in those terms, however, in order to suggest that Hegel's philosophy was so obviously mistaken that sooner or later Germans would reject it. For autobiographical reasons, he understood its immense persuasive power, and elsewhere in "Philosophy" he admiringly referred to it as "the mightiest of all modern systems."[71] Droysen and Duncker, in their own ways, showed the same ambivalence. Haym therefore believed that an imposing power had been required for its overturn, and he cited a "historical reaction" caused by the "vital drives of the German national spirit (*lebendigen Triebe des teutschen Volksgeistes*)."[72] His language shows that he saw this change as decisive for Germany's moral and political future, but he believed that Hegel's defeat alone was insufficient to produce practical results. Because institutions reflected the spirit, "a new philosophy" was also needed.[73] That philosophy had to encourage moral action by taking adequate account of empirical data. Haym did not overestimate his own abilities as an expounder of philosophy, but he tried to provide at least the elements of this philosophy in three works that, despite some obvious differences, contained a set of common and consistent ideas: *The Authority that Falls and that which Remains*, which he optimistically subtitled *A Popular-Philosophical Essay* (1846); *Feuerbach and Philosophy: Towards a Critique of Both* (1847); and the aforementioned article "Philosophy."

His effort at philosophical reconstruction rested on the observation, offered in *The Authority,* that there was "something" in everybody that was "simply incommensurable with the concept (*etwas schlechthin für den Begriff incommensurables*)."[74] Here his criticisms of "absolute idealism" as anti-empirical and ethically insufficient came together. In its abstractness, this idealism made the individual impossible to comprehend and made individuals unsuited for ethical decisions in actual circumstances. Haym wanted a philosophy that offered valid and binding guidance to real people in real situations. His basic task, as he described it in a letter in January 1845, was to demonstrate "the identity (*Identität*) of the ideal and the real."[75] This meant explaining in philosophical terms what was in any case actually occurring in modern German history, as, in fact, the national rejection of "absolute idealism" to which he pointed was a historical case in point of a whole population seeking to create such an "identity."

Haym's discussion of these matters was often murky, and it would be a mistake to make him seem more lucid than he really was. Nonetheless, the outlines of his argument and its implications are clear enough. The "ideal," he believed, existed in the realm of the spirit, the "real" in the realm of nature. He wanted to make these identical in the sense that the former could validly guide and explain actions in the latter. This "identity" would not be empirical in the sense that the ideal was merely an accurate description of the real, but it would be empirical inasmuch as the ideal could now take account of the concrete and contingent circumstances that individuals faced. He wanted not just a valid definition of the true and the good, but specific ethical guidance for the actual conduct of affairs. In other words, and here too he strongly resembles both Droysen and Duncker in their criticism of Hegel, his motivation was fundamentally moral. It was also essentially historical because, in supplying the "identity" that idealism had failed to produce, he believed that he was carrying out a historical necessity.

More precisely, and roughly in the way of the Christians viewing the relationship of the New to the Old Testament, he thought that he was completing and perfecting what "absolute idealism" had offered in a preliminary but now unsatisfactory way. That is, he admired Hegel and Schelling for making the first modern attempts at solving the problem of identity, but he faulted Schelling for producing an "identity" so purely ideal that it could not apply to particular actions in the day-to-day world and blamed Hegel for simply borrowing and adapting Schelling's useless theory.[76] He was encouraged in his own attempt by the growing recognition of these failings and by the fact that Feuerbach had moved away from "absolute idealism" by "pressing toward the concrete" in an evident desire "to establish reality and humanity." He did not, however, believe that Feuerbach's philosophy was really an improvement, because he had so heavily stressed the "ego" at the expense of everything else that he was just as one-sidedly trapped in the real as Schelling and Hegel had been in the ideal, but he was pleased that Feuerbach was a symptom of philosophical change.[77]

Haym thought that he had found the needed way to move between these two extremes. He tried to present the results in *The Authority*, where he discussed the possibility of individual ethical activity. He reasoned that no action could properly be called ethical unless it were freely chosen by the actor, that is, unless the ideal informed the real. Because the standard was rational and absolute, all ethical people would make the same ethical decision in the same circumstances. In that sense, ethics would be authoritative. This authority, however, had to be freely accepted, rather than imposed. That was a problem because, Haym maintained, simple observation showed that until the present, human history "consisted solely in the collision of freedom and authority." A convincing demonstration of identity would change all that. With real and ideal reconciled, it would be possible to find an "authority . . . in response to which I freely renounce my freedom once and for all and which I recognize or obey by this very act of renunciation."[78] This "authority," once discovered and defined, would also have major political implications because it gave individuals what, in Haym's as well as in Droysen's and Duncker's opinion, was required for political life, the ability freely to choose to obey. Haym began his search for this authority by pointing out that it had to be a "spiritual power" (*geistige Macht*) because only a faculty of the spirit could decide or obey. He then argued that the faculty in question could not be "reason" (*Vernunft*) because reason was essentially the same as freedom, and it would be a contradiction in terms to try to reconcile freedom and authority solely from the side of freedom. That had been the error of Schelling and Hegel in establishing a merely "ideal identity."[79] Haym therefore turned to what he defined as "the need for ethical activity; the authority that abides, that which is certain without a concept—it is the conscience (*Gewissen*)."[80] The conscience seemed perfectly suited to Haym's purposes, because as it was spiritual, it was in the realm of freedom, yet at the same time it was nonrational and, so, in needed contact with nature and necessity. It alone could reconcile the free and the unfree, the ideal and the real.

This is not a persuasive demonstration. Haym barely defined his key abstractions and, more serious, he did not try to prove that the conscience, as he defined it, actually existed. At best, the subtext of his argument runs as follows: Ethical activity occurs, but it cannot occur without a requisite human faculty. The conscience is the only conceivable faculty; therefore, because ethical activity does occur, there must be such a thing as conscience. The important point, however, is that Haym himself believed that his demonstration was a success and that he had based ethics on the "character" and the "points of subjectivity" that he found missing in Hegel's philosophy. Behind, and largely concealed by, the philosophical jargon of his time and place was Haym's belief that people were good in the sense of being conscientious and wanting to submit to rules that were both objectively valid and freely chosen. Behind it, too, was a historical optimism that argued that at last, in the Germany of Haym's time, it was possible for people to recognize and act on true moral authority. Haym thought history would soon reach its predestined goal, and he meant to help it get there.

Thus he tried demonstrating the authoritative nature of the conscience, but he did not stop at the basic level of individual ethics. He tried to apply his theory. In fact, he believed that it was historically necessary that he apply his theory at the collective or public level. To this end, he developed his theory of "real identities" and the urgent defense of historical empiricism that it demanded. Real identities were actual instances of the reconciliation of identity between ideal and real. As such, they were historical events, though Haym's relative ignorance of history forced him, in most instances, to leave it to his readers to supply cases in point. He did, however, supply a typology of these identities, for which he adopted a Hegelian terminology. They occurred in three "moments" that, in rank order, proceeded from "speech" through "evolving concrete morality" to "art," all of which were subsumed as "abolished [yet 'raised' and therefore 'preserved'] moments" (*aufgehobene Momente*) in "religion," the highest form of human endeavor. This listing at first seems apolitical, but that appearance is misleading. Religion was the "highest form of action by the ego" (*Form der Thathandlung des Ichs*).[81] This wide definition could and did include politics.

Haym did not fault absolute idealism solely for its ethical insufficiency. He also condemned it for scanting historical empiricism. The two criticisms were part of the same case inasmuch as it was the inability of the ideal to take adequate account of the real—that is, the empirical—that caused its ethical failure. The real identities were empirical cases in point of the identity that Haym sought and, like Droysen and Duncker, he thought of the empirical bent of the German present as a promising sign of its ongoing moral and political progress. Thus, comparing the age of absolute idealism with his own, Haym claimed that the preceding generation had been "fortunate" in its calling "freely to translate the life of the mind into a world of ideas," but he believed that the "present generation" was even more fortunate because it was called to exchange the intellectual essence of the old metaphysic "for the gold of real existence." He therefore noted hopefully the interconnection between the "ethical tone of the present" and the "increased earnestness of empirical research." As a consequence of this "devotion to the concrete," he and his contemporaries had "invincibly rescued . . . freedom" and would therefore be able "to steer through the conflagration of history into a safe harbor."[82] As his choice of a nautical metaphor implies, Haym had in mind collective as well as individual redemption and expected practical historical results.

The immediate means to this progress was historical inquiry. Philosophy, he maintained, had done its part by expounding the idea of freedom and analyzing the "vital, developing interpenetration of man and nature (Durchdringung von Mensch und Natur)." Now empirical research had to provide the "full sense of the historical," without which "real identity" could not be achieved.[83] He insisted on the specifically historical character of this research by pointing out that the otherwise admirable Feuerbach, though empiricist in approach, had ignored "the historical moment . . . almost completely." That was a snare for the "true empiricist" to avoid because there was no such thing as a "universal human being." There were only "nationally, temporally, geographically, and individually determined human beings."[84] With the partial exception of his article "Philosophy," which was a very detailed history of the development of truth from the ancient Greece to nineteenth-century Germany, Haym could not himself present the results of such inquiries. He could, however, encourage others to do so and indicate how history could be put to moral and political use, and he did have at least a general interpretation of the past from which he, also in general terms, projected the future.

At first appearance, admittedly, Haym's criticisms of absolute idealism seem to have little to do with each other. His claim that its identity theory was too purely ideal to affect individual actions and his demand to take empirical account of history seem related only in the loose sense that both required close attention to the concrete and the particular. Haym never really integrated these claims adequately into an internally consistent philosophy. For all his good intentions, he was simply not a successful synthesizer and not an effective exponent of his own ideas. Some of his statements, however, give reasonably clear indications of what he wanted to say. His discussion of Kant's ethics and his scattered remarks on historical progress since the sixteenth century give a reasonably clear sense of what he took truly ethical action to be, of why he urged contemporaries to the study of history, and of how he expected the future to look.

His discussion of Kant is quite informative. Haym argued that Kant achieved "practical and empirical . . . mediation" between philosophy and history. This claim at first seems surprising, but all that Haym really meant was that Kant "derived from his doctrine of the categorical imperative—discussed in Kant's *The Metaphysical Foundations of Morals*—the obligation to intervene as a member in the historical process."[85] This is a plausible and illuminating way of looking at the categorical imperative, that is, at the idea that in ethical activity properly so called, people act in such a way that their actions could be framed to the maxim of a universal law. After all, if individuals at all times employed the categorical imperative, their actions would continuously and freely produce a binding system of laws contained in the empirical data of history, that is, the sum of their actions. The result would, of course, also be an instance of that combination of freedom and necessity that he so greatly admired and would be what he termed a "real identity."

Haym was less convincing, at least as an interpreter of Kant, when he asserted as a supposed requirement in Kant's ethics that "philosophy . . . prove its imperative *as such* through the observation of the historical process." After all, Kant's insistence that motivation rather than result is the true test of ethical action meant that ethics were invisible to empirical examination. This assertion, however, is good evidence for what Haym had in mind. Haym wanted both the assurance that people could find binding ethical standards to guide them in their actions and that an observer could chart these actions in history. He unintentionally distorted Kant's meaning in order to gain the latter assurance. Haym therefore believed that it was possible to avoid the danger of seeing in history merely "what has happened for the realization of the noumenal moral law" and of simply "establishing the imperative as a lifeless fact." That is, it was possible to go beyond the lifeless history of the spirit that he found in Hegel to "seeking . . . traces in history where the imperative is present as a vital drive, not as externality but as strength."[86] In other words, research could find real cases of real individuals performing really ethical actions. In Haym's terms, "real identities" could be validated both before and after the fact.

The purpose of this search was not simply to supply examples of good and bad actions for imitation or avoidance. In 1842 Haym had abandoned his belief in timeless truths in favor of a Hegelian vision of progress that he kept long after rejecting Hegel's identity theory and embracing empiricism. He wanted to historicize ethics in order to keep a watch on ethical evolution through time. Just as ideas gained and lost validity over time, so the ethical content of history changed, and changed purposively. In Haym's view, things were getting better. Change was a necessary and beneficent part of history, even when it destroyed the old to make way for the new. In that attitude, he used the term "right of history" in Droysen's sense.[87] Given his weak grounding in history, he was not able to discuss such matters at length or in much detail, but he shared Droysen's and Duncker's views of the content and direction of modern history. Again, he devoted his major works to providing philosophical legitimation of that content. He, too, dated the beginning of modern history from the Reformation and saw the task of the present and immediate future as a resumption and completion of the Reformation's "energetic drive toward a restoration of the dissolved unity . . . [between] the moral and the intellectual."[88] That claim, obviously, made his own philosophizing seem a centrally important contribution to the assigned tasks of the present. He was, of course, joining Duncker and Droysen in seeing in the Reformation a change in ideas that would ultimately lead to a change in practice, including political practice, now that the intellectual requirements for such change had been met.

Germany's present and future politics interested him deeply, because in the future German state, he believed, Germany's new ethical discoveries would find their complete realization. He did not himself say very much about political questions, however, because his ignorance of history made him diffident. He preferred to be guided by the senior and more knowledgeable Duncker.[89] Unsurprisingly, therefore, his few remarks on recent history and on present and future politics are entirely in line with the latter's as well, of course, as with Haym's philosophical excursions. He aided Duncker in his 1846 agitation over Schleswig-Holstein and over the meeting of the Prussian United Diet the next year.[90] At Duncker's urging, he reviewed Georg Gottfried Gervinus's pamphlet "The Prussian Constitution" and came to much the same conclusions about it that Droysen did. He admired constitutional government, but he did not agree with Gervinus's call for a Prussian constitution both out of a fear that too rigid a constitutionalism would impair cooperation between king and people and in the belief that, in any case, a Prussian constitution was too limited an objective. The object was to unify Germany as a constitutional state.[91]

The meeting of the diet excited him because he believed that it was the beginning of a major transformation that would, in political terms, complete Germany's ethical progress. He accordingly followed newspaper accounts closely and repeatedly turned to Duncker for advice and instruction.[92] In mid-November he prefaced his *Speakers and Speeches of the First Prussian United Diet*, which he prepared at Duncker's instigation, with a plausible description of his initial and eventual estimation of the diet's significance:

Just as, after the barren winter, the spring strengthens the earth and enlivens it to new birth, so a power of spring ran through us and the entire German nation when Prussia's estates were gathered into their first parliament. The remembrance of so much nullity vanished before the hope that mightily seized us: we too would now develop laws, we too would become a powerful and respected people (*Volk*), we too would live in the enjoyment of an ordered freedom. The inspired word of our representative drove with convulsive effect into the core of our life, and we younger ones, who were not blessed to see the war-like rising of the nation (*Nation*) at the beginning of the century, for the first time experienced the significance of a moral movement seizing the entire people (*Volk*). In the wide-spread ground of intellectual strivings we saw this movement lead like a fresh stream along whose banks the grass again stood green; we drank from it thirstily as from a well of life.[93]

The language is florid, but it conveys quite well his sense not just that something very important was happening but that something inevitable was in process that would revivify Germany in moral and political terms. His key hopes were the simultaneous possession of national power and "ordered freedom" (*geordnete Freiheit*). The image of spring following winter, as Haym employed it, was not meant to suggest cyclical recurrence but to signal a long-anticipated blossoming.

He recurred to seasonal images when he discussed his realization, months later, that he would have to wait a while longer for unification and freedom. He claimed then that he had earlier mistaken "a single, premature spring day" for the "late appearance of spring" and also compared his original analysis to the use of a "bad star chart" that made it impossible correctly to identify the stars and track their courses.[94] In their own way, these analogies were also hopeful because, of course, even a delayed spring eventually arrives, and the stars can be tracked with the right star chart. This was Haym's assertion of the possibility of certain prediction, in fact it was itself a prediction. Just as in "The Prussian Constitution" Gervinus wrote of a "silent force of affairs" (*stille Gewalt der Dinge*) that was at work in Prussia and Germany in 1847, so Haym wrote of a "power of affairs" (*Macht der Dinge*) that worked through individuals and toward the unification of Germany as a state. This time, he reasoned, it had not produced the right individuals in the right place and at the right time. The next time it would, and he hoped his book would help them learn from the mistakes of their predecessors.[95] He was confident about the future, and it made sense for him to be. By his analysis, the ethical preconditions for statehood in Germany already existed and the signs of change seemed plain to see.

Heinrich von Sybel

Heinrich von Sybel followed his own, rather different, path into what became the Prussian School, and these differences in the course of his development help explain the distinctive features of his mature historical and political thought and practice. Even before 1848, for example, he was cautious in offering predictions, though he did possess a theory of progress and thought he knew where German history was headed. Further, he was an early believer in compromise, in not letting the best be enemy of the good, an outlook he associated with the admired English tradition of politics. Finally, his designation of Prussia as the destined agent of political reform in Germany was relatively opportunistic. He thought that, for reasons of tradition and self-interest, Prussia would unify Germany under a suitable constitution, but this was a fairly cool-headed calculation unmixed with any special affection for the Hohenzollern monarchy. The fact that in other, and more important, respects he shared their views suggests, of course, that the real driving force behind the creation of the Prussian School was a common desire to advocate unification and the active collaboration between government and citizens on the basis of historical certitude.

His social and geographical origins partly explain these differences. He was more socially secure than Droysen, Duncker, or Haym. His ancestors belonged to the urban patriciate of the formerly independent Westphalian city of Soest, and his father earned the family a hereditary patent of Prussian nobility for years of diligent work in the Prussian administration.[96] His degree and professorship did not bring him into the elite; they merely determined what branch of it he served in, and he seems not to have felt, as the others sometimes did, a need to prove himself through the possession and display of special knowledge. He also had less reason to feel antagonistic to the old order. Moreover, he was not a Prussian except in a legal sense. During his lifetime, to be sure, Soest was a part of the Prussian Rhineland, but this was a recent acquisition far to the west of the core provinces of the monarchy. As a Protestant in an overwhelmingly Catholic area, he felt some affection for the Protestant Hohenzollern dynasty and was profoundly distrustful of the Catholic church, but he was a westerner as Droysen, Duncker, and Haym were not. He viewed Prussia from an emotional as well as a geographic distance. It also surely made some difference that, until 1849, he was not in contact with the other three. From 1843 onward, Droysen and Duncker knew each other at least by correspondence and exchanged common political views. Duncker and Haym worked closely together from 1845 onward and, through Duncker, Haym was at least tenuously in contact with Droysen. Sybel seems not to have made their acquaintance until 1849 and to have worked on his own before that date.

His formal education also followed a different pattern. It provided him with the intellectual materials necessary for historically based predictions of the national future, but his arguments had distinctive emphases and nuances. For example, he was as devout an empiricist as any of the other three, but his empiricism was unproblematic. He invoked it to fault careless scholarship, not as a triumph of the German mind toward which history had toiled. This was because he never fell under the spell of philosophical idealism and studied under Leopold Ranke at Berlin from 1834 to 1837. He attended Ranke's lectures in each term of his study, and his six-semester membership in Ranke's seminar set a record never again matched by a Ranke student.[97] Ranke used the seminar not just to have students report on their own and comment on each other's research but to persuade them of his views on how to study and teach history. Sybel was deeply enough impressed that he himself established a historical seminar modeled on the original as soon as he became a professor at Bonn.[98] Sybel meant more than a routine compliment when he wrote Ranke in 1874 to describe those seminar meetings as "unforgettable" occasions from which his "academic life took its beginnings."[99] Ranke's effect on Sybel went beyond instilling a habit of meticulous attention to document and detail. Sybel also acquired a dogmatic certainty that there was one right way, the Rankean way, to research and write history. He was, by his lights, merely stating an undeniable truth when in 1844 he told Georg Waitz never to let "the positing of grand hypotheses impair strictness and method in the treatment of individual sources" and never to "make current a preconceived view too early in the consideration of the surviving data."[100] This self-assurance is all the more remarkable because Sybel was then engaged in a serious fight with his friend Waitz over the origins of early German political institutions. In any case, these were sentiments with which Droysen, Duncker, and Haym would have agreed but which they would never have stated so flatly. They defended empiricism against the competing approach, which in many ways they still admired; for Sybel it was a dogma so certain as to invite statement without supporting argument.

This self-confident empiricism assured that when Sybel turned his hand to prediction, his predictions would be grounded in historical data, but another of Ranke's legacies threatened to keep his attention safely riveted on the past rather than on the present and future. Ranke, who was a conservative opposed to national unification in any case, consistently argued that history could not instruct the present for the benefit of the future. He had excellent grounds for making that case. On the one hand, he believed that God worked fundamental changes in history, so that the experience of one epoch was not relevant to another. On the other hand, and more important in this perspective, he did not believe that there was progress in history. Without that belief, it was not possible to project tendencies observed in the past into the future. If Sybel had remained entirely true to Ranke's teachings, he would not have ventured to predict, and, in the event, his predictions were tentative and cautious.

Droysen, Duncker, and Haym, of course, variously adapted elements of Hegel's philosophy of history to arrive at a theory of progress. Sybel, for several reasons, did not. He appears to have been temperamentally averse to philosophy, though he later said that it was "unfortunate" that he had not studied it "with the same diligence" as history and at the end of formal study he tried to read Hegel.[101] Nothing much came of the exercise, though one of the theses for defense appended to his 1838 dissertation on the historian Jordanes and the origins of the Getae read: "The historian cannot write history without philosophy." Even if he believed that, as opposed to offering it for the sake of debate, the proposition is too vague to indicate a definite philosophical orientation. Another of the appended theses is more suggestive. In a clever reversal of Tacitus's often quoted dictum in the *Annals* to have written "without anger or passion" (*sine ira et studio*), Sybel asserted that historians do or should write "with" (*cum*) those qualities.[102] Again assuming that he did not offer this solely for the sake of argument, it reads like an early indication of a strong wish to put history in the service of present and future needs, a wish that more or less called for a theory of progress.

Sybel did, in fact, develop such a theory, or perhaps one should say outlook, as he did not systematically articulate or defend it. He borrowed the materials from a surprising, though actually reasonable, source, the teachings of the great legal historian Karl Friedrich von Savigny. This source is surprising because, from the time of his famous debate with the legist Thibaut over the wisdom of revising and codifying German law, Savigny has been a byword for a sort of legal conservatism. It is not possible to do justice to Savigny's views in a short space, but it is possible to describe his basic argument. He believed that laws do, or anyway should, reflect the developed condition of the "national spirit" (*Volksgeist*) and should not, therefore, be amended or replaced according to the ahistorical dictates of reason. Argued in those terms, the view is hard to refute unless one wants to say that laws should not fit time and place. A corollary of this view, however, is more problematic, namely, the notion that laws and legal institutions that had existed for some time have a presumed right to continue to exist. Droysen's contrast between the "right of history" and "historical rights" was an assault on just this corollary.

It was, however, possible to accept Savigny's basic claim without going on to argue against deliberate legal and institutional change. The arguments that Droysen, Duncker, and Haym each made against the Enlightenment, for example, were quite consonant with Savigny's attack on Thibaut's theories without being arguments against progressive reform. Nor was Savigny simply and single-mindedly against change. The *Volksgeist* was a historical product that changed and brought changes over time, though Savigny had no reason to stress this obvious implication. Sybel did. In 1888 he recalled that, as a student at Berlin, he attended one of Savigny's lectures "half by accident" and was delightedly surprised by the "plenitude of ethical and cultural historical wealth" that a careful study of the pandects (the digest of decisions and opinions of Roman jurists) supplied to him. He began to study under Savigny in the belief that "a full quantum of juristic education is the indispensable precondition for the comprehension and presentation of political history."[103]

Sybel evidently liked finding a legal complement to the more narrowly political history studied under Ranke, but it also seems to have had the wider effect of accustoming Sybel to thinking and judging the suitability of institutions and practices in terms of the needs and cultural level of the people and country in question. This mental habit could, of course, easily become a standard by which to appraise contemporary practice and ascertain future necessities. Once he was practiced in that habit, once he was accustomed to thinking of change, even gradual change, as normal, Sybel was able to think of progress as a norm and, so, to judge even sudden and major changes as desirable as long they contributed to progress over the long term. He argued this case in the first of several scholarly disputes that checkered his career. (Though he was always polite to his adversaries, he was pugnacious enough really to enjoy a good fight.)

This first fight grew out of his earliest scholarly publications, his dissertation on Jordanes and the Getae (1838), the *History of the First Crusade* (1841), and *The Origins of German Kingship* (1844).[104] These works all dealt with early German history and let him employ both the techniques of political history learned from Ranke and the techniques of legal history learned from Savigny. This combination led him, in the last of these works, to the inescapable but at first alarming, and for some time controversial, conclusion that the major political institutions of medieval Germany were borrowings from the late Roman Empire rather than products of slow, indigenous development. This conclusion at first disturbed him, and it subsequently angered some of his readers, much in the way that any discussion of possibly beneficial effects of imperialism might outrage a postcolonial population today. French military successes and legal innovations in Germany, earlier in the century, were humiliating, and many Germans did not want to read about how much their forebears learned from the Roman legions. Moreover, Sybel's thesis contradicted the published views of the great Germanist Jakob Grimm and threatened to cost Sybel the friendship of his fellow medievalist and Ranke student Georg Waitz who was publishing contrary findings in the same area.[105]

Sybel, however, felt forced to his conclusions, because the evidence pointed to them and he felt governed by evidence. He read the evidence that way because his study of legal evolution made him mindful of the relationship between laws and cultural levels. In this case, he found that German political practice in the early Middle Ages, though roughly suited to actual needs, was too advanced to have been produced by their primitive society. Obviously, then, it had been borrowed and adapted. This meant, however, that he had modified Savigny's model of legal evolution in two ways, neither of which actually contradicted Savigny. First, and in a manner analogous to Droysen's idea of the "right of history," he implicitly legitimated sudden and profound change by accepting as justifiable German borrowings from the Romans. Second, and relatedly, he legitimated such innovations by reference to their long-term as well as immediate effects. In a revealing passage in a letter to Ranke, he admitted that he was putting early Germans on a level with the "West Indian negroes" of the present, and then pointed out that it would be valid if the negroes of the West Indies, centuries hence, reached the high cultural level to which Germans had now attained. (In fairness, he did not rule out that possibility.)[106] The letter showed both continued affinity to, and new independence from, Ranke. There was nothing in the Rankean approach to contradict instances of sudden change and borrowing in history, but, from Ranke's point of view, to validate change in terms of benefits over the long run was to introduce an exiguous standard of historical judgment. Sybel needed such a standard because he really wanted, as Ranke avowedly did not, to use history to instruct the present in its tasks.

In principle, this view of history called for the analysis of the present and the anticipation of the future in terms of tendencies seen to be unfolding in the past. In practice, Sybel (like Droysen and Duncker and Haym) often started from his understanding of the present and his hopes for the future in posing questions to the past. This present-mindedness was only natural, and it was theoretically defensible as long as its results were scrupulously tested with historical evidence. Sybel discussed this matter in July 1846 in "On the Tories," one of the lectures that he gave each year on the elector's birthday after leaving Bonn in 1845 for Marburg in electoral Hesse:

History and the present are not only linked by a temporal band. They stand to one another like lesson and deed, like knowing and willing. The strivings of the present should orient themselves and base themselves spiritually (*sich orientieren und geistig begründen*) with reference to the completed stages. For his part, the historian can win only from a vital rapport with the present the moral warmth (*sittliche Wärme*) needed to make a new artistic existence blossom from the past. . . . More than any other discipline, therefore, is history forced from her proper tracks when one wants to direct her solely to the learned circles. She is made to prosper in the open air and among the drives of the market place. If as a result she is sometimes dissipated or falls into error, that is only a sign that she has not yet reached her full strength and not at all that she has been seized by a sick deviation.[107]

These remarks show both what Sybel had in common with Droysen, Duncker, and Haym and what was distinctive in his conception of the tasks of the political historian. The obvious and important similarity was Sybel's clearly stated belief that history is inherently progressive, that progress unfolds in "stages," and that historians should be partisans of observable progress. In logic, this meant that Sybel, too, had to think of the winning side as the right side. This standard, moreover, left no room for nonhistorical standards of judgment.

Sybel also included some ideas that were more strictly his own. His claim that only a "vital rapport with the present" allowed the historian to write good histories was original, although the others certainly possessed that rapport, and the role of present-mindedness in research was an important question for Droysen years later in his lectures on historical method known and published as the *Historik*. This idea seems to be an application of the previously noted thesis appended to Sybel's 1838 dissertation that the historian should write "with anger and passion."[108] Sybel also wanted to write readable histories to be read by large readerships. Obviously, the strategy of all four historians required them to reach out to the largest possible publics, because, in the nature of things, it would have made little sense to have reserved moral and political preparation to a few, highly specialized readers. Only Sybel, however, described writing history as making "a new artistic existence blossom." He did not want moral earnestness to compromise the aesthetic demands of his craft. On the contrary, he believed that the one led to the other, and his most politically charged prerevolutionary writings are also his most enjoyably readable. Droysen, Duncker, and Haym did not yet take the time to worry about such matters.

In other respects, too, Sybel tried to follow the standards that he proclaimed. After publishing his controversial *Origins of German Kingship* in 1844, he turned away from medieval history and wrote on modern history for the literate lay readership. Just as Droysen in 1843 stopped working on antiquity and turned to modern history, so Sybel now produced works designed to tell readers about the prospects for change and to teach them how to behave in a changed political system. He complemented these with polemics against ideas and practices that he thought inimical to progress. It is easy to infer from these works a clear, if general, picture of the German future as Sybel envisioned it. He also offered vicarious experience in practical politics, perhaps because, for reasons of social antecedents, he could imagine wielding power to a degree that they could not.

Thus, one of the main points that he made in his previously mentioned lecture, "On the Tories of Today," was that even in the England that he deeply admired, the land of "slow progress" where "not one of the old forms is broken" even while "their content is completely changed," progress had often resulted from "countless conflicts" and from the "mixing of struggling forces."[109] If that had been true of England, it was even more true of the Continent. He pursued this idea further in his second, 1847, address on the elector's birthday, "On the Relationship of our Universities to Public Life." For example, he discussed the often violent expansion and consolidation of absolutist monarchies that Droysen had described as the rise of the "powers" to make the same point that Droysen did. He confessed that when one studied the victory of absolutism in Germany, it was impossible to "defend oneself from a deep regret . . . [for] the personal freedom, the colorful freshness, and the exciting variety" destroyed in the process. He then reminded his audience that history had called the princes to "hew from the rubble of German nationality the first stones" for the construction of the future. He pointed to "the new discipline and stark effectiveness of sovereignty" that they had introduced and that would be necessary in the ultimately unified Germany and to the "inevitability" of their achievement.[110] What happened was justified both by its happening and by its contribution to the future.

Sybel was calling for more than resigned acceptance of what could not be avoided. He wanted people to welcome the inevitable, and he maintained that history provided the winners with the necessary consciousness of their historical rightness. For example, he praised the absolutizing princes in Germany not merely in terms of their long-range and unintended effects but because their exertions were "borne along by the consciousness of a great and world historical superiority (*Bewußtsein einer großen und weltgeschichtlichen Überlegenheit*)" that would not have been present had their work not been necessary and that further excused the often violent and unlawful means they employed.[111] The converse of this attitude was his contempt for, and even anger at, those who took the wrong side in history, presumably on the grounds that they might have known better than to stand in the way of progress.

Three clear examples of this disdain appear in Sybel's writings before 1848. In 1843 thousands of Catholic pilgrims converged on the Trier cathedral to view what they believed was Jesus' robe. Sybel, along with J. Gildemeister, another professor at Bonn, responded by publishing a pedantic and often sarcastic treatise, *The Holy Robe at Trier and the other twenty Holy, Unsewn Robes. A historical Investigation*.[112] Sybel's dislike and distrust of

Catholics and Catholicism was consistent and unrelenting, but he was angrier at their anachronism than at anything else. He was equally harsh in the next year in the pieces that he wrote for the prestigious daily, the *Kölnische Zeitung,* on the Rhenish *Autonomen,* the privileged corporations of former imperial knights and their descendants. Despite his own legal status as noble, he had no use for legalized privilege. His irritation at the *Autonomen,* however, was at their misplaced nostalgia for the Holy Roman Empire.[113] In his better-known *Political Parties in the Rhineland described in their Relationship to the Prussian Constitution* (published in 1847, but with the main text written before the summoning of the Prussian United Diet) he was equally severe in attacking the so-called feudal-clerical party for trying "to shatter the creations of twelve generations and reverse the world of the present."[114]

To try to reverse progress was not merely wrong but criminal. That, in his view, was a mistake that Edmund Burke, his political hero, would never have made. To many nineteenth-century Europeans who studied England, Burke was not the conservative that a later generation of ideologues made him out to be. His pragmatism (and his eloquence) in dealing with revolution in Ireland and America and his horror (and his eloquence) at the revolution in France endeared him to those who wanted progress without upheaval. Sybel, who used Burke's career as a model for progressive statesmanship, was no exception. In order to correct the political inexperience of his readers, Sybel published two long essays on Burke—"Edmund Burke and the French Revolution" (1847) and "Edmund Burke and Ireland" (1848)—in Adolf Schmidt's politically congenial *Zeitschrift für Geschichtswissenschaft.* The point of these accounts of Burke's thoughts and actions during two revolutionary crises was to show how to handle major historical change when it finally came. Sybel therefore continually interrupted his narrative and analysis to address readers in his own voice in order to make sure that they had not missed the morals that he wanted to draw.

He heavily underscored Burke's talent for supporting, hence channelling and controlling, timely change while averting hasty and radical measures. In doing so, he singled out for praise Burke's "practical standpoint" and pronounced "empirical tendency."[115] He also admired Burke's "poetic love for the given material" and characteristic habit of "never asking about system and principle" but only about "creation and effect."[116] These compliments reflect a general dislike on the part of German liberals for doctrinaire politics. More specifically, they imply a claim that successful statesmen possess the empirical and practical virtues that Sybel recommended, a case in point of the affinity that Sybel desired between the historian and his history. Sybel, of course, wanted his readers to acquire

these qualities through critical emulation of the models he presented because he thought that they would soon be called to the unfamiliar exercise
of self-governance in Germany. He also wanted to give them a compass to
steer by. That compass was his interpretation of Germany's past and future history, but the readers had to know enough history to read its bearing. Here, too, Burke provided a useful model, and Sybel accordingly
praised him for considering matters in a "world-historical manner" and
for understanding the great truth that in the broad context of world history, "the life of a nation (*Leben eines Volkes*) follows general laws independent of the arbitrary will of individuals." Great men like Burke
accommodated themselves to these laws and thus knew how to behave because "past and future" were linked "in uninterrupted connectedness"
inasmuch as "political like linguistic development possesses an inner necessity."[117] In so arguing, Sybel was employing the vision of historical
progress that he had adapted from Savigny years earlier. His affinity for
Burke made him attribute to him his own theory of progress and to portray him, surely incorrectly, as someone who navigated the present with a
map of the future spread before him. That was what he wanted his readers to do as well, and he was ready to chart the future for them—if only
somewhat sketchily. As the linguistic analogy suggests, Sybel was more
modest than, say, Droysen, in predicting the future. At least, it seems a
more uncertain exercise to determine the future development of a language than, thinking of Droysen's favorite metaphor for prediction, to
guess where a river is headed by noting the direction of its flow. Sybel obviously did not think that the task was impossible, whatever its difficulties
and uncertainties, and he extrapolated from the past at least the general
shape and content of the future. These anticipations consistently appear as
points of reference in his writings between 1846 and the outbreak of revolution in Germany in 1848.

He, too, dated the beginning of modern history from the German Reformation, which "sunk in the prepared earth . . . the seeds of a new world
history." Like Duncker and Droysen, he insisted that the Reformation was
as much a political as a religious event. The reformers, he believed, sought
a comprehensive reform of "faith and morals" and therefore directed their
appeals to "the mass of the people who thirsted for salvation, rather than
to the potentates of the Church." The fortunate result was that they had
"not fallen into one-sided enthusiasm but had united all the achievements
of scholarship, art, and politics in the rebuilding of the times." He explained this sweeping quality of their efforts by pointing out that "state
and society were enclosed in the Church," so that religious renewal required "a critique of the collective political and social situation."[118] He also
pointed to the linkage between classical antiquity and the Reformation,

whose political goal, he explained, was the selective creation, obviously under greatly altered circumstances, of the "antique state."[119] By this he meant primarily the return to active political participation of the citizenry. More generally, he, too, thought of political life as the necessary completion of the moral emancipation begun in the sixteenth century.

Luther, that is, began a "movement" in which "progress" would follow in the "state and profane knowledge," though not all at once and not without more or less painful reverses from time to time. These short-term costs were the price of long-term benefits, and Sybel readily admitted that the immediate effect of the Reformation was the prevalence in Germany of particularism and princely absolutism. He made the same case that Droysen and Duncker did, namely, that this unhappy coincidence was the necessary effect of the demonstrable "impotence" of the imperial government and the manifest impossibility, given the "general disunity" among the territorial princes, of achieving fundamental reforms through consent. These factors came powerfully into play during the reign of Charles V. Sybel acknowledged the cost to Germany of continued, in fact of increased, weakness and division. He also believed that this cost was worth paying because the "sole means to escape the misery of general decline" and to hasten national unification was the "total rejection of the old, wasted imperial unity (*Reichseinheit*)" and in the temporary increase in particularism. In a parallel and closely related fashion, the increase in the arbitrary powers of the triumphant princes cleared away the remnants of feudal privilege and, thus, prepared the way for subsequent freedom.[120]

Sybel, then, thought of the sixteenth, seventeenth, and eighteenth centuries as periods of major historical progress in and for Germany. Outward expansion and internal integration of some German states meant that "large masses were integrated, strong enough to represent worthily the national spirit (*Nationalgeist*) at home and the national strength (*Nationalkraft*) abroad and to prepare forcefully for a future unification of the Fatherland."[121] This analysis shows several characteristic features of Sybel's analysis of recent German history. First, he, too, distinguished between the real content of history and the conscious motives of historical actors. The princes thought that they were acting in their own interests, but, in fact, they were preparing for national unification. As Sybel had remarked in praise of Burke, history follows an "inner necessity."[122] Second, he looked forward both to internal freedom and external strength. Both were ends in themselves while being means to each other. Finally, and quite clearly, the great goal toward which history was moving was national unification.

Sybel was, unsurprisingly, especially interested in more recent history, and his discussions of the late eighteenth and early nineteenth centuries reveal a clear belief that the historical wind had set in for the establishment of a special kind of constitutional order in Germany. Thus, he greatly admired Frederick the Great but noted that, for historical reasons, he was the last of the great monarchs.[123] Elsewhere, and on a more general note, he commented that toward the end of the century, "life seemed to go out of" absolute monarchy, which had, in any case, by then completed its necessary tasks.[124] The occurrence of the French Revolution proved that something more timely and vital was needed, though Sybel thought that both the theory and practice of the revolution were no better than what they tried to replace. The former was flawed because "the complete individualism of *natural rights* makes impossible a rational and effective organization . . . of rule." This is a curious criticism in view of the tremendous military power that the revolution unleashed, and Sybel's judgment was obviously more affected by his belief that trust between citizens and government is the source of strength than by the actual evidence of the historical record. He also deplored the revolution's practical effects. For its first years, he pointed to terror, tyranny, and foreign conquest without explaining how individualism led to these. Over the longer term, it was responsible for what he thought of as the chief features of contemporary France. His indictment of it reads like a list of his own social fears: the revolution had resulted in "plutocracy" and the prevalence of "competition, social war, and ever-present egotism."[125]

Germany had another path to follow and began to advance along it in the early nineteenth century. With foreign troops on their soil, Germans came to understand that "the time had come to dissolve the absoluteness of the individual state (*Absolutie des Einzelstaats*) on the one hand and to strengthen the national consciousness of great Germany (*Nationalbewußtsein großen Deutschlands*) on the other." Germans, that is, now rejected particularist loyalties and became intensely aware of their common nationality. They wanted political freedom and political unity. The first practical result of this changed consciousness was the "fresh greatness of Prussia" shown in Stein's reforms to which, Sybel maintained, the "life of the nation" still resonated.[126] In other words, Germany in general and Prussia in particular were ready, or almost ready, to resume the task of unification necessarily put aside long before during the reign of Charles V. This movement ceased during the Restoration, but Sybel expected its speedy and successful resumption. Like Droysen, Duncker, and, more vaguely, Haym, Sybel looked to Prussia to lead in this work, but his designs for Prussia had some distinctive characteristics.

He made this case in *The Political Parties of the Rhineland* (1847), the main text of which he completed before Frederick William IV issued the February Patent but the foreword to which he drafted when the Prussian United Diet was already in session. He used the work to trace the struggles of a hero, the "constitutional-liberal party" against a villain, the "feudal-clerical party." The former, as the representative of inevitable progress, would ultimately prevail and, when it did, Prussia would get a constitution and, after a time, Germany would be unified. In fact, he thought of a Prussian constitution as a precondition for national unification. As a westerner who had taught in the Rhineland and in Hesse, he keenly appreciated German distrust of Prussia. He therefore judged that a Prussian constitution was "in the interest of German unity" because it would eliminate "the difference between Prussia and the other German states" and thus quiet the latter's fears. He also believed that only a constitution would fit Prussia for her tasks. By heightening "the political education and dedication" of Prussian citizens, it would release their energies into the state. It was, he believed, "a truth of history" that "the strength of the Prussian state can only be created through the free activity of its people."[127]

These findings, though in principle based on historical evidence, are really derived from Sybel's basically Aristotelian assumption that people "are called not merely to family life."[128] State power and dynamism would increase under a constitution because political activity and engagement were basic human needs. This fundamental belief had a major practical annex. Sybel, characteristically if somewhat self-deceivingly, declared himself free from the "despotism of theory" and correspondingly aware of the "rich variety that the historical development of politics displays." In other words, different nations with different pasts needed different constitutions. The Prussian and, later, the German constitutions were not exceptions to this rule. In a partial contradiction of his argument from human nature, therefore, he called for a Prussian constitution "not as an inherent right of men and peoples but on account of its utility in the Prussian and German circumstances of today."[129] In other words, the political capacities of Prussians and Germans had to be exercised in ways and under forms that were in the Prussian and German political interest.

It was, for example, essential that the power of the Prussian monarch remain intact because of the presence of "powerful neighbors" and because the growing conflict of rich and poor required "a strong and steady central government" of a sort that no democracy could provide. For Sybel, as for Droysen, this did not entail centralism on the French model. The diversity among the Prussian provinces and within Germany as a whole ruled out that possibility. Moreover, Sybel believed that a decent respect for individual needs and local peculiarities would actually increase the strength and cohesion of the state.[130] It certainly did not require excluding the people from political power. Sybel reasoned that capitalism and the consequent conversion of all property into liquid form gave a large portion of the population sufficient wealth and leisure for informed and active participation in state affairs.[131] (Almost needless to say, he favored a property qualification for the franchise). The object was to tap the energy of this loyal and monied citizenry for the good of the state, as "utility" was, after all, the standard by which to judge constitutions.[132] To that end, he argued that "a free and reciprocal recognition of monarch and parliament is the essential, the basic condition of constitutional life."[133] He, too, saw political freedom as willing cooperation rather than as contest and conflict, though with the important qualification that his standard was a "state power that is strong enough for the conduct of national affairs without annihilating the sphere of individual rights."[134]

In stating that pious hope, Sybel simply did not imagine that there could be any rights contrary to state power or that state power, in a unified Germany, would trample on legitimate rights. This outlook led him to distrust formal, legalistic guarantees as much as Droysen and Duncker did. He was especially hostile to the idea of the separation of powers, which he compared to an attempt to separate "the light from the lamp." In his view, such separation was not possible and, even if possible, not desirable. He denied vigorously that it existed even in England, its supposed homeland.[135] The real cause of his objections was probably less its alleged unfeasibility than its threat to weaken the state by setting part against part. His fear on this point made sense in light of his belief that freedom and strength were reciprocal qualities in the state. On those grounds he argued that the constitution would have to rest on a "deep and free trust" among all parts of the state, including government and citizenry. He therefore also urged "moderation" on all parties and a determination to achieve reforms with the least possible break with the past.[136] It will come as no surprise that he thought it "impossible to found a constitutional monarchy through revolution."[137]

It followed, of course, that change would have to come from above, and Sybel joined the others in looking to the Prussian monarch to constitutionalize Prussia by voluntarily sharing his sovereignty.[138] Interestingly, he gave no reasons why the monarch should choose to do this, though by implication he had in mind precedents under Frederick the Great and Stein and, more generally, the supposed royal self-interest in gaining the access of strength that constitutionalism, rightly conceived, was bound to offer. He was correspondingly excited and delighted in 1847 by the promise of the February Patent. He described it as an "immeasurably important step" because simply by issuing the patent, the king had "declared and determined irrevocably" the necessity for future change that would lead through a Prussian constitution to national unification. He believed that this harvest could be gathered quickly if the "seed" just planted were properly tended and the "natural development of this germ upset by no new hindrances." Even if something unforeseen should go wrong, the patent and the diet would have indicative significance. Accomplishments to date showed an increase in "political sense" that meant that development could not be delayed much longer.[139] This tranquil optimism did not, could not, survive the events of 1848.

4

Expectation and Action: March to May 1848

Droysen, Duncker, Haym, and Sybel misread their situation and prospects in spring 1848 for understandable reasons. A brief glance at the political world in which they moved will explain why this was the case. On 22 February the barricades went up in Paris. Two days later, Louis Philippe, France's Orleanist monarch since 1830, fled to London while Alphonse Lamartine, author of a four-volume history in verse of the French Revolution of 1789, formed a provisional government for the Second Republic. With memories of that revolution very much in mind, the German princes hastily introduced reforms and installed popular governments when unrest spread into Germany. These new governments sent relatively national-minded delegates to the Confederate Assembly (*Bundestag*) at Frankfort, which, in late March, impaneled the Seventeen Trustees (*Vertrauensmänner*) to draft a constitution for a unified Germany. In the same period, though without official sanction, fifty-one persons associated with the prerevolutionary opposition met in Heidelberg and called for the convening of a Pre-Parliament (*Vorparlament*) to meet later in the month at Frankfort in order to prepare for an elected assembly that would unify Germany. Before either the Seventeen or the Pre-Parliament met, revolution struck both Vienna and Berlin. On 14 March, Metternich was dismissed and fled to England, and on the twenty-first, Frederick William IV, sickened by three days of street-fighting in his capital, ordered his troops from Berlin and promised his support for constitutional government and national unification.

Things seemed to be changing, quickly and profoundly. The significance of these events certainly seemed clear to Droysen, Duncker, Haym, and Sybel: in a few weeks, every barrier to Germany's unification as a constitutional state had been leveled. If only the revolution could be kept in hand, all that they had wanted and expected seemed certain to be accomplished very soon. It seemed that their predictions for the German future were about to be realized, and the question now was not how to bring about change but how to keep it moving in the right direction and at the right speed. When, in these changed conditions, they sensed danger, it came more from the left than the right. Their optimism was entirely understandable, but there was a good deal of self-deception in their appreciation of the situation. They were too ideologically blinkered to see that, in fact, less had changed than they imagined.

Official Germany no longer resisted change and now actually sponsored it, but this shift in policy was a result of panic and temporizing rather than of a change in heart or, more damaging to liberal and nationalist hopes, of a real change of who really had power. The princes hoped to avoid the worst and to preserve some of their power by forestalling the revolution with timely concessions. Despite their present fears, however, the princes were still there, and so were their armies. In March, and for some time thereafter, they were either afraid to use those armies or, as happened in Berlin and Vienna, used them badly by deploying field troops in city streets against urban crowds of the soldiers' fellow citizens. Later, however, the princes would recover their nerve and their generals would make the needed changes in tactical doctrine. Later, too, they would regain the confidence, or at least the acquiescence, of a majority of their subjects. Many of those who took to the streets in March were not really interested in the national questions that preoccupied the deputies in Frankfort, and the princes' defense of the sovereign rights of their states was genuinely popular even among many liberals. In the spring, however, it would have required prescience to see that the conditions existed for a successful counterrevolution. Change seemed unstoppable, and to Droysen and the others, change meant the constitutional unification they had long predicted. They were, of course, pleased with this conclusion.

Haym nicely captured the spirit of those first weeks in a letter to his parents. He wrote the main text on 16 March, after the revolution in France and during the first stirrings in Germany. He registered some anxiety when he noted that "the Fatherland is also shaken," but then added confidently that "the long-sought regeneration will proceed out of the peculiar spirit and feeling of German nationality." In a postscript written on 18 March, after he had learned of Metternich's fall from power, he apostrophized: "God be praised that we have seen this day; I have great hope that He will be of further help!"[1] He was delighted to witness the outcome that he had expected, but witnessing was not enough. The politics of expectation now had to give way to a politics of action. Before 1848 Haym and the others had been condemned, willy-nilly, to approach the history of the present mainly as onlookers and commentators. They had done what they could, but for the most part, they watched and waited. At last they could do something. Politicking was legal, and there were meetings, official and unofficial, to attend and address. Men like Haym were well placed for such activities. They were literate, articulate, and energetic. Unlike most Germans in 1848, they had a program and were used to thinking of politics in national terms. Moreover, they were notables of a sort. They were known in their localities, at least in a general way, for their political views, and their publications gave them something of a national reputation. It was also to their advantage that they had moved to the right just by standing still. Before the revolution their views were unacceptable to most of official Germany. Now there was less to choose from, for those with power and privilege to preserve, and their views seemed relatively moderate. Their calls for a unified, constitutional Germany were now not very different from what could be heard in the Confederate Assembly. It also helped that they wanted to act.

In Droysen's case this wish was satisfied fairly quickly. In Schleswig-Holstein a provisional, German nationalist government had constituted itself at Rendsburg on 24 March with the avowed purpose of bringing the duchies fully into Germany. On the twenty-seventh, it nominated Droysen, prominent for years in local German nationalist politics, to represent it at the meetings of the Seventeen in Frankfort, where he arrived on 2 April. On the sixth he began to attend the meetings of the Seventeen, despite the initial reluctance of the Confederate authorities to challenge Denmark by recognizing the credentials of a representative of the Rendsburg government.[2] The move from provincial Kiel to Frankfort—formerly the site of imperial coronations and now the seat both of the Confederate Assembly and the unofficial but authoritative Pre-Parliament—was a major change of milieu for Droysen. He loved it. Now he met almost daily with such political luminaries as Anton von Schmerling and Franz von Somaruga of Austria and Max von Gagern of Wiesbaden, as well as fellow historians such as Gervinus and Dahlmann. He occasionally talked with Franz von Colloredo-Wallsee, Metternich's old antagonist and now Austrian delegate to the Confederate Assembly. Droysen's letters and the diary that he now kept sparkle with dropped names. This was very different from giving a political edge to his lectures at Kiel, addressing gatherings in the duchies, and lobbying by mail with old friends and associates now placed in Prussian ministries. If only for reasons of unchangeable temperament, he still found much to deplore, but he was unquestionably happy. In one letter he even remarked that he felt as if all his "members and faculties were increasing in keenness."[3] His letters in the following weeks show that he thought that he was close to the center of power, and he took it as a matter of course when the electoral committee for the fifth district of Schleswig-Holstein chose him for the National Assembly.[4]

Duncker's entrance into national politics was nearly as rapid as Droysen's. When the revolution reached Berlin on 18 March, he was in Halle and engaged in the initial research for what eventually became his *History of Antiquity*.[5] He now put his work aside and hurried to the royal court of Prussia in order to offer whatever advice he could. There is no reason to suppose that he had any important effect on royal policy or action, but circumstances had changed enough that he at least received a friendly hearing at court. He became closely enough acquainted with Augusta, Prince William's liberal and anglophile wife, that he was able in coming months to use her as conduit for suggestions on royal policy and as the personal contact who years later secured his appointment as tutor to the Prussian heir apparent, Frederick. He also met with Rudolf von Auerswald, Prussian minister-president until 29 March, who saw in Duncker two qualities especially valuable in the present circumstances: a record of opposition of sufficient standing to win the trust of revolutionaries and a commitment to monarchy deep enough to make him a reliable representative of Prussia at Frankfort. Auerswald consequently sent him west to the Pre-Parliament, though in the absence of direct rail link between Berlin and Frankfort, Duncker arrived only twenty-four hours before that body adjourned.[6] He was actually en route to Frankfort when the Provincial Diet of Prussian Saxony elected him representative to the forthcoming National Assembly on 2 April, and the final session of the Pre-Parliament that he attended threw his mandate into doubt by decreeing that representatives to the assembly were to be elected in indirect elections with a nearly universal male suffrage.[7]

Duncker's reaction to this sudden turn of events was mixed. He was delighted at his election. "Let us thank God that we have seen this day," he wrote to his wife, and added that he believed it would be possible to "build a good house for the Fatherland." He felt bound by the Pre-Parliament's election decree, however, and doubted the legality of his election. He decided to hold on to his seat, but only until valid elections were held. On 10 April the Provincial Diet reversed itself and declared its earlier election of deputies null and void. Then, several days later, the committee of electors at Halle, in accordance with the resolution of the Pre-Parliament, selected Duncker by a heavy majority. In slightly more than two weeks, the professor and editor had been endorsed by the Prussian head of government, the Prussian Saxon Diet, and the electors at Halle. Duncker was only telling the truth when he described his second, definitive, election as "the happiest day of my life."[8]

Haym was no less eager to enter national politics, but he found it harder to do so because he was younger and less well known. As the revolution spread into Germany, he rushed to complete his article "Philosophy" for the *Ersch and Gruber General Encyclopedia for the Arts and Science* in order to gain the leisure needed for full-time political activity. At the same time, on 13 March, he wrote to offer his services to David Hansemann, a celebrated Rhenish liberal who had been pleased by Haym's favorable account of him in *Speeches and Speakers of the First Prussian United Diet.* Hansemann replied on the eighteenth by asking Haym to join him at once and to come prepared for a long stay. This was an encouraging response, and the two met on the twenty-fourth in Cologne and, a few minutes later, boarded the train for Berlin, where Hansemann hoped to be asked to form a new ministry. Five days later, Hansemann was indeed asked to form a new ministry along with Ludolf Camphausen, whereupon Haym received the distinctly less gratifying task of clipping and filing newspaper articles that might interest Hansemann.[9] His credentials qualified him for something better than that. On 1 April, through Hansemann's influence, he became a writer for the *Nationalzeitung,* a new Berlin daily that favored constitutional monarchy and national unification. Haym's appointment was good for Hansemann because it gave his government increased access to the still volatile public opinion in Berlin. It was also good for Haym because it gave him increased scope for his energy and talents, though it still left him in the position of an onlooker rather than an actor. He was correspondingly pleased when the electoral committee for the Mansfeld Lake and Mountain District of Prussian Saxony, following the advice they had solicited from Duncker, elected Haym to the National Assembly.[10] He owed his new position to a friend's influence and to the peculiarities of an electoral system in which voters elected electors empowered to choose whomever they thought best, but at least, though only twenty-four years old and still obscure, he had been elected.

Sybel was less fortunate. He was well enough known and connected to be invited, along with his father, to the Pre-Parliament in which southern and western liberals like himself were in any case overrepresented, but he failed to win the seat he craved in the National Assembly. There were two reasons for this. First, the economist Bruno Hildebrandt also wanted a seat, and Hildebrandt had been on the Marburg faculty longer and was better known. Second, Sybel displayed a candor that was morally admirable but politically ill advised in the present excitement. During the campaign, he spoke strongly and repeatedly in behalf of limiting the franchise to those who paid a direct tax. This not only excluded the poor but also those who rented property. Some of his potential constituents responded by gathering around his house on successive nights to break his windows, and the voters chose electors known to oppose Sybel's candidacy.[11] As a result, Sybel had to be content with a seat in the Hessian assembly at Cassell and, in 1850, in the short-lived and futile Erfurt Assembly. For the time being, he was stuck in Hesse, though he followed events at nearby Frankfort as closely as he could and was an active leader in the Marburg Fatherland Union (*Vaterlandsverein*), an organization of three to four hundred members that was generally friendly to Prussia and favored both national unification and constitutional monarchy.[12]

All four men experienced much more than just a change in position and powers, important though that change was. They had thought about politics for years and had a clear sense of what had to happen and what had to be done, but of course they lacked practical political experience, and despite their frequent and fervent defenses of historical empiricism, they thought of politics in generalities rather than in concrete detail. Moreover, they had thought of someone else doing history's work, and therefore had put most of their effort into preparing people morally and intellectually for what was to come. Now they faced a changed situation in which they had to carry out the day-to-day tasks of politics. They had good intentions and their basic confidence in their predictions remained intact, but they had to develop and apply different tactics for a changed situation. This required thinking about events on a day-to-day basis and in great detail. There had simply been no reason to do this before. There were millenarian strains in their thinking, especially in Droysen's, but they were not utopians who attempted an exact and complete portrait of the future. It had been enough to sketch its outlines. Now they felt partly responsible for its finished appearance, and this responsibility tempered their optimism with a measure of anxiety. This anxiety was most in evidence either when they had to deal, conceptually if not directly, with social groups unlike their own or with people who refused against all reason—so it seemed—to see matters as they did.

Before the revolution, for example, they had simply not given much thought to those at the bottom of the social scale, though their repeated expressions of horror at the French Revolution and continual insistence on the special dignity of their professional calling certainly bespoke at least a diffuse social fear. Now they wanted to help govern and remake a Germany in which popular risings of some magnitude had occurred and were still occurring. They were glad that there had been a revolution, but they wanted it to stop before it became radical and violent. Furthermore, they believed that Germany was shortly destined to become a national community. Both halting the revolution in time and constructing a community required them to deal somehow with lower social classes, about which they knew very little. Their received ideas offered a little guidance by ruling out, at first, outright repression, but their initial tolerance was limited and fragile and, at varying rates of speed, they moved from incomprehension to active antipathy. This is not surprising. As Duncker recalled a year later, they wanted a national constitution that would be "democratic and honorable," not limited to representation of the bourgeoisie in which an overly powerful centralized administration "controlled the balance." He meant a fairly broad franchise in a constitutional monarchy run by a strong monarch.[13] Here Duncker expressed a naïve hope shared by all four that with the right constitution in place at the right historical moment, social conflict would disappear as a matter of course. When the prospect of receiving such a constitution did not immediately quiet unrest, it was logical, though socially narrow and uncompassionate, to conclude that whoever was still in the streets was somehow unworthy of belonging to the real national community by reason of defying plain historical imperatives.

Droysen reached this conclusion almost at once. His trip to Frankfort at the beginning of April led him through the restive Rhineland, and in a letter dated 4 April, he remarked: "The people are even worse than I have always said, rootless, entirely materialistic, without a trace of piety or any but the most trivial interests."[14] If Droysen had always thought that, he said it only in private and unrecorded conversation. To be sure, he may long have had an academic's sniffing contempt for others' "trivial interests," and at least from the time he wrote the commentaries to his 1832 translation of Aeschylus he dated the start of world history from Athens' ruinous experiment in democracy, but the anger and hatred in his letter are new and contrary to his prerevolutionary expectation that in politics Germany would succeed where other nations had failed by constructing a free and stable national community. Nor was his attitude limited to a remote detestation of people he did not like or understand. In another letter written the next day, he pointed to republicanism in the German south and to sporadic looting and rioting elsewhere and speculated that everything might be wrecked by continued revolution. That was his real fear and the cause of his hatred. Germany at last faced the near prospect of freedom and unification, and the mob threatened to wreck this opportunity. He began to call for official vigilance and timely action.[15] Unwisely, he feared the people while trusting the princes.

Haym, and almost certainly Duncker, at first thought in terms of a gentler approach. The key document is the statement of political program that Haym sent to the electors at Mansfeld that he later claimed was "linked as closely as possible to Duncker's."[16] Most of the statement is given over to the constitutional questions that really interested Haym and Duncker, but Haym also included an interesting discussion of the situation of the poor. He proposed, first, extending to them a modicum of relief through a "more equitable division of tax burdens." Although he did not explain what changes in taxation he had in mind, it is at least clear that he evidently did not want the state to use its fiscal powers in a way that would actually increase poverty. He further proposed applying the "principle of association between employer and employee." This proposal is tantalizingly vague. Haym may have been looking backward to guild regulation of production and trade or, relatedly, forward to later corporatist attempts to still social unrest.

In any case, it is clear that Haym did not think of differing economic interests as irreconcilable and therefore thought that willing cooperation could remove any major sources of conflict. In his view, then, social and economic reform had the same moral prerequisites of good will and civic dutifulness that political reform did. He went on to moderate even these mild suggestions by adding that "in no task must the helping hand draw back more quickly than in this, and the one thing that I know for certain is that this danger will not bring us down helpless if we hold fast to the prin- ciple of morality."[17] If Haym had been practiced in seeking elective office, this would read suspiciously like an attempt to reassure through lofty vagueness. After all, Haym wanted to be elected and he had no way of knowing what the electoral committee in Mansfeld wanted to be told. It is more likely that he was guilelessly stating his few thoughts on the matter: he was liberal enough not to want the state unnecessarily to intervene in society's affairs, and, as his prerevolutionary writings clearly show, he re- ally believed that sound morality had major practical effects.

Despite his brevity and consequent imprecision, Haym seemed hon- estly hopeful. His hope was largely a result of ignorance. Reminiscence is weak historical evidence, but a recollection from his memoirs about his at- titudes in this period rings true. Just after his election to the National As- sembly, Haym was approached by a man who had opposed his election:

He was a member of the poorer agrarian classes, a downtrodden, perhaps indebted man. What did he care about high politics, a unified Germany, and its future con- stitution? After the speeches of the enthusiasts, which had beaten upon his ears, he expected the abolition of duties and fees that burdened the rural population and the levelling of all privileges of the land-holding aristocracy. Would I, then also work for that? *So little had I thought about these matters, I was all the more moved by the modest countenance of the man;* I could not promise him exactly that his difficulties would be ended in Frankfort, but I could not refuse a few pages on the subject that he had put together using a dictionary . . . as valuable material for my information [my emphasis].[18]

Haym's memory may have played some tricks on him. For example, his claim that the lower classes were uninterested in national affairs was a commonplace in Imperial Germany but not in early 1848, and Haym may have been less tactful with his interlocutor than he would have his readers believe. There is no reason, however, to doubt his claim that he just had not thought much about these matters. His recollection of his ignorance is probably correct, and his description of his response is suggestive of his real attitudes. He was moved by the man's situation and "modest countenance," yet he had only pity and good-natured contempt at the idea of such a person drafting a statement. He could feel sorry for the poor, but he could not quite take them seriously.

His contempt remained, but his good nature soon disappeared. When there was a riot at the Berlin Arsenal on 14 June, he wrote to David Hansemann with angry advice. Matters, he claimed, had "come to a point where either a decline into terrorism by the masses begins ... or where once again and for the last time there is an opportunity to beat hard upon the head of this madness and violation of law and freedom." In other words, the alternatives were stark. Either the "madness of the rabble" (*Wahnsinn des Pöbels*) would prevail or the "rational development of the state" (*vernünftige Staatsentwicklung*) would continue.[19] It is, of course, hardly surprising that Haym was appalled at mob violence, especially as in his view the revolution had been completed, but several points in the letter are significant. First, his language was uncharacteristically violent. Second, he did not blame just the rioters but used the word *Pöbel* as a collective noun to suggest the existence of a numerous and dangerous underclass of riffraff. Third, and most important, he analyzed the situation in terms of a historical cleft stick: *either* the "rabble" would have its way *or* political development could continue. By implication, constitutional government and national unification, despite their historical inevitability, were now in doubt. Continued unrest and too yielding a stance by the authorities might lead to catastrophe.

Sybel combined elements both of Haym's initially conciliatory mood and the distrust that Droysen expressed in his April correspondence. He began with the assumption that at least some reforms were in order, and in a declaration of program drafted on 28 April, for a newly formed liberal and nationalist group at Marburg, he called for recognition of the principle of "association" in economics as in politics. He did not mean only association between employers and employees, as Haym did. In his view, anyone should be free to join with anyone in behalf of common ideas and interests. This view held the potential for legitimating the division of society into competing interest groups and parties, but that was certainly not Sybel's intention. He, too, thought of a unified Germany as a basically unitary community, and he had a liberal's confidence that people, left to themselves, would learn to agree. Specifically, he invoked the principle of "association" in order to invite the lower classes to join the Fatherland Union. He was still conciliatory enough to hope that the people would soon see things his way.[20] He nevertheless hedged this trust with nervous skepticism. When he looked down the social slope, he worried about renewed revolution. Elsewhere in the draft he stated that between 6 and 11 March, the Hessian people had attacked their government with "irresistible force." He justified this attack on the grounds that the government had violated freedom of conscience and had closed all legal avenues to improvement. Further revolution was unjustifiable, however, because all that had changed, and Sybel now found it "urgently necessary . . . to declare: The *revolution, that is the time for forceful change in the state, is finished in and for Hesse.*" The time had arrived to seek "legal betterment of our circumstances." Evidently his language was a little too strong for others in the union. In the final version, his "urgently necessary" was changed to "equally necessary," a revision that left his basic thesis unaffected but moderated its force by justifying it on the same grounds as the original revolution.

A further sign of Sybel's social nervousness was his advocacy of the limited franchise, for which he paid the price of a lost election and broken windows. He associated democracy with misguided efforts by the poor to despoil the rich, and in a speech on 28 April, the same day that he drafted a program for the Fatherland Union, he claimed that republicans sought to appeal to "the poorer inhabitants" by promising them gains "at the expense of the well-off."[21] Unlike Droysen, Duncker, and Haym, he was explicit in linking his demand to halt or moderate the revolution to the defense of property. This linkage, by the way, led him into a historiographical venture of major importance for his postrevolutionary career. He concluded that a historically informed populace would be immune to republican enticements and decided, probably after losing the election, to write a small work for the literate members of the lower classes that would "tell the people into what wretchedness the great French Revolution brought the lower classes themselves through its communist tendencies." Specifically, he planned to show that the French Revolution had gone astray because of "insufficient regard for the rights of property."[22] By analogy, of course, the same danger existed in present-day Germany. Sybel did not publish the work in this form. Other claims on his time prevented its early completion, and the continual discovery of relevant materials led to repeated expansions of its scope. Its first installment appeared in print in 1853 in his *History of the Revolutionary Age 1789–1795,* which ran to five sizable volumes by 1879.[23] The multivolumed, finished work retained the original thesis of the little pamphlet.

- Fear of social conflict and continued revolution, however, occupied only a fraction of these men's attention amid the unfamiliar situation of spring 1848. Although they remained basically optimistic through these early months, they were aware of other threats to the realization of their program and had a heavy sense of the magnitude of the task before them. Looking back from the distance of one year, Duncker recalled a political consensus in which he had joined:

Constitutional monarchy appeared to us as the required demand of the time, as the historical necessity of our epoch, as the reconciliation between the north and south of Germany, as the compromise between absolutism and freedom. The conquered principle was to be offered acceptable conditions, a proper peace was to be concluded between the contending parties. Constitutionalism, as we wanted it, was to be democratic and honorable: it was not to be limited to the representation of the bourgeoisie in which an overly powerful centralized administration controlled the balance; it was to proceed from the self-government of the provinces and to be fulfilled in the rule of a German parliament. We did not want to preserve monarchy as a rule by families but rather as that great and protective institution which, rooting itself in the past, could also assure the future, which stood above and beyond the parties and their conflicts, guaranteeing the permanence and stability of the state, which expressed and represented the majesty of the government.

This program was simple enough in principle. Monarchy was to retain much of its authority, but it was now to act in the national, rather than the dynastic, interest and was to share power with representative bodies. Old and new would be reconciled, and monarchy would guard the civil peace by standing above the parties and representing the state as a whole. The question was how to turn this vision into a reality. "Never," Duncker averred with pardonable exaggeration, "in the whole course of history was there a greater, never a more difficult assignment." It was, he rightly believed, necessary to overcome divisions of sovereignty, religion, and economy of centuries' standing in the virtual absence of central institutions while fighting against republicanism and reaction.[24] Moreover, the general agreement that Duncker described left unanswered important questions of tactics that the completion of the draft constitution of the Seventeen on 26 April posed in acute form.

This draft constitution was actually the work of a subcommittee of the Seventeen composed of Dahlmann, Sylvester Jordan, Friedrich Daniel Bassermann, Wilhelm Eduard Albrecht, and Max von Gagern, though the Seventeen as a plenum discussed and approved both individual provisions and the document as a whole. In brief, Germany was to be a constitutional monarchy with a hereditary executive and a bicameral legislature. The lower house was to be elective and the upper house was to consist of reigning princes, representatives from the free cities, and appointed "men of proven service to the Fatherland." The national monarch was to be hereditary and, in addition to holding executive powers, would possess the power of legislative initiative and an absolute veto. It was also generally assumed, though nowhere actually stated, that the national monarch would be a Hohenzollern.[25] It was questionable whether this constitution, however admirable in design and provisions, could command both the broad popular support and the assent of the German princes needed to reconcile old and new. It was also questionable whether Prussia or, more accurately Frederick William IV, could be counted on to do the right thing at the right time. In the immediate aftermath of the Berlin revolution, he had declared in an important phrase that, from this moment forward, "Prussia merges into Germany" (*Preußen geht in Deutschland auf*). Unfortunately, the promise was imprecise, and the changeable king might renege.[26] Finally, it was also questionable whether the rest of Germany really wanted a Hohenzollern ruler, especially now that Frederick William had discredited himself first by resisting and then by appeasing the revolution in Berlin.

Droysen said no to the first question and yes to the second, though he did so on his own terms. He was a member of the Seventeen, but he was harshly critical of its political approach in general and of the draft constitution in particular. This reaction was in part a consequence of outlook and temperament. His historical optimism had always been a matter of awaiting a happy outcome in the long term; when his euphoria weakened after the first weeks of revolution, he reverted to finding and censuring human failings in the shorter term. He was also unhappily aware of what he took to be immediate and mortal dangers to Germany. There was the continued danger of republican anarchy.[27] Moreover, Germans were already fighting Danes in the northwest and might, he imagined, have at any time to face invasion from France or Russia or both.[28] The National Assembly was being elected and would soon convene at Frankfort, but he took no comfort in this prospect. He complained that no adequate preparations had been made, and he worried about how Austria and Prussia would regard this first German parliament.[29] He also had a presentiment that the princes and the right more generally might be uncooperative, even though cooperation was in their real interest and could have been attained if only the other members of the Seventeen had been clever enough.[30]

He therefore complained of feeling "quarrelsome and irritable" and, in a letter to his close friend Wilhelm Arendt, written the day before the Seventeen made their draft public, disgustedly and immodestly condemned the Seventeen in biblical language for not taking his advice:

We Seventeen are nothing; despite my best efforts, we took our task as narrowly and in as doctrinaire a fashion as possible and have brought into existence a draft that, because and insofar as it is good, will be a stumbling block to the Jews and a thing of derision to the heathen. For it is certain that most princes will disavow us and the deputies on the right will scorn us. What is to be done! We would have had to have had fewer professors and more men of action among us in order to do a reasonable job; now we are squeezed-out lemons, more's the pity.[31]

Droysen's criticisms seem almost paradoxical at first. He regretted that there had been too many "professors" and too few "men of action," yet the only good advice came from Professor Droysen. The draft constitution was really good, he thought, but this goodness was a real defect. The great chance was seemingly now lost, but in the weeks that followed, Droysen acted as if everything could still be put right if others would only follow his advice. This reaction was not only a product of irritability and self-dramatization; Droysen thought that he could see into the future better than most others, and it alarmed him when they failed to take his advice.

His distress was both apparent and real. It was real insofar as, for the present at least, events were not following the course that he expected, but his underlying hopefulness was even stronger, because he thought that he knew how to get history back on its track. Like Duncker, he wanted to reconcile the old with the new, and he, too, thought that this required a national constitutional monarchy of the sort proposed by the Seventeen. He was entirely sincere when he praised the draft constitution in principle, but he believed deeply that the princes, and especially the Prussian monarch, had to be similarly persuaded of its excellence because, really, nothing could be done without them. He was angry at his fellow members of the Seventeen because they had done too little to persuade the old authorities and their potential supporters on the German right. The preamble to the Seventeen's draft made some pleasant-sounding overtures to these needed allies, but that was not enough.

At first, Droysen thought in terms of habituating the princes to national governance. On 16 April, for example, he had unsuccessfully proposed to the Seventeen that they join with the Confederate Assembly in creating a provisional national executive to meet the dangers facing Germany and, equally important, to "anticipate a bit of the future national unity (*Reichseinheit*)." On the seventeenth, he raised this matter again, with greater urgency. The period before the National Assembly met would bring "endless danger," which would continue even during the "interregnum" that would commence with its opening. Germany therefore needed, right now, some form of provisional government.[32] His colleagues did not follow his suggestions, however, and national affairs remained under the tenuous control of the Confederate Assembly and the Committee of Fifty (*Fünfziger-Ausschuß*), a standing body with loosely defined powers of oversight created in a compromise when the Pre-Parliament adjourned in early April.

Under these circumstances, Droysen decided to act on his own, and his actions give a clear indication both of his estimation of Germany's historical situation and of his analysis of present German politics. In late April he was preparing a general situation report for his government in Rendsburg when he met Heinrich von Arnim, the Prussian Foreign Minister. He was encouraged enough by their talk that he arranged for a second meeting on 29 April with Hans von Bülow, an undersecretary in the Foreign

Ministry, also in attendance. Droysen rewrote his report for this occasion in order to make it a close review of the German political situation that led to compelling conclusions about the policies that Prussia must now adopt and follow.[33] The result was a closely reasoned appeal to Prussian self-interest that moved ineluctably to its conclusion through the successive elimination of all other policy options. This appeal is especially interesting because it shows Droysen's calculations clearly and in detail. The fundamental fact in current German politics, Droysen maintained, was the "sudden and disgraceful (*jähe und schmähliche*) collapse of the system that has prevailed in Germany and her individual states . . . this system of German impotence and self-sacrifice . . . [that] was nothing more than the artificially sculpted keystone in that construct of international law, the Holy Alliance." He insisted that it was superficial at best to treat the outbreak of revolution in the German states as an accidental byproduct of the upheaval in France. The Paris rising was the occasion, but the real cause lay in German history. As proof for this contention, he pointed to the speed with which the system of 1815 had fallen and added pointedly that any attempt to return to the state of affairs that had prevailed before March would surely fail.[34] In terms of his received theory of history, then, an irreversible and irrefutable judgment had been passed according to the "right of history." Backward movement was impossible, and an indefinite continuation of present dangers and uncertainties was intolerable. That meant that further progress was necessary. Germany had to be unified and have a constitution, and Prussia really had no choice other than to lead the way to both results.

Droysen admitted that this course entailed major difficulties, even though it was the only policy suited to present circumstances. He accordingly termed the Seventeen's draft constitution "impractical," but added that "every other possible combination seems to be so to an equal degree." He elaborated this thesis by posing a series of disturbing questions: Would the smaller German states accept rule by either of the two German great powers? Could Austria and Prussia agree to partition Germany between them when it had value for either only in its entirety? Could Austria reassume the imperial title without war with Prussia and strenuous objections from Bavaria? If, conversely, Prussia tried to rule Germany alone, would not Austria withhold the Tyrol and Bavaria? Should Germany, then, have an elected president? Would not that encourage the states to become republican cantons, internally weak and easy prey to foreign invasion? Or might it not bring back the difficulties of the Holy Roman Empire as the several dynasties turned the elections to their own advantage by extracting concessions in return for support? "In a word," Droysen concluded, "there is a danger that Germany, as it reaches out for its long-sought unity, loses it completely, yes, and even its thin remnant, the confederation of the princes."[35] It was a danger that Droysen thought possible to avert if Prussia would only play its historically necessary role. In order to persuade Arnim and Bülow to put Prussia on its proper course, Droysen pointed to the good features of the draft constitution. It provided for a constitutional monarchy that would offer the advantages and avoid the disadvantages of democracy and absolutism because, under that system, "hereditariness holds the state with anchor-like firmness, and the ministers, the premier, their president, come from the representative majority, a continual indirect election of the best men."[36] Monarchy, that is, would assure continuity with the past, and representation would unite state and society and secure the most talented citizens for high public office. A Germany so unified would be stable and secure. It would also be powerful, and Droysen no doubt thought that this prospect would appeal to the two men from the Foreign Ministry.

His basic thesis was that Germany "must be strong, as strong as the danger and our hope." Here Droysen sounded the cosmopolitan note that often accompanied his most stridently nationalistic utterances. A German constitutional monarchy "in the heart of Europe," he insisted, would be strong enough to "end the oligarchy of the great powers" that he detested. He valued German strength as good in itself, but he also justified it in terms of its service to European peace. Germany, once unified under a constitutional monarch, would "create and secure" a "peace of the peoples" because it would have no reason to attack any other country and would itself be too strong to invite attack. Moreover, it would win the friendship and alliance of most of the lesser powers on its periphery.[37] Droysen was entirely in earnest in so arguing. Power was important to him, and he certainly had no objection to the deliberate use of force in the pursuit of legitimate national interests, but he also plainly thought that a German nation-state would be pacific in inclination and pacifying in effect. Thus, in a protocol submitted to the Confederate Assembly on 18 April, he had made the same points and further argued that the United States (the world's first "state" properly so called) would be Germany's "natural ally" and that a unified Germany, like the United States, would have no need for the "huge standing armies" characteristic of the old order. If necessity arose, an armed citizenry would fight well and gladly in the national defense.[38] Droysen omitted those two final points from the memorandum that he prepared for Arnim and Bülow, probably because of his current belief that, in the immediate future, Germany needed Prussia's existing military establishment and whatever naval strength she could muster for the war with Denmark and for use against possible invaders.[39]

It was therefore urgently necessary for Germany to become a constitutional monarchy, and Droysen thought that it was just as necessary for the Hohenzollern to become the national dynasty. He thought it self-evident that only they or the Habsburgs were serious contenders, and he did not seriously consider selecting a dynasty from one of the small or middle states as a compromise solution. He recognized it as a difficulty that either dynasty could be expected to oppose the other's candidacy and argued that a compromise between them was impossible because joint dominion by both over Germany would amount to a return to the system of 1815. He had already argued that this was neither desirable nor feasible. Droysen deliberately portrayed the situation as nearly hopeless in order to show that hope remained as long as the Hohenzollern were willing to do the right thing at the right time. In destroying the system of 1815, he reasoned, the revolution had also destroyed the Habsburgs' power. They were no longer serious contenders for national leadership because their empire was now in dissolution and, in the future, at most a "purely personal union" would exist among their crownlands and other territories. As a result, and here Droysen was being wildly optimistic, Bohemia and the German-speaking provinces could be had for Germany, while the Hohenzollern could safely make their bid for German supremacy.[40]

"To the degree that Austria progressively declines and attempts combinations that bear the old signature of dynastic politics," Droysen declared, "Prussia will reveal herself to be a purely German state." In other words, simply by being herself, Prussia would stand in shining contrast to Austria and attract support throughout Germany. Prussia had to take advantage of this opportunity by adopting "a constitution based on provincial representation" (*provinzial-ständische Verfassung*) in order that she "be able to merge into Germany (*in Deutschland aufgehen*). To the Hohenzollern will fall the office left vacant by the Hohenstaufen." Droysen tried to make it seem easy and, by invoking a return to lost medieval splendor, he tried to make it seem glamorous, but in fact he was asking a lot from Prussia's rulers. The enormity of his request explains why he troubled to dismiss all other proposed solutions before offering his own. The "constitution based on provincial representation" that he demanded in fact meant that there would be "no more Prussian monarchy; let her dissolve herself into three or four territorial states, each with its own representative institutions, with its own administration, in personal union nonetheless with the previous ruler." This was the "sole condition" under which it was "now possible" to unify Germany and under which Prussia could cease being the least among the great powers.[41] Stated baldly, Frederick William had to break up the state that he ruled.

Harsh though Droysen's criticism of the work of the Seventeen had been, he was himself a prisoner of theory. To be sure, in his memorandum he had tried open-mindedly to take close and adequate account of detail and contingency, and he had deliberately appealed to Prussian self-interest as well as high-mindedness. His contentions, however, made sense only in light of his prerevolutionary reading of the logic and tendency of German and world history and, more specifically, of his analysis of Prussia's situation. These rested as much on still unshaken faith as on evidence. Despite the angry complaints that he continually made in April, his historical optimism was still intact; indeed, it was the basis for his complaints, just as his seeming responsibility for the national future was his occasion for offering them.[42] He would fundamentally reassess his ideas only months later, when it became undeniably clear that many Prussians valued Prussia and that Austria was stronger than he had imagined.

Duncker and Haym also retained their optimism, though they did not criticize the work of the Seventeen or call for the voluntary dissolution of the Prussian state as Droysen did. Without denying that the course might entail serious difficulties, they simply recommended the speedy adoption of the Seventeen's draft constitution.[43] Of course, they may have been more worried than they seemed. Most of the evidence for their ideas in late April and early May comes from the campaign statement that Haym drafted and modeled on Duncker's, and it would have been only natural for him to display confidence rather than anxiety, cheer rather than gloom.[44] After all, Droysen wrote his angriest statements in his diary and in his copious private correspondence. Still, Haym (and presumably Duncker before him) let some expressions of worry slip into his formal statement, though he does not seem to have been very worried about the major question of how to make the draft acceptable to the princes in general and the king of Prussia in particular. The likeliest explanation is that Duncker and Haym had read the draft, agreed with its provisions, and thought that it offered useful guidance for the forthcoming National Assembly.

In fact, Haym's agreement with the draft constitution was so strong that the sections in his statement dealing with constitutional questions often borrowed its language, though he tended to defend its provisions in terms of the historical theory that he and Duncker had articulated before the revolution. Thus, he argued that Germany's future constitution could not be designed according to the canons of pure reason because it was not possible "to assure the happiness of states nor to bind the spirit of nations through the rigid order of an artificial system of government." It was, instead, necessary to consult history and, then, adopt the most appropriate of "the forms of government discovered and developed over the centuries." In Germany's present circumstances, this meant constitutional monarchy at both the state and federal level. Haym's advocacy of constitutional monarchy, which had the advantage of being continuous with Germany's political tradition while assuring that the revolution would go no further, was enthusiastic and unqualified: "I declare myself to be in favor of constitutional monarchy with my entire soul and complete conviction. I hold that to be the wisest way to make popular freedom and princely rule compatible on a large scale. I see no risk in introducing this system on a broad and popular basis; for it lies in the nature [of this system] that the dignity and security of the princes increases . . . as the spirit of purified freedom penetrates more deeply into the lower level of the population." The object was to assure "popular freedom" with as little risk as possible. Constitutional monarchy evidently made unnecessary the limitations on the franchise that Sybel proposed, because it would actually strengthen the princes who would now have a contented citizenry behind them and would teach citizens, even those at the "lowest level," that they were part of the state and had consequently to work for its welfare. "Harmony" would be the result of the combination of "princely rule" and "popular freedom."[45]

Haym's statement went beyond these generalities to offer a sketch of Germany's future institutions. The monarch, and especially the national monarch, was not to be a figurehead. The king of Germany would have both legislative and executive powers and would be able to define policy and defend national interests. The bicameral legislature would be the "seat of . . . [the] spirit of harmony." As in the draft constitution, the upper house would be composed of reigning princes and "men of the most proven patriotic worth." Haym added his own touch to his description of the lower house. It would be elected on a broad, though not universal, male franchise and would be the gathering point for "the power of intelligence and moral culture" in Germany. Now as before, Haym associated the intellect with morality and saw both as indispensable to Germany's political reconstruction. He simply assumed that these were the qualities that German voters would value in candidates. From both chambers, he further argued, "the purified will of the nation (*Nation*) shall . . . emerge and find no other obstacle than moderation and ever renewed examination."[46] Germany was, evidently, soon to possess the most thoughtful legislature in history. In terms of his philosophical vocabulary, the new German state would be a "real identity."

This confidence must have been a little less serene than it appears, and Duncker's recollection that the task of creating a constitutional monarchy seemed overwhelmingly difficult even in the spring of 1848 is probably an accurate description of their actual feelings at the time.[47] Aside from fearing further revolution, Haym understood that the princes and the states would have to accept constitutional monarchy. He employed a curiously reflexive construction to pose this matter: "A national power will constitute itself over the various states, and their independence will raise itself within its proper bounds while they freely move themselves into the presented unity." His language makes the process seem automatic, as, given his historical theory, it should have been. He also wrote of constitutional monarchy being "transposed from the parts to the whole," after which the newly achieved national unity would "work upon the members." This may explain his optimism, because by 1 May all the German principalities were more or less constitutional monarchies. That is, the essential precondition already existed. Haym's statement, however, left two further matters open. He wanted the monarchy to be hereditary—"if possible." In choosing a monarch, he claimed, "the eyes of all Prussians naturally turn to the House of Hohenzollern." That is, his own preference was clear, but he implicitly admitted that conditions might require another choice.[48]

Sybel took a very different view of affairs. He was still confident that Germany would be unified on acceptable terms, but his reading of historical necessity led him angrily to reject the work of the Seventeen and to reject it in terms quite unlike Droysen's. In his pamphlet "On the National Constitution of the XVII Trustees," he claimed to have read the draft "with intense regret." "So much talent, so much uprightness and love of Fatherland" had been wasted on a document that at "every point stood in bitter contradiction" to actual conditions."[49] He based his criticism on his reading of the tendency of German history and voiced two major complaints. He objected, first, to the attempt to institute constitutional monarchy at the national level and, second, to the separation of powers that he thought he detected in the draft. He did not accuse its authors of being ahistorical. He conceded that they had tried to take history into account, but he believed that they had lamentably misread its real demands:

The foreword to the proposal is entirely correct when it assumes monarchism in most of the German peoples. It is equally certain that in most, even when the feeling for German unity momentarily shines forth, the spirit of locality and state lies deeper in the blood. We do not wish to praise this or count it good fortune, but that is the way it is, and after the history of the last eight centuries it cannot be otherwise. In such a context, it is not statesman-like and [not] practical wisdom to draft a constitution that is a slap in the face to the most prominent aspects [of that situation]. It would be revolutionary if one wished to use all the means at one's disposal toward that end; and as it is, it is doctrinaire and nothing more than doctrinaire.[50]

It is not clear whether this was a new insight on Sybel's part; his prerevolutionary comments on future German unity showed that he expected Prussia to play a major role in achieving unification but did not indicate clearly the actual shape of the new constitution. In any case, his criticism was realistic and perceptive, and he, faulting the draft for being "doctrinaire," also insisted on constructing the future along lines set by the particularities of past and present. He fully accepted the premisses of the Seventeen's draft, but he inferred different conclusions from them because of his greater appreciation of the vitality of particularism in German politics. Because Germans, in their great majority, were loyal monarchists, they would not accept the national dominance of a dynasty other than their own. Constitutional monarchy in the form proposed by the Seventeen was unlikely to be accepted and, even if briefly tolerated, would be subverted by the jealousy and discontent that it aroused. That is, it would at best be a source of weakness rather than strength.

Sybel linked this to a second criticism. On the national level, he argued, the Seventeen's draft "offered only the image and appearance of true monarchy without the substantial possession of true power."[51] It was wrong for Germany to have a national monarchy, and, furthermore, the proposed national monarchy was not monarchical enough. In order to make this case, Sybel recurred to his earlier theoretical objections to the separation of powers and sought to demonstrate that idea's falsity in a way that allowed him to describe the sort of constitutional arrangements that were well suited to a unified Germany. The Seventeen, he noted, accorded executive and limited legislative powers to the monarch, purely legislative powers to the parliament, and judicial powers to the national court. He did not object to the division between legislative and judicial powers, but he was deeply distressed by the proposed relationship between king and parliament. Specifically, he disliked the fact that the former could initiate and veto legislation while the latter actually made the laws. This seemed to him too sharp a division between the executive and legislative powers. "In practice," he assured his readers, "such a separation is as unfeasible as if one wished to separate the light from the lamp because one can separate them in theory."[52]

This criticism seems curious at first because the Seventeen had given the monarch a share of the legislative as well as full possession of the executive power, and it would have been uncharacteristic for the monarchist Sybel to want an elected parliament to possess executive authority. Sybel would have replied that the fault lay in draft constitution, not in the terms of his argument. Germany needed to be a unitary state in which executive and legislative power were in the same hands, and the draft did not provide for this. He developed this case as a reply to those who cited the Belgian and, especially, the British constitutions to justify the separation of powers. He found such citation to be poorly informed and therefore misleading. In England, for example, the separation of powers had been a useful political slogan without practical content. The executive and the legislative had in fact always been united there, whether in the king in the seventeenth century, in the House of Lords in the eighteenth century, or in the Commons in Sybel's own day.[53] This led him to a further observation, namely, that England's supposedly constitutional monarchy was as much a fiction as her separation of powers. England at present, he argued, had parliamentary government, not monarchy, although he acknowledged that the queen did play the valuable role of embodying the nation in her person. That function was suited to British historical traditions, but could not be replicated in Germany where national monarchy, for reasons already mentioned, would be divisive rather than unifying.[54] Sybel's own patrician background no doubt helped incline him to this view.

Germany therefore needed a union of executive and legislative powers suited to her spirit and traditions. Sybel advised government by an aristocratic college, and noted that the cases of Venice, England, and the Roman Republic showed that such colleges, rather than monarchs, provided the greatest degree of strength and steadiness in government. Without specifying the actual composition of such a college in Germany, he explained that, in keeping with the dominant tendency in modern history, it would be necessary to "connect such colleges to a great democratic force" in such a way that "at every moment the state power may appear to be the product of free *popular will* . . . without sacrificing it to the accidents of *popular whim.*" This was the same Sybel who placed his political career at risk by calling for a limited franchise in the midst of Germany's first national elections. He wanted the constitution to be democratic only in a very special sense of the term. It was to protect individual freedoms and provide for an elected lower house, but real power would reside in the aristocratic upper chamber, which would act as a brake on democracy. He wanted to capture the people for the state, not the other way around.[55] Moreover, he expected most governmental business to be carried on in the states, which would remain strongly monarchic. He was as resolutely in favor of strong, monarchic government in the states as he was opposed to it for the nation as a whole.[56] The constitutional form that he proposed offered Germany more than what he termed a "blossoming freedom at home." Although he did not develop the point in any detail, he believed that the collaboration of an aristocratic college with an elected lower house would also secure to Germany "the most powerful military strength," and that mattered to Sybel as much as it did to Droysen, Duncker, or Haym.[57] As historians, they were all acutely, and understandably, aware that disunity had made Germany in recent centuries the battleground of choice for Europe. He was, more specifically, uneasy about the course of the fighting with Denmark and, like Droysen, feared that France and Russia might attack at any time. His anxiety added force to his comments: Germany had to adopt the right constitution and do so quickly in order to ward off foreign invasion.[58] In this connection, he was especially bothered by Germany's lack of a navy, and on 17 May he cosigned a strongly worded leaflet that called for contributions to construct a powerful fleet to protect Germany's coasts and commerce.[59]

Sybel's insistent preference for an aristocratic college as the center of national government obviously put him, for the time being, at some distance from Droysen, Duncker, and Haym, but it would be a mistake to overrate the difference between his view and theirs. His attack on the draft constitution rested on assumptions that he shared with them. Like them, he shared the drafters' hopes and wanted the same kind of unified Germany. His criticisms had to do only with the means or, more specifically, with the shape and composition of the national government. Such disagreements about matters of contingency were bound to erupt once Sybel and others passed from the generalities appropriate to a politics of expectation to the continual judgments and recommendations that a politics of action required. In this sense, at least, his attack on the draft was similar in kind to Droysen's, different though their criticisms were in substance. Equally marked differences of opinion would occur in the following months.

Moreover, Sybel qualified his support for government by an aristocratic college by explicitly identifying an unwelcome but possible situation in which government by a national monarch would be not only permissible but also indispensable. Much of his objection to the Seventeen's proposal had been based on the jealousy that he foresaw between dynasty and dynasty, and he was evidently most worried at the prospect of a contest between the Hohenzollern and the Habsburgs. He therefore speculated that, if Austria were to break up or, alternately, to regain its original strength and then refuse to enter a unified Germany, a national monarchy would become "possible" and at least a "temporary dictatorship" would be urgently necessary. In either of these cases, only the House of Hohenzollern could provide the leadership that Germany would need and serve as the "firm anchor of salvation" in the calamity that would deprive the nation of "one quarter of its best peoples." Sybel hoped that neither situation would arise, though in considering the possibility of an Austrian revival, he showed a livelier and more astute political imagination than Droysen with his confident predictions of Austria's approaching collapse. He looked on these possibilities as little short of catastrophic and as cases in which there would be "no more talk of natural and healthy circumstances" and in which it would no longer "be a question of an enduring constitution for our smiling Fatherland." "It would then," he warned, "be a question of saving whatever is to be saved." Germany would be forced to substitute a "field commander" for a "constitution."[60] This was a telling insight because, in the following autumn, Radetzky's occupation of Vienna marked the substantial reconquest of Austrian power and the new

Austrian government under Felix zu Schwarzenberg pursued precisely the policy of refusal that Sybel had feared. Those events led Sybel fully into the camp of Droysen and of Duncker and Haym with whom he now worked closely. In effect, Sybel had anticipated the political minimum program of the later, postrevolutionary Prussian School. In the spring of 1848, however, this anticipation was still faint. He was largely alone in voicing this warning, and even in his pamphlet it served as an analysis of the worst case included to underscore his chief contention that, under normal circumstances, national monarchy was not right for Germany. Here, too, Sybel resembled Droysen. Both complained angrily about major aspects of the Seventeen's draft but did so within an ambient optimism. The National Assembly was soon to convene, and in public discourse the question was how, not whether, to unify Germany.

5

In the National Assembly: May to August

On 18 May the National Assembly began its sessions in Frankfort's St. Paul's Church, a recently built and ungainly red-stone structure never actually consecrated for divine services. Germany had no real parliamentary experience, and the confusion and disorganization of the early sessions should have been depressing, but Droysen, Duncker, and Haym—who were attending deputies—were again optimistic during the first weeks of the assembly's existence. It gave them a focus for their political energies, and the fact of its meeting served as a measure of how much things had changed since March.[1] Droysen's correspondence and diary entries nicely illustrate the change in mood that the convening of the assembly occasioned. On 16 May he was still complaining about the lack of adequate national leadership and compared Germany to a "ship driven before the storm."[2] On 19 May, however, he noted that he, like everyone else he knew in Frankfort, felt the "highest satisfaction" and believed that events at last were moving along the "right track."[3] This was high praise from him, because it showed that he thought Germany was again following the dictates of history. In a letter to his close friend Justus Olshausen on 20 May, he went further and claimed that the course of affairs in Frankfort now gave him "all the best hope for the future" and, in a letter of Wilhelm Arendt on 9 June, he went further still by describing "the course of our affairs [as] sublime and worthy of admiration." It was, he urged, necessary only to raise one's head in order "to hear the distant thunder of a great history."[4] He had wholly regained the high spirits that he felt in March.

The opening of the assembly put Duncker and Haym in the same glad frame of mind. Haym, the fourth youngest deputy in the assembly, admitted to David Hansemann in a letter that he felt a little out of his element among the older and more knowledgeable men around him, but added that the meeting of the assembly gave him "the best hopes for the future."[5] Similarly, Duncker later recalled his "inspiration" when the assembly came

into session and his accompanying sense of "uplift at the joyous com-
mencement" of its work.[6] It was not the prospect of prolonged parliamentary activity that stirred them. Duncker, for example, modestly acknowledged at the beginning of the assembly's work that he was a worse
parliamentarian than most of his fellows.[7] He acted on this belief, and only
twice addressed the assembly as a whole. Similarly, Haym took the floor
only in January 1849 and afterward never spoke again. Although he later
described himself as the "most attentive listener" and "most diligent visi-
tor to the sessions," he also recalled that his determination "to follow, to listen, to observe, to criticize" was a product of the reportorial habits that he
had acquired when he researched his book on the Prussian United Diet.[8]
However attentive he may have been, he admitted in a letter to his parents
in early July that he found most of the speeches tedious and unimportant.[9]
This was also Droysen's finding. He was little inclined to listen carefully to
others' addresses, and he never addressed the assembly himself.

This behavior, which at first seems strangely at odds with their professed hopes for the assembly, was not the result of shyness or of a disinclination for public address. For all three men, public speaking had been a
major tactic before the revolution, and Droysen and Duncker were gifted
and spirited lecturers. No doubt they disliked having to listen to others.
Furthermore, they were as outspoken in committee meetings and at the
political clubs that gathered nightly in Frankfort's inns and public houses
as they were silent in the assembly. Although Droysen never spoke before
the assembly, Heinrich Laube in his informative and circumstantial memoir on the National Assembly recalls Droysen in debate as "a victorious
fighter, a tough opponent with inexhaustible resources" who was "so spirited and so many-sided" that he "gave the impression of superiority" even
when his opponent mustered the better arguments. In part, Droysen was
being playful. He attended "almost daily" the meetings of groups on the
left with which he had "nothing whatever in common" chiefly to goad
them into arguments on major questions.[10] He was also matching his tactics to the situation as he understood it. As Droysen remarked in a letter
written on 8 July, he believed that he could "be more useful in a small
circle" than in speeches to the plenum.[11]

This assertion fitted his understanding of the assembly's historic function. He did not think of it as a constituent body invested with full powers
to draft and implement a new German constitution. To have done so
would have been to accept the theory of popular sovereignty that he ab-
horred and to have contradicted his own historical theory according to
which unification had to come about through a reconciliation between old
and new and, more specifically, through voluntary Prussian actions. This
view of affairs obviously diminished for him the importance of debates in
the assembly, but it certainly did not mean that the assembly itself was

unimportant. Apart from being a legal embodiment of Germany's nascent unity and constitutionalism, it was a forum in which the interests of the states could be noted and reconciled with the national interest without lengthy and parallel negotiations. That was Droysen's view in late April, and he still held to it once the assembly was in session.[12] It was also the view taken by Duncker, Haym, and—though he was not a deputy—Sybel. This was why they were so interested in the early discussions about the competence and legal standing of the National Assembly.

This view of the assembly's functions of course ruled out the favored thesis of the German left, namely, that the assembly should proceed "solely and alone" (*einzig und allein*) in the political reconstruction of Germany, but it also excluded the German right's "contract principle" (*Vereinbarungsprinzip*), according to which the assembly had the task of drafting the constitution but the states as well as the assembly would put it in force through multilateral contracts.[13] The former was too radical and seemed to threaten Germany with republicanism and continued revolution. The latter, by contrast, was too conservative and seemed equally dangerous. The "contract principle" was actually a significant constitutional innovation, inasmuch as it gave the nation as a whole, represented by the National Assembly, the right to negotiate as a legal equal with the several states, but in practical terms it left the states with the power to veto the new constitution in whole or in part. Droysen and the others wanted some means to obtain the assent of the states, but this means left the states with too great a power to obstruct. Moreover, this principle was fundamentally at variance with their reading of Germany's current historical situation.

These considerations became evident in the debate over the Lepel Protocol. On 4 May, Viktor von Lepel, who represented Hesse-Darmstadt in the Confederate Assembly, submitted a formal proposal to create a standing committee of states' representatives to report on the assembly's actions to the states and to communicate the states' wishes to the assembly.[14] Although the proposed committee's powers were purely reportorial, it was possible to see in the protocol an attempt to undermine the assembly's independence vis-à-vis the states, and it consequently called forth a number of angry rejoinders. In any case, Lepel's motion demanded a reply because the assembly could do little as long as its position and authority remained open to question. Droysen accordingly prepared a lengthy memorandum for Guido von Usedom, the Prussian delegate the Confederate Assembly. He hoped to persuade Prussia to declare for the assembly's independent competence and, in his habitual thoroughness, drafted a detailed explanation of the assembly's historical and legal position.[15]

Droysen sent the memorandum on 14 May. It began by posing this central question: "Does the Assembly possess the right to frame the German constitution, or has it been summoned to contract one with the states?" He argued strongly in favor of the former proposition in a combination of precise legal language along, however, with items of historical theory that made legal niceties irrelevant to the current situation. In the legal portion of his argument Droysen derived the assembly's authority from the collapse of the old system that had been signaled, first, by the appearance of new policies and personnel in the states and, second, by the virtual cessation of the confederation, the "keystone" of the old order. The confederation had "not merely become theoretically unviable" but now was "already superseded, in fact and with the full recognition of all parties." More specifically, Droysen meant that the election decrees issued on 30 March and 7 April by the Confederate Assembly on demand from the Pre-Parliament amounted to a tacit surrender by that body, and the states that it represented, of any legal right to determine Germany's constitutional future. The National Assembly, therefore, did not have to contract with the states because they had already delegated to it their rights in the matter.[16]

Droysen based the historical portion of his case on his concept of the "right of history." He suggested as much when he claimed that the confederation had "in fact" been superseded, and he made that point explicit when he argued that the revolution had occurred because of Germany's longing for unification, with the consequence that the National Assembly, when convened, would embody that unity. This drive toward unification, Droysen believed, was the central tendency in German history and therefore legitimated both the revolution that it caused and the assembly that was, so far, the revolution's major accomplishment. To give added force to this contention, Droysen pointed out that the authority of the assembly was the same in kind as that possessed by the princes in and after 1815. That is, the post-Napoleonic political map of Germany had been drawn arbitrarily and without the consent of the affected populations, but it had been legitimate insofar as it was historically necessary and for as long as the governed obeyed their governors. By the same token, the revolution and its achievements were legitimate because they were now historical facts created by historical necessity.[17] Though he did not expressly use the terms, Droysen based this argument on his essential distinction between the legitimist "historical right" and his more revolutionary "right of history."

This simultaneous use of arguments that, in logic, contradicted each other, was not the result of carelessness. Whether by design or not, this combination of arguments was rhetorically persuasive, because it both reminded Prussia and the other states of their earlier undertakings and pointedly informed them that a revolution had occurred and that they were, in consequence, under siege. They had promised unification, and they could, if necessary, be forced to keep that promise. The combination also reflected Droysen's sense of historical reality. The legal implications of the states' earlier actions mattered because the states still existed, their consent was still required, and they were still bound by what they had said and done. The revolution was also a reality with its own logic and implications. It had long been axiomatic for Droysen that legal formulas, however important they might be, could not invalidate history. The National Assembly, therefore, was authoritative whether the states approved of it or not. Thus, two separate sets of considerations led to the same result, and, in Droysen's analysis, they reinforced each other in yet another way.

The states, and Prussia in particular, could catch up with history and defend their remaining legitimate interests only by keeping to their undertakings and supporting the National Assembly, which, in turn, could fulfil its historic task and grant Germany a stable unity only by working with the now transformed states. They needed the assembly's backing, and they could gain this only in exchange for good behavior. Droysen therefore wanted the states to allow the assembly as much latitude as possible. At the same time, he wanted the assembly to be as considerate as it could be of the states' interests. Once its authority was unquestioned, therefore, he expected the assembly to be prudently mindful of the states' sensibilities as it designed the nation's institutions, and he did not object to its consulting with the states as long as this consultation was voluntary. To that end, and consistent with his long-held views on truly representative government, he wanted the assembly to create national institutions for Germany that would be responsible only for those areas vitally necessary to the nation's internal cohesion and external strength. Everything else would be left to the state governments. He reiterated these points in the memorandum and other papers and publications in the following weeks.[18]

This view, of course, had important implications for the standing of the assembly. On the one hand, it gave that body dignity and central importance, so that Droysen logically concluded that "the assembly itself is the first and decisive fact of the completed unification of Germany in public law; it will discuss and decree as to the form and constitution in which this political essence shall henceforth operate." By so doing, it would demonstrate beyond cavil that in Germany the era of princely property in power had ended and real statehood had begun. On the other hand, Droysen's analysis made the states, Prussia in particular, especially important. "Now," he insisted, "is the moment in which Prussia can and must assume her position." This claim had urgent importance for him: "Only through the good will of the current governments in Germany, above all Prussia, can the vast danger to which we are so close be removed."[19] In Droysen's vision of how history moved forward, this complementarity of opposed interests was the assurance of coming progress.

Droysen was not the only one to draw these conclusions, though it was possible to reach them on purely pragmatic, less elegantly theoretical grounds. Most deputies in the political center felt as he did, and Duncker and Haym record in the their postrevolutionary memoirs having the same reactions to the Lepel protocol.[20] In Marburg, Sybel cosigned and probably authored an appeal to the Hessian government that took the same line. It responded to the Lepel Protocol by admitting that the new constitution "would come into existence through solid harmonization between the princes and peoples of Germany" and therefore urged the assembly to study the political situation carefully and to consult with the state governments whenever possible. It also stated that if any or all of the states took exception to measures in the national interest, then "no other answer is possible than that the National Assembly should have the sole right to decide."[21] These rationalizations explain the popularity in their camp of the somewhat mystifying thesis that the constituent power lay neither with the people nor with the princes but arose instead from the "sovereignty of the nation" (*Souveränität der Nation*).

This important phrase achieved currency in a major speech by the liberal nationalist leader Heinrich von Gagern in which he accepted the acting presidency of the assembly on 19 May 1848. The concept it stated, however, had obviously been mooted among sympathetic deputies somewhat earlier, because it appears in Droysen's diary entry for 17 May: "Sovereignty of the nation, not popular sovereignty, not sovereignty of the parts."[22] Gagern himself justified the concept in terms of its utility, namely, the "difficulty . . . not to say the impossibility" of unifying Germany except under the assumption that the assembly had the last word in constitutional questions.[23] As a concept, "sovereignty of the nation" assured the assembly a basic minimum of authority without raising the ghost of the French Revolution of 1789 by invoking popular sovereignty and without risking counterrevolution by conceding to the states. The term's very vagueness seems to have attracted Haym, no doubt because it allowed the assembly to gain its point without dangerous concessions to the left or the right.[24]

This view of the assembly's authority implied both delight in its existence and a tendency not to take its proceedings very seriously at most times. Supporting it placed Droysen, Duncker, and Haym solidly in its right center, and they were early members of what then and since has been called the *Casinopartei*. Because national politics had hardly existed in Germany before 1848, deputies arrived in Frankfort without political affiliations and in considerable ignorance of one another's political views. Groupings of political opinion quickly sorted themselves out, however, in continual meetings, usually held at night, at various hotels and cafés in the city (as a consequence of which Germany's first political parties are named after long defunct bars and cafés in Frankfort). The right center first gathered at the Mainlust and Weidenbusch but by late June had situated itself at the Casino Café, from which it took its name, the *Casinopartei*. This party, though the term *party* is somewhat misleading given the initial lack of discipline and the tendency of many deputies to float among groupings, was the largest in the assembly. It variously recorded 150 and 166 members throughout the summer, and though it deferred drafting a program until the September Crisis, it distinguished itself from the Café Milani on its right by rejecting the "contract principle," and the Augsburger Hof party on its left by being more conciliatory toward the states even while defending the independent authority of the National Assembly.[25]

Parties define themselves in terms of what they do not agree about, and the German parties initially defined themselves in response to the combats over the powers and position of the National Assembly.[26] Given the variety of reasons that one could have for taking a particular position on the assembly's authority and the early tendency of deputies to attend more than one party meeting, to say that someone belonged to a particular party is to say little about his actual politics, especially in the first weeks of the assembly's existence. Over time, however, party labels came to have greater meaning as changing circumstances led to increased clarity about long-term objectives and this clarity, in turn, led deputies to choose party allegiance with care. Thus, in the late summer, the right wing of the *Casinopartei* deserted it to form the *Landbergspartei*, and in December its particularists and pro-Austrians broke away to form the *Pariser Hofspartei*.[27] Even so, internal disorganization in the *Casinopartei*, of which both Droysen and Haym complained, remained a continuing problem that the eventual introduction of party discipline in September only partially remedied.[28]

Under these circumstances, a tendency toward differentiation within party groupings appeared as a result of which like-minded deputies clustered together and, at times, worked against the larger party of which they were nominally members.[29] Droysen, Duncker, and Haym, for example, belonged to what Droysen termed the "narrower circle" (*engere Kreis*), which variously met at the Weidenbusch, Hirschgraben, and Englische Hof.[30] Its larger membership included, among others, Heinrich von Gagern, Friedrich Daniel Bassermann, Gustav Mevissen, Hermann von Beckerath, Karl Jürgens, Adolf Lette, Friedrich Römer, and Karl Mathy.[31] Even this smaller group was not always able to achieve or maintain unity, however, and its meetings often became the scenes of long and heated debates. Droysen, Duncker, and Haym also belonged to a small, and presumably more informal, group that Haym labeled the "professors' circle" (*Professorenkreis*), though he was himself not a professor (nor, as his postrevolutionary career unfolded, did he ever become one, though he wrote many fine intellectual histories and edited the prestigious journal *Preußische Jahrbücher*).

Aside from Droysen, Duncker, and some others whom he did not identify, Haym recalled as its members Georg Beseler, Dahlmann, Gervinus, Andreas Michelsen, and Waitz. To a degree, this may have been more a social than a political grouping in which academics, now removed from their families and universities, continued their prerevolutionary acquaintances, but the grouping surely had a political dimension as well. In 1848 conflicting political loyalties overbore old social ties. For example, Duncker and Haym broke with their old friend Arnold Ruge because of his connection with the Frankfort left.[32] Furthermore, their political and historical ideas were too closely interlinked for them neatly to compartmentalize their professional and partisan lives. No doubt it seemed quite natural for them to spend time when possible with people who not only supported the same political program that they did but also held the same tenets of historical theory. It is an indication of this that in Frankfort Droysen, Duncker, Haym, and Gervinus (to whom they still felt politically close) lived within one block of one another on the Bleichstraße, whereas no other deputies had lodgings there.[33]

The initial euphoria lasted a while because their view of the National Assembly as the duly empowered agent of mediation between old and new in Germany met no serious challenge during the first eight weeks of its sessions. The assembly's authority still appeared assured, and its capacity to conduct business in an efficient and orderly fashion visibly increased. The election of Heinrich von Gagern to the acting presidency of the assembly symbolized for them the necessity of what had already been achieved and suggested that unification and constitutionalization would soon be completed.[34] Their statements at the time suggest that they were both impressed with the likelihood of success and awed by the immensity of the task still facing them.[35] This contentment distorted their political perceptions, however, to the extent that they measured the significance of the assembly's proceedings chiefly in terms of probable effects on Prussia and the other states. In addition, their historical philosophy disposed them to doubt the significance of merely legal reforms.

For this reason such evidently important matters as the framing of guarantees as "basic rights" (*Grundrechte*) bored them. This was true even of Droysen, who as a leading member of and recording secretary for the assembly's Constitution Committee (*Verfassungsausschuß*) was busily engaged in that very work. They knew that enactments of this kind were important in their own way, but could not by themselves determine the success or failure of unification. In any case, purely formal guarantees did not seem as a sufficient condition for true freedom. Accordingly, during the relevant committee sessions Droysen spoke only once, characteristically to make a case for free schooling for German youth, and took the general position that the statement of rights should be drafted with an eye to its probable effects on the states.[36] When the draft on basic rights came before the whole assembly, he complained of being bored.[37] Only tactical considerations made the issue seem at all interesting: they hoped that the proclamation of these rights would weaken the appeal of the assembly's left throughout Germany.[38]

Their interest was correspondingly greater in the debates that followed the submission of two motions, each proposed by a deputy on the left and each designed to set major precedents through the disposition of a specific issue. The first motion was brought forward by Franz Raveaux on 19 May and ostensibly dealt with a recent Prussian decree that stipulated that Prussian citizens holding seats both in the German National Assembly at Frankfort and the Prussian National Assembly at Berlin would have to step down from one or the other. If only for the reason that it was impossible to be in Frankfort and Berlin at the same time, the decree obviously made a lot of sense. The difficulty was that a state government had issued a regulation dealing with national representation. Raveaux's motion to overturn the decree contained the implication that he had made explicit in his speech to the assembly: only the National Assembly in Frankfort possessed the right to distribute authority in the nation (*Competenz-Competenz*).[39]

This motion was understandably troubling to Droysen, Duncker, Haym, and, more generally, to most of the right center. They agreed with Raveaux in principle because he was upholding the standard that they had themselves proposed in response to the Lepel Protocol and had affirmed in the principle of the "sovereignty of the nation," namely, the assembly's final right of decision in constitutional matters. They strongly disagreed, however, with Raveaux's present application of it, because they did not want to offend Prussia and because too clear and emphatic a statement of their own principle would have the undesirable effect of blurring the distinction between their position and the left's claim that the assembly should work "solely and alone." It was immediately clear that the issue that Raveaux had raised would have to be settled and that settlement would be difficult.[40]

Before any settlement could be achieved, however, the deputy Franz Heinrich Zitz of Mainz offered another motion of equal importance. Mainz contained a confederate fortress with a mixed garrison of Austrian and Prussian troops. On 21 March some citizens made insulting comments about the House of Hohenzollern in the hearing of Prussian soldiers. Disorders broke out and the garrison command imposed martial law on the city, but not before four Prussian soldiers had been killed and numerous citizens injured. Zitz had a number of harsh things to say about the Prussian component in the garrison and called on the assembly to discipline the offending troops.[41] This motion was problematic for several reasons. First, the accuracy of Zitz's charge seemed doubtful, and it was easy to see him as a troublemaker. Further, given Mainz's strategic location and the widespread if unfounded fear of French invasion, this hardly seemed the time to trouble the resident military. Finally, and especially worrisome to Droysen and the others, Zitz's motion, if carried, would not only offend Prussia but also imply that the assembly claimed active governmental as well as constituent power.[42]

These considerations were weighty enough that the assembly decided not to follow Zitz's lead. His motion was referred to a special committee that reported back on 26 May with a much diluted version of the original text. Even in this form it was not acceptable to Prince Felix Lichnowsky, who spoke against it in sarcastic terms, or to Anton von Schmerling, who persuaded the deputies to vote a return to the order of the day.[43] On 27 May the deputies turned to the altogether more difficult matter of the Raveaux motion. Since its introduction eight days before, numerous amendments and alternate proposals had been offered, but their number was now reduced to four. None of these dealt explicitly with the original question of Prussia's decree on double mandates and all of them were attempts to establish precisely the upper limit of the assembly's competence. In the course of the day's proceedings, the majority of the deputies finally voted for Johann Peter Werner's version, which stipulated that "all provisions of the individual German [state] constitutions that do not agree with the general [national] constitution . . . are to be considered valid only insofar as they accord with the latter, notwithstanding their existing efficacy until that time."[44]

This ingenious compromise nicely demonstrates the determined moderation of the majority in its dealings with the states. The Werner motion preserved the assembly's claim to supremacy by proclaiming its right of final decision in constitutional questions, but it left the states free to make any determinations not directly opposed to those of the assembly and it postponed any possible conflict with the states until the national constitution was actually completed and in force. Until that time, the states could do as they liked. This was just what Droysen, Duncker, and Haym wished. They voted with both majorities and applauded the assembly for its wisdom, though Haym later expressed a slight regret at the abstractness of Werner's language.[45] Without seeming to arrogate powers at the states' expense, the assembly had maintained its claim and had given its work some needed protection against the concurrent constitution-making of the constituent assembly in Berlin.[46]

They were almost jubilant in their belief that the disposition of both motions marked a great victory in the drive for unification.[47] It was as if finding the right language in Frankfort could settle the destiny of the whole nation. Haym, for example, wrote to Hansemann on 29 May to tell him that "in an affair [the Zitz motion] that lay outside our legal sphere we rejected any intervention out of hand; there [the Raveaux motion], where we moved upon our most particular legal basis, we expressed our supreme (*übergreifendes*) legislative power in a deliberate statement." Haym felt good about this, and concluded: "We have finally moved out of our original insignificance, we have finally occupied ourselves with something besides mere preliminaries and formalities."[48] Actually, the assembly's actions were preliminary and formal, but Haym's delight was genuine, and this was an excellent chance to point out the assembly's essential moderation to the joint leader of the Prussian government. Droysen reached the same self-congratulatory conclusion. In a letter he noted that in voting down the Zitz motion, the deputies showed "what we do not want" and in voting for the Werner motion, "what we do want."[49]

Circumspect though both votes seem now, these men were respectful enough to established authority that the assembly's actions also struck them as courageous as well as principled and prudent. Haym subsequently described these decisions as the assembly's "vote of confidence" in itself.[50] Writing at the time, Droysen professed to see in them strong indications that history was still moving along its appointed course: "Nowhere in Germany [is] there a doubt of our dignified but earnestly expressed confidence; the territorial all-mightinesses . . . part before us, in Berlin the government wishes to support itself upon us. This upsetting of power would be unwholesome and incurable if the organs of our unitary power were not constructed here at the seedbed of our future. God first gave us the wish, the hope for national unification; now the facts force it upon us."[51] This confidence was still heavily influenced by his providentialism, and the assembly's recent treatment of two difficult motions confirmed for him that the achievement as well as the desire for unification were historical necessities in accordance with God's plan. There are strong, though more muted, hints of the same view in a contemporaneous letter of Haym's.[52]

The next matter that engaged their passionate interest and, at its conclusion, further confirmed their optimism was establishing a provisional central government. The need for doing so was obvious and urgent to anyone who wanted Germany unified. It was clear that it might take months to complete a constitution, and Germany had to be governed in the meantime. The assembly was too large and unwieldy to perform this task by itself and had in any case foresworn such a role when it tabled the Zitz motion. These considerations called for a speedy decision, but there was also a reason for caution and some consequent delay. Even though the government would be provisional in form as well as composition, that is, even though it would exist only until a new constitution could be put in force, it would set an important precedent and probably influence the assembly's deliberations on the permanent form of national government. For that reason, discussions of this subject were engrossing and at times heated.

Proposals for the creation of a provisional executive started coming from the floor as early as 23 May. On 6 June the Priority Committee, a group entrusted with scheduling the business to be brought for the plenary sessions of the assembly, permitted Ludwig Simon, a deputy from the left, to address his colleagues on this issue. The assembly followed his advice to the extent of creating a special committee, chaired by the historian Dahlmann, to study the motions already submitted and then to report back with its own recommendation (*Prioritäts-Ausschuß über die Anträge auf Bildung einer provisorischen Centralgewalt*).[53] The same divisions that would plague the assembly as a whole when it handled this difficult question also troubled the meetings of the special committee. When it reported on 19 June, it had no single recommendation to offer; instead, it had a majority report to which Duncker, a committee member, subscribed, and two widely varying minority reports.

There might as well have been no special committee, because in the following debates the three original proposals became many. Day by day, new and incompatible proposals reached the chair and continual amendments changed beyond recognition proposals already under discussion. At the same time, the disunity among the deputies became increasingly and distressingly evident.[54] These divisions were of considerable force in further distinguishing and identifying the still forming political parties.[55] They also reflect the marked tendency, directly contrary to the stated beliefs of most, to act as if the revolution's fate hung on finding just the right phrase in a piece of legislation. Three questions were really at issue in this case.

The first concerned the shape and composition of the provisional executive. The left, in the interest of popular sovereignty, wanted a committee of deputies elected by the assembly. Many, however, preferred what they called a *trias* of three members, a Hohenzollern, a Habsburg, and, to represent the middle and small states, a Bavarian Wittelsbach. Some of its supporters hoped that this would also be the form of the executive in the finished constitution, whereas others simply wanted to conciliate the states for the present and left open the question of the final form of the national executive. Then there were those who, anticipating eventual constitutional monarchy, wanted one-man rule, with the executive chosen from among the reigning dynasties. Second, and also troublesome, was the question of the source and legitimation of the executive's authority. Three basic options existed that could apply to any of the three proposed forms. It could be claimed either that authority derived from the assembly alone, or from both the assembly and the states, or just from the states. As one would expect, the answers divided largely along the lines of left, center, and right, respectively. Finally, there was the question of the exact extent of the provisional executive's powers. This question was thorny because it touched on cherished notions about the ideal limits of state power, tested deputies' adherence to federalism, and would foreseeably affect the states' attitudes toward the assembly.

Droysen, Duncker, and Haym approached these questions with a strong sense of their urgency, although they were not always in agreement with each other. They were, however, clear about certain matters from the outset. They recognized Germany's need to have a provisional government as soon as possible and they wanted to make certain that its form would neither exert an unfortunate influence on the assembly's final decisions nor exacerbate its ongoing relations with the states, Prussia in particular. In consequence, they were profoundly opposed to all schemes that called for the election of the executive or for the appointment of a committee of deputies because these implied republicanism.[56] They were just as unwilling to countenance the appointment of the executive by the states or, as some proposed, using the Confederate Assembly as acting executive. They did not want to suggest an unbroken continuity with prerevolutionary times and, furthermore, believed that the confederation no longer had a useful role to play. They were able to invoke notions from their historical theory to argue these points.[57]

It is rather more difficult to explain what they did want. The *trias* scheme embodied in the special committee's majority report, in which Duncker had joined, had two attractive features. It promised to grant an equitable share of influence to the states and, so, to reassure them about the assembly's benevolent intentions. Further, the fact that the three representatives would, in all likelihood, be close relatives of reigning monarchs would be an important concession to the principle of monarchy because its acceptance by the deputies would suggest a determination to preserve both states and princes.[58] In one of his two addresses before the whole assembly, Duncker rose to defend this proposal in a fairly theoretical disquisition. He claimed that the problem before them was the six-centuries-old ailment of German disunity and insisted that its solution was possible only through thoughtful "mediation" (*Vermittelung*). As in his prerevolutionary speeches and writings, he used this term in a more or less Hegelian sense to mean a synthetic combination of old with new. He correspondingly urged the deputies that they work "in the sense of a center, in the sense of a vital creative middle, not that middle that anxiously holds itself apart from the extremes but that middle that synthesizes the divided and opposing forces into a creative and formative motive power" (*die auseinanderstrebenden Kräfte zusammenfasst zu einer schaffenden und gestaltenden Triebkraft*). The assembly could play that role only by orienting itself to the tendency of history.[59]

In making that claim, Duncker had a particular and practical objective. His great fear, he explained, was that the assembly, in view of its great potential power, would attempt to decide the issue "all by itself." In Duncker's view, that approach was both "unpolitical" and "impractical": "I hold it to be unpolitical because it is a mistake to destroy completely a by-passed system [or] the elements and carriers of a principle (*ein überwundenen System, die Elemente und Träger eines Principes ganz zu Boden zu werfen*). It is politically correct in such a situation to carry along in the movement, to continue the old elements that were so long maintained intact in the previous circumstances." His understanding of the operation of the historical process, that is, now dictated tactics. Were his advice ignored, he believed, the old elements in German political life would actually gain strength from the one-sided opposition to which they were subjected and thus be able to obstruct unification. Again, this conclusion was required by the laws of history.[60] His finding was, of course, entirely consonant with his assumptions. It shows that he believed that the assembly could succeed in its task as long as it made no fatal error. It also reflects his belief that historical progress occurred through mediation between old and new, so that if unification was the goal toward which progress had now to move, then unification would not occur if the new ignored or crushed the old. His argument could also be stated in simpler, more pragmatic terms: if the assembly offended the states, then the states might block its efforts. For these reasons he urged the deputies to approve the *trias* plan.

So persuasive did the case for the *trias* seem, that Haym, persuaded by Duncker's reasoning, mourned its abandonment for some time.[61] As the discussions in the assembly continued, however, opinion began to run toward the *monas*, or one-man rule. Droysen presents a case in point of this shift. On 6 June, that is, while the special committee was at work but nearly two weeks before it reported, he wrote to Arendt: "I look forward with some confidence to the discussions on the creation of a central power . . . *a directory of three as the essence of all the collective powers of the German governments*, chosen by them and appointed by the parliament; that is, installed by a vote of confidence from the nation and creating a national ministry (*Reichsministerium*) responsible to us [my emphasis]."[62] He was as firm a believer in trialism as Duncker or Haym. On 19 June, however, he recorded in his diary the previous day's "preliminary discussions in the narrower circle at Jürgen's, where among others were Lette, Duncker, Kierulf, etc. I strove to clarify the purpose of the establishment and to demand speed and decisiveness in the decrees; not just executive power but government; *by no means three but one*—the divine order of the world has so prepared our affairs that our Washington will not be lacking [my emphasis]."[63] Evidently, even God now inclined to executive monism.

Droysen had changed his mind in the hope that Germany would providentially find a single ruler with heroic qualities, though he almost certainly also wanted to set a precedent for a subsequent constitutional monarch. Even in his 6 June letter praising the *trias* plan he had warned against making too great concessions to particularism now that the states, as he believed, were so weakened.[64] He had probably taken that warning more to heart in the following days. This turn in his opinion, however, forced him to deal with the question of who the single ruler would be. He wanted a Hohenzollern, but that was impossible. The March events in Berlin and the recent storming of the Berlin Arsenal had brought the dynasty into such serious disrepute that when, on 20 June, the deputy August Ernst Braun suggested that the assembly vote Frederick William IV of Prussia national executive by acclamation, his colleagues actually collapsed into laughter and the motion failed even to get the twenty votes needed for formal consideration.[65] Under those circumstances, one further attraction of the *trias* plan, at least for Duncker, was that it promised to put a Hohenzollern at the top, although only as one of three.[66]

Droysen therefore tried to turn necessity into opportunity. He looked for the happy aspects of the situation and sought ways to improve on it. If the choice had to be a Habsburg, not a Hohenzollern, he wanted the situation exploited in such a way that it would tighten the bonds between Frankfort and Berlin. He was partially consoled in any case by the knowledge that the probable choice among the Habsburgs was the now aged Archduke Johann. Still a national hero by virtue of his leadership of the Tyrolean uprising against Napoleon in 1809, he seemed more a German than an Austrian figure. Droysen was also comforted by his continuing belief that Austria was on the verge of collapse. Perhaps with Johann as executive it would be that much easier to salvage Austria's German provinces and Bohemia for the unified Germany. He further reasoned that Prussia could gain moral credit throughout Germany by a ready acceptance of Johann's investment with office. He hoped that this would benefit the Hohenzollern case when it came time to institute a permanent, not provisional, executive. He also wanted to make sure that only an "ostensible honor" fell to the Habsburgs and tried to assure that the cabinet officers who served the executive would be Prussian by origin and German in inclination.[67]

Duncker and Haym, again, did not share this outlook, and their attachment to the *trias* plan in fact grew stronger in the wake of the June Days in Paris and the storming of the Berlin Arsenal on 15 June. Further revolution seemed to be in the air, and one-man rule smacked of republicanism.[68] Judging from their votes, they were disappointed and resentful when, on 23 June, Heinrich von Gagern momentarily stepped down from the president's chair and used his very considerable moral authority to persuade the deputies to save time and to avoid useless debate by simply naming a national administrator (*Reichsverweser*) on their own authority.[69] This was what contemporaries called Gagern's "bold stroke," and his open appeal to expediency—which Haym erroneously interpreted as a statement of "principle" and "a huge concession to the left"—should have taken much of the sting out of what otherwise might have seemed an assault by the assembly on the states' remaining powers. Certainly Droysen applauded the action. Even before this he had urged that it was wiser "to be practical than to hawk principles." He agreed that the times were troubled, that it was necessary to act quickly and decisively, and, anyway, he wanted the *monas*.[70]

Droysen, Duncker, and Haym were, however, in agreement in the third major area of concern, namely determining the limits of the executive's power. That was only natural inasmuch as their differing views on its composition was an instance of choosing different means to the same end, and the question of executive competence was a question of ultimate objectives. First, they believed that he should be responsible to the nation as a whole and, hence, accountable to the assembly. Although Haym and Duncker had been distressed by the assembly's seeming arrogation of power on 23 June, on the twenty-eighth they voted against Georg von Vincke's motion that the election of the national administrator by the assembly be subject to the formal approval of the states.[71] It cannot have helped that Vincke spoke for the political right, and their principled view was that the majority of deputies had voted their conviction and that the thing to do now was loyally to maintain unity.[72] The matter was less problematic for Droysen, but he also took the same position.[73] They did not, however, want the new executive to be the mere agent of the assembly, and they accordingly joined in the slender majority that voted down a motion requiring the national administrator to "publish and execute the decrees of the National Assembly."[74] The proposed measure seemed to approximate too closely the detested centralism of the great French Revolution and was, therefore, a threat to the future authority of the states.[75] Their reverence for the states, nonetheless, had definite limits. They wanted Germany strong and they wanted effective national government, right away. They consequently voted for those measures that gave the national administrator full powers to represent Germany diplomatically, to conclude (subject, of course, to the consent of the assembly) treaties with foreign powers, and, most important, to exercise supreme command over the nation's military forces. Because these forces were state, really royal, armies by tradition and by oath, this was a major challenge to the princes and the states. The deputies appear not to have anticipated that in this area the assembly would, before very long, first clash unsuccessfully with the old powers. Given their agenda for Germany, and more specifically the value that they attached to tangible national power, they in any case had little choice. Unification would have little meaning if the states retained independent armies while the national government remained unarmed.

These developments confirmed and increased their original optimism. In keeping with their historical outlook, Duncker and Haym quickly made peace with the defeat of trialism. They had been bothered at first by Gagern's intervention of 23 June, but Duncker quickly concluded that it had all been for the best. Germany would now be able to defend herself against foreign dangers and enjoy a foretaste of unification while the assembly continued its labors on the new constitution.[76] Haym also felt reconciled. In a letter to his parents on 6 July he announced that "Gagern's way was the boldest and the best" and went on to offer some reflections on what these events showed about the current rate of historical progress. He now took the recent defeat of the trias plan as an encouraging sign that showed that it is "not men with their wit and clever political calculations who make history." History, he urged,

makes itself above the heads of men; the result, such as has appeared here, came about through a miracle and as through a higher determination of destiny. No principle, no article, no party has triumphed; on the contrary, the instinct for unity, the drive toward establishment and preservation of monarchy has conquered. Seen from that point of view, the establishment of the position of the National Administrator and the election of the Archduke Johann has something thoroughly sublime about it; and all of us felt this sublime quality as we, the prince-electors of the nineteenth century, elected the "emperor" and as our president led the first cheer for the elected.

This satisfied accommodation with historical reality was, of course, a logical consequence of their historical theory. As men determined to help effect the historically necessary, there was simply no way to be right against history. Haym approached without quite expressing Droysen's overt providentialism. If the *trias* plan had failed, that meant that it was good for it to fail and right to be happy about what replaced it. Later, it would become harder to sustain optimism in the face of defeat when more was at stake than having a provisional government headed by one person rather than three. The recent outcome, paradoxically, also confirmed Haym in his disdain for parliamentary proceedings, and in the same letter he again pointed to the boring, even trivial, character of most sessions.[77]

Droysen took the same satisfied reading of recent events. "Everyday," he noted in his diary on 9 July, "the fact presents itself more compellingly that the unity and strength of Germany finally wants to become a reality." He commented further on the "mysterious" decline of the "republican party and specifically the left side of the Assembly."[78] He evidently believed that these events were interrelated strands in the weave of historical necessity. Like Haym, he thought that history itself, not individuals in the assembly, was responsible for what had happened. Thus, in a letter to Arendt written the day before, he argued that history had taken "a giant stride forwards" in the settlement of the provisional power question and now was "finally at the point where it can conduct a little politics and . . . we will be happier than ancient Greece which was equally cultivated and equally divided." His personification of history was no mere figurative device, as his reference to ancient Greece shows. He evidently believed that at last, after a "little politics," world history would complete in Germany its central task of creating stable human freedom. He expected to see this occur in a short while. He confessed that he found it hard in the "hurly-burly of battle" to find an "overview and connection," but he was absolutely certain that the "best part of this vast movement occurs according to its own laws." "Matters," he insisted, "are just ripe."[79]

This confidence could not last because it was based on an interpretation of history that some sharply contrary evidence was about to call into question. Their optimism sprang from a vision of history as progressive and purposive and, more specifically, from two beliefs about the German present to which they appealed continually in the spring and early summer, namely, that most Germans really wanted unification in a constitutional monarchy with a Hohenzollern at its head and that the princes and governments of the states would accept the loss of sovereignty and curtailment of their powers in exchange for guarantees of remaining autonomy and in the national interest. Disillusionment was approaching on both scores, especially the second. The states did not take recent events, especially the creation of the provisional executive and the first attempts that his government made to exercise its nominal authority, nearly as well as they had expected. Prussia's reactions were especially alarming because of the confidence that they reposed in her and because of the centrally important role that they expected her to play.

Despite the political naïveté they often displayed, they fully understood that they were asking Prussia to make sacrifices that she would find difficult to make. That was why they had tried to concede to her interests and sensibilities whenever possible, even while insisting when necessary—as in asserting the assembly's ultimate competence or in giving diplomatic and military supremacy to the provisional executive—on the irreducible primacy of the nation's claims. They thought that Prussia would fall in with their plans, first, because those plans were historically predestined and, second, because historical evidence seemed to be on their side. In a heavily autobiographical passage from his recollective history *The German National Assembly* (1849–50), Haym wrote of deputies like himself during this period: "They correctly believed that it would be good if Prussia's royal house and people endured for a time yet and patiently submitted themselves to an idea that could only manifest itself as rough and painful in its first fury. *Was not such an approach itself grounded in the entire course of Prussian history?* [my emphasis]"[80] This idea had a prehistory in the prerevolutionary speeches and writings of Duncker and Droysen, and it later became a common theme in the mature histories of the Prussian School. In the early summer of 1848 it possessed obvious relevance: Prussia was so great a state that it would do what had to be done, just as it had done so many times before. Then, to make the assurance even surer, there was the matter of the states', especially Prussia's, self-interest. In a newspaper article written in early June, Droysen had argued that the states would make the needed "sacrifice" because there was "no longer any separation between the governments and the nation." Therefore, "only the dynastic interests" could be offended. He did not take these very seriously because the "Viennese court was broken for the second or third time . . . Or does one fear the Prussian cabinet? It is so far gone that it seeks its support in Frankfort."[81] In fact, Prussia was neither as selfless nor as helpless as they supposed, and was increasingly willing and able to assert its interests against the assembly.

Warning signs began to appear right away. Haym learned from Hansemann of Prussia's reservations about a national government in which she would not be directly represented, and more public indications quickly appeared.[82] On 29 June the Confederate Assembly granted merely de facto recognition to the provisional government, obviously an indication of the attitude of the states. On 4 July, Rudolf von Auerswald, Prussian minister-president since 25 June, sent an official note to the National Assembly in which Prussia recognized the new government but qualified this recognition by stipulating "that no consequence for the future be drawn from the National Assembly's procedure in this extraordinary matter." Despite the conventionally polite official language, this declaration threw doubts on the assembly's powers. On 8 July, Hannover submitted a declaration that recognized the government but expressly complained that its creation injured Hannover's sovereignty. On 12 July, a number of the states went beyond expressions of doubt of the assembly's competence and, in effect, began to undercut the authority of the new government itself. The new government had asked the states to send military contingents to Frankfort to swear allegiance to Johann and his government. Austria, Prussia, Bavaria, and Hannover refused outright, and only a few of the small states actually complied.[83]

From their point of view, the situation continued to deteriorate, though neither then nor later did they appreciate the real popularity of the particularist reaction, especially in Prussia.[84] For example, Droysen hoped to compensate Prussia for the assembly's unilateralism in setting up a provisional executive and then appointing a Habsburg by creating a government staffed by Prussians and sympathetic to Prussia. Berlin was initially receptive to such plans, but for reasons unacceptable to Droysen and most of the National Assembly. Prussia wanted to use the appointees as a counterweight to Austrian influence and to centralism, whereas Droysen wanted a means to bind Prussia to the German nation. The tension between Berlin and Frankfort with respect to this matter became strong enough that the favored candidate for national minister-president, the Rhenish liberal Ludolf Camphausen, felt obliged to decline because he could not do what both Berlin and Frankfort wanted. Droysen was greatly upset because a Prussian of equal stature at home and equal presentability in Frankfort simply did not exist.[85]

Meanwhile, the Foreign Ministry in the provisional government went to the Austrian Anton von Schmerling and the Ministry of the Interior to J.G. Hecksscher of Hamburg. The only Prussian in the new ministry was General Eduard von Peucker as minister of war, and his early actions only further alienated Berlin. The refusal of the larger states to permit their armies to swear allegiance to the national government offended his sense of discipline, and his response was an order on 16 July for the armies to parade before the national colors and to pay homage to the national government.[86] The state governments took principled exception to the centralism that this implied. More to the point, the loyalties of their armed forces were at issue. Droysen was thoroughly alarmed at their reactions, and Duncker, using his contact with Princess Augusta, prepared a memorandum that defended the assembly and its action in moderate terms while trying to appease Prussian anger. He especially sought to convince her that Prussian self-interest itself dictated warm cooperation with the assembly at Frankfort.[87] Apart from the immediate ill will that the Peucker affair caused on both sides, it meant that no candidate acceptable to Berlin would also be acceptable in Frankfort. The nearest approximation to such a compromise was the appointment of Hermann von Beckerath to the Finance Ministry, and he aroused no enthusiasm in Berlin. The naming as minister-president of Prince Karl von

Leiningen, author of a recent article in the *Frankfurter Oberpostamts-Zeitung* in favor of future centralism, was positively offensive to Prussia.[88]

That these events were beginning profoundly to undermine their initial optimism shows in some of Droysen's observations. He was in despair and termed 9 August, the day of Leiningen's installation, "the worst day I have ever lived through."[89] By that date, other, equally disturbing signs of polarization between Berlin and Frankfort had contributed to this mood, though it was hard for them to acknowledge these signs of hostility. Their whole understanding of German history told them that it should not exist, while what they observed showed them that it did. The period from mid-July to early August was a time of mounting and finally successful assaults on the high optimism that they achieved at the end of June. The shocks that they received occurred through personal intervention in politics as well as through distressed observation of official events.

On 12 July, for example, Droysen tried to improve matters by writing to Hans von Bülow, an under-secretary in the Prussian Foreign Ministry whose acquaintance he had made in late April in a meeting with then Prussian Foreign Minister Heinrich von Arnim. He evidently wanted to use this personal contact to tell the assembly's side of the story to official Berlin, and he began the letter by admitting that the steady drive toward unification might be less visible in the Prussian capital than at Frankfort. He assured Bülow, however, that this drive was "irresistible" and that the election of the national administrator was therefore better explained by the "general conditions" in Germany than by any special "virtue of the National Assembly." In other words, the assembly had only done what history required of it and was not bent on demeaning Prussia. He then discussed the need for self-denial in the present moment. His tone became wheedling. He found Prussian irritation understandable because, as "a Prussian born," he had himself required "self-conquest" to vote for Archduke Johann. He now expected similar resolution on the part of official Prussia. He wrote that Prussians were rightly proud, but their pride would be especially justifiable if they now continued their long tradition of sacrificing themselves for the greater national good.[90] With these preliminaries completed, Droysen made his major point: "It is completely clear that if Germany is to become a real federation (*Bundesstaat*), along with military affairs, above all foreign relations must be purely German and treated as such." He consequently urged Prussia to take "a bold but at the same time worthy step" and "remove the foreign politics of Germany from Prussia completely and place them in the hands of the central power." This action would bring two major benefits to the Prussian government, he believed. First, it would allow it to outflank the increasingly uncooperative Prussian National Assembly in Berlin because the Prussian throne would be openly allied with national unification. Second, the Hohenzollern dynasty would regain in a moment the confidence of Germany lost in the preceding months, and its future in the unified Germany would be assured.[91] In his optimism, Droysen was once again asking of Prussia more than she would give, though on this occasion he did not ask her to dissolve herself into smaller territorial units. Even so, he was asking Prussia, whose troops were taking the brunt of the war against Denmark, voluntarily to surrender control of its foreign policy. That Droysen asked for these things at all, however, shows his continued confidence in his prerevolutionary theorizing about Prussia and her historical mission.

He cannot have been altogether surprised by the reply, however, both because of the skepticism that Prussia had already expressed about the assembly's recent creation of a national government and because of current rumors—they turned out to be correct—that Prussia contemplated a separate peace with Denmark.[92] Certainly the reply was harsh. Bülow did not reply in person and instead commissioned Heinrich Abeken, a university acquaintance of Droysen's, to respond. Abeken's lengthy note bristled with a Prussian particularism offensive to Droysen and showed consistent hostility to the policies being pursued in Frankfort. As he accurately informed Droysen, the monarchy's reservations toward the provisional government did not come only from a few well-placed reactionaries but instead reflected the deeply held views of the government, the Berlin Assembly, and a majority of Prussians in all the provinces. Prussians, he insisted, had "the most decided German inclination," but "there has in addition to that been expressed with equal decisiveness the consciousness that Prussia must not cease to be Prussia when it does or wants something for Germany."[93]

Abeken offered these general observations to rationalize a specific proposal. Because the world knew Prussia but not Germany, why not let Prussia take over the control of foreign affairs for the nation as a whole?[94] This suggestion, though a mirror image of Droysen's suggestion, would not by itself have horrified him. Droysen had himself mooted it several days earlier in the Constitutional Committee as a less desirable, nonetheless possible, way of concerting a common national foreign policy.[95] It was the reasons that Abeken supplied that were unacceptable to Droysen. They entailed perpetuating Prussia's separateness. In his diary Droysen noted bitterly that Abeken's note had given him a "penetrating view" of the "misconceptions and pettiness of affairs" current in Berlin.[96]

Then followed the politely phrased official Prussian protests during the Peucker controversy ominously followed by publication of the pamphlet, "The German Central Power and the Prussian Army." The work was anonymous but had in fact been written by Karl Gustav von Griesheim, a Prussian general on active duty. This fact was known to Droysen and almost certainly to Duncker and Haym. The work, then, might be a less polite way of making official Prussian views known. It was worrisome enough just as an indication of Prussian military views. Griesheim advised against yielding Prussian forces to national control and suggested instead that they be used at an opportune moment to seize territories north of the Main River for Prussia. He also made the same point urged in Abeken's letter, namely, that Prussia not cease to be Prussia even in a unified Germany.[97] Droysen, Duncker, and Haym were understandably troubled by this display of unabashed Prussian particularism.[98]

Under these pressures, their moods changed, though not all at once. In July, Droysen began to record in his diary his discouragement at reports arriving from Berlin. At first these entries were short and noncommittal, but then he began to record his feelings in longer, more emotional passages.[99] Similarly, Haym used his correspondence with Hansemann to defend the authority of the assembly and to declare its readiness to cooperate with the Prussian government, but with time his points became at once more insistent and less assured. By the end of July, in marked contrast to his statements only a few weeks before, his nervousness and lack of certainty were unmistakable.[100] Their basic confidence was beginning to break, though it would be some time yet before they arrived at a fundamental reappraisal of the situation.

As late as 1 August, Droysen composed an essay in which he remarked approvingly on the evident growth of sentiment in favor of unification and professed special pleasure in the assembly's recent decision to retain Posen (Poznan) for Germany, a move which to him seemed a milestone in the evolution of a national foreign policy. Germany had at last learned "the proper egotism" in the conduct of its affairs.[101] In its pages he did not shy away from the increasingly strained and worrisome relations between Frankfort and Berlin, but he still tried to find grounds for continued hope. That is, he acknowledged that further progress depended on Prussia's unreservedly embracing federal unification and admitted that Prussia's historical pride and fear being submerged might for a time prevent Berlin from adopting and following the correct policies, but he assured his readers that these difficulties would soon disappear. The Hohenzollern monarchy was already completely German and would soon acknowledge the fact and act accordingly. Simply by feeling a need to explain and excuse the delay he had moved some distance from his earlier optimism, and his closing words show that his confidence was shallow: "Once again," he stated, Prussia held "the fate of Germany in its hands—perhaps for the last time."[102]

That was wishful thinking, and Droysen's growing fears were more evident in another draft of the essay, where he said that it was obvious to observers that Prussia had to be dissolved into smaller units in the interest of unification, and then asked: "But will this be attainable? Will the dynasties, the states, the tribes (*Stämme*) agree? We stand on the brink of the only reaction that Germany has to fear. Not an Austrian . . . It is essentially a Prussian question that is at stake. Prussia has a history; therefore, Prussian particularism, the most justified kind, is beginning to assert itself. Prussia's retreat from full, complete, unreserved freedom would be a legal title for every other dynasty to demand the same. A new miscarriage would only leave Germany the more impotent."[103] Not only was Droysen more fearful in private than in public, he also feared different things. He was worried not merely about delay but about failure, a failure caused by Prussian particularism. For the time being he had stopped worrying about the republican left and had sensed the danger of "reaction" in Prussia itself. However understandable Prussia's current attitudes were, they threatened a revival of particularism in all the states that would not only halt progress towards unification but would actually leave Germany worse off than it had been before March. If that were true, it meant that Droysen had been wrong about many things and that it was time to rethink his ideas.

He was only partly able to do so. In a diary entry made on 7 August, he freely expressed his anger and disappointment without quite admitting that, perhaps, he had been wrong and that, perhaps, he had expected the impossible. In keeping with a vision of historical necessity in which history was never wrong though individuals might err, he disgustedly tried to find out what might yet be salvaged:

On this day I felt the entire impotence of our situation. It is hopeless that the activity, yes, the existence of our assembly and our work can always appear to be called into question anew. *If there is so little conquering truth in our activity, then history is just in permitting German unity to be purely diplomatic* . . . The Prussians have a justified attitude but it is overstretched and exaggerated . . . The whole object of controversy is accorded a position that . . . puts us at a distance from what we should be doing. Precisely the non-dynastic, precisely the March movements, however else they may be judged, were the basis for unification for all. This is being increasingly surrendered. *Perhaps very necessary and wholesome.* For if I judge this assembly correctly, it will never create a constitution out of its plenary powers. *Events will intervene first and necessarily ripen* and then a constitution will be decreed [for] the poor Fatherland, in the best and most salutary case a Prussian [my emphasis]![104]

It is important to note both what he did and did not admit. He admitted that history was not turning out as he had expected, though he did not actually say that he had misread it or that it had been unreadable. This was entirely consistent with his view of history as a passer of judgments that were beyond appeal. He did not conceal his own unhappiness, but he could not blame history and therefore could not blame Prussia, which, after all, was merely acting as history's agent. He was consequently prepared to accept whatever happened, although he still thought some form of unification was inevitable and hoped that at least this would occur through a constitution dictated by Prussia and, presumably, including a degree of Prussian hegemony in Germany.

This crisis in Droysen's thinking is important both as an indication of the quandary in which these historians' theory placed them when they faced unwelcome events and as a foreshadowing of their future political program. No one was more passionately attached than Droysen to the idea of Germany's unification as a constitutional monarchy created through Prussian sacrifice. Yet faced with evidence of the unfeasibility of this program, he had to beat down his anger with deliberate stoicism because there was no defying history. It was an attitude of accommodation, but it was a principled accommodation. Now, as in later years, this took the form of seeking unification on any terms and, in the best case, as a virtual Prussian takeover of Germany that would have horrified him not long before. This was not simply a scaling down of demands in the face of adverse circumstance; rather, it was a taking of the best that history had to offer as the best because history offered it.

Droysen's August despair quickly passed, but it left him shaken and sobered, and later disappointments at Frankfort brought its return with more enduring effects. On 7 August he toyed briefly with the notion that perhaps the republican left had been correct in arguing that the assembly should act on its own, but he quickly dropped that radical line of speculation, and his depression deepened by the ninth. By the tenth, however, he hoped that history might, after all, cunningly provide a means to the sort of unification that he once confidently expected.[105] He wrote to Arendt, as he often did in moments of excitement. He laid much of the blame for the current situation on Prussia, though he also criticized the assembly for treating Prussia like a petty state like Nassau. He continued this partial exoneration by observing that Prussia "must either destroy or be destroyed" and then, without mentioning who the adversary would be, expressed his hope that through war Prussia would find an "occasion" to make herself "indispensable to Germany . . . [for] without war everything will become confused." Before this war broke out, the National Assembly had to rush to complete its constitutional draft so that there would be "organic institutions of unity" that Prussia could put into force at the moment of her choosing.[106] Then this idea, too, dropped from sight for a while, and he returned to counselling appeasement of Prussia by the assembly. He cannot yet have abandoned all his earlier hopes because even in the autumn he had not wholly given up the belief that Prussia might break voluntarily into smaller states in the service of unification.[107] Where else could he turn except toward Prussia?

There is no evidence about Duncker's views specifically in August, although his 31 July memorandum to Princess Augusta shows the same fears that led Droysen to his crisis.[108] In any case, the degree to which he was scandalized when the deputy Lorenz Brentano suggested that the republican rebel Friedrich Hecker was no worse than Prince William (he was angrier than either Droysen or Haym) suggests an anxiety about Prussian sensibilities, as well as loyalty to Augusta's husband.[109] Haym went through an evolution like Droysen's, but without its suddenness or intensity. The first sign of a change on Haym's part appeared in a report that he sent on 12 August to his constituents at Mansfeld in which he explained that the particularist reaction in Prussia required that "the politics of trust make way for the politics of negotiations and transactions." Like Droysen, he blamed Frankfort as well as Berlin for the impasse that had occurred, and he wanted restraint and conciliation on both sides. He really wanted Prussia to play the part for which he thought her cast. Successful unification was possible only if the "people and government of Prussia" willed it and therefore resolutely supported the National assembly. At the same time, the assembly had to accommodate Prussian feelings: "If we are prepared to relent in the harsh assertion of the idea of German unity, then those on the other side will relent in the exaggerated and poorly understood assertion of particularism."[110] If only because he was writing to those who had elected him, he expressed himself with guarded optimism, but the change in his outlook since late June was obvious enough. Unification now seemed contingent rather than ineluctable and had probably to be achieved in a compromise form.

The change in Haym's outlook was more evident in a letter that he sent to his father on August 28 in which he admitted that everyday he had to learn "to modify the ideal according to the conditions of reality." This was the same note of stoicism that Droysen had sounded: Haym was willing to let history dictate to him, though two particular matters left him feeling uncertain. First, he was troubled that the eventual rule of the Hohenzollern over a unified Germany was not "already more securely in the sack" than was in fact the case. Second, he complained that "world events are now so confused that no one can know what even the immediate future will bring us."[111] He was puzzled because history had not behaved as he had supposed it would. He nonetheless still took it as axiomatic that he would follow the "conditions of reality" and seems to have trusted that whatever happened would somehow be good. His complaint about the present confusion of events also shows that he continued to think of predictability as the normal condition of history. He was mentally prepared for the accommodation that he, too, would have to make.

6

Crisis and Reconstruction

By late summer, unexpected events had severely stressed the optimism that Droysen, Duncker, and Haym felt after the question of the provisional executive had been resolved in late June. In several important respects, Droysen had briefly changed his political program, though not yet his vision of history, and Haym now thought that unification could be achieved only with greater difficulty and after greater compromise than he had earlier supposed. These changes in outlook, however, were only partial and, to some extent, temporary. It took more than Prussian obduracy in the face of the provisional government's decrees to force them to revise ideas long and fervently held. Their historical theory at first blinded them to unwelcome facts, and it also enabled them to find some hidden good in seeming bad when disappointing evidence became too obvious to disregard. From September onward, however, successive dashings of their hopes forced on them important and lasting changes. These disappointments were too severe for them to absorb without some fundamental rethinking and reconceptualization. They altered their political program and, more important, revised both their historical theory and their interpretation of history's course.

This revision was sparked by a change in Prussia's policy toward the ongoing war with Denmark over Schleswig-Holstein. Retaining these territories for Germany and exploiting the struggle for their retention as a means of binding Prussia to the national cause had been a major interest of theirs since at least 1844. They had, consequently, been greatly encouraged when Prussia, partly in an attempt to recoup some of the prestige just lost in capitulating to the revolution in Berlin, made a major declaration of policy on 24 March 1848 that committed her forces to maintaining the territorial integrity of the duchies, to preventing their incorporation in whole or in part into Denmark, and to maintaining them as a unit in a newly unified Germany.[1] That declaration, however, and the subsequent dispatch under General Wrangel of by far the largest contingent in the mixed German force in the duchies were the actions of a sovereign state acting on its own initiative in what it then saw to be its own interest. Even before the frictions caused by the creation of a provisional executive, the assembly tried to nationalize the war in the north and, thus, by implication to control the disposition and use of the Prussian contingent. Specifically, the assembly insisted in a motion passed on 9 June that it alone had the right to conclude any binding treaty with Denmark. Droysen, representing a district in Holstein, voted for this measure. Duncker and Haym, representing Prussian districts and surely understanding that the bill was, in the nature of things, aimed to tie Prussia's hands, voted against it.[2] This measure completed an anomalous and politically dangerous situation: Prussia, potentially as strong as ever, bore the brunt of the fighting and assumed the risks of war in the Baltic, whereas the National Assembly at Frankfort claimed the credit and denied Prussia the right to supplement military action with diplomatic measures that might seem to be in her interest. (Of course, the assembly could hardly have claimed to embody national sovereignty while conceding to a single state what amounted to a deciding voice in national foreign policy).

Prussia's apparent willingness to accept this situation was encouraging while it lasted, though Prussian discontent surely was one reason for her summer protests over the provisional government's claims to independence in foreign policy and her refusal to allow her army to swear allegiance to the national government. Droysen, Duncker, and Haym evidently missed these clues, or else refused to recognize them as a result of wishful thinking. From Prussia's continuing military participation they drew the incorrect conclusion that this was a sign of her real willingness to accept heavy burdens on behalf of Germany and a promising indication that, when the time came, she might still do whatever was necessary for unification. Droysen claimed this in his 1 August essay and, again, in an article written after the preliminary truce between Prussia and Denmark, on 29 August.[3] Duncker suggested the same thing in more general terms in a speech before the assembly, and both he and Haym recalled this as a basic belief during the late summer.[4] Given their strong initial support for Prussia's action in the duchies and their lingering hopes that Prussia would finally cooperate in unification, their continued faith was understandable though quite mistaken. As a matter of principle, they disbelieved rumors about a Prussian separate peace with Denmark.[5]

They were surprised and embarrassed, therefore, when Prussian and Danish representatives at Malmö in Sweden agreed on 26 August to a preliminary truce. They, and the rest of the deputies in Frankfort, now faced a dilemma. If the National Assembly ratified the truce, as Prussia wished, it would involve itself in the odium of an agreement that many in Germany thought shameful and would appear to be subservient to Prussia. If it rejected the truce, however, it would prolong a conflict that was hopeless now that Prussia had withdrawn and would worsen relations with Berlin beyond repair.[6] Either way, the assembly would lose. This situation was especially painful for Droysen, Duncker, and Haym because it demonstrated the wrongness of their earlier estimation of Prussia. Thus, on 11 July, when Duncker addressed the assembly on the rumors of Prussian plans for a separate peace, he had remarked that "if [the] reports were true, then the foreign politics of the *old* Germany would be stronger than those of the *new*, then the politics of the *unified* Germany would be weaker . . . than those of the divided Germany."[7] In July he had pointed to those implications because he thought that their very gravity showed the implausibility of the rumors. Now that Prussia had made peace, he was forced to accept these evident but very unwelcome conclusions.

While they considered the implications of Prussia's action, they had to decide how to vote when the truce came before the assembly for ratification. That is, they had either to involve themselves in approving a treaty they thought disgraceful or in continuing a now unwinnable war while angering Prussia. They would have much preferred to be allowed to stand aside, and at first they actually hoped that the national government would spare the assembly embarrassment by signing the truce on its own authority and then presenting the deputies with a welcome fait accompli.[8] That course of action was probably illegal, however, and the Provisional Government declined to try it. Their only comfort was that they would not actually have to vote for or against the truce itself but only for or against its temporary "arrest" (*Sistierung*), and this was a distinction without a difference because a "no" vote meant that the truce would go into effect.[9] Duncker and Haym were sure that Prussia had made a disastrous error, but they did not want the split between Berlin and Frankfort to become irreparable and they voted against the continuation of the arrest.[10]

Droysen faced more of a predicament. He thought that Prussian good will was indispensable for national unification, but he had been involved for four years in the politics of the duchies and he sat in Frankfort for the fifth district of Holstein. Possibly in the belief that the majority would vote to end the arrest in any case, he voted for its continuance in the first vote and then was stricken to discover that his side had won and that the assembly had, in effect, repudiated the truce. He knew that his decision had been untenable. Before the vote he had opined that rejection of the truce would mean that "Prussia or at least half of Prussia will be against us."[11] Ten days later he wrote to the wife of a friend in Kiel that "the question itself has for a long time not concerned our lovely land [Schleswig-Holstein] but Prussia."[12] In his remorse, he now switched sides. Along with Karl

Philipp Francke, Richard Jens Ernst von Meergard-Brunn, and Andreas Ludwig Jacob Michelsen, he drafted the compromise resolution that would let the truce come into force and was part of the slender twenty-one-vote majority that passed it on 16 September.[13]

All three were no doubt relieved at this outcome, but they could take no satisfaction in it. In their correspondence, both Droysen and Haym noted that the assembly had lost much of its moral authority in the process, and they were also depressed by the revulsion with which many deputies now regarded Prussia.[14] In fact, resentment over what, as the deputies saw it, Prussia had done to the assembly by making peace had grown so intense that Duncker, despite his own pronounced misgivings about Berlin's decision, made it a point of principle to say nothing critical about Prussia.[15] Because Prussia still seemed the key to unification, it was necessary to follow her even when she acted against vital national interests.[16] As Haym put it in a letter to Hansemann on 17 September, the "honor of Prussia" had been at stake in the preceding day's vote.[17] That was why he had voted as he had and why, despite considerable disenchantment, he continued to defend Prussia.

Droysen was of the same mind, though he added a note of moral pride about the self-mastery that it took him to support Prussia.[18] In fact, he felt as if he and his fellow deputies now faced a devil's alternative. In a letter to Wilhelm Behn on 15 September, for example, he explained histrionically that

if we reject the armistice, then Prussia will break with us, then we will be excluded from international relations, then we must revolutionize and anarchize in order to fight against I don't know whom, then we must expect the hungry French in Baden and even give up the duchies . . . If we approve the truce, then the central power and the parliament will be morally broken, the agitators will cry treason, the red republic will appear first in Baden and Württemberg and Rheinhessen and the French will march quickly to its aid.[19]

Despite these feelings, he helped prepare the compromise resolution that approved the truce the next day, as he evidently thought that it would also bring renewed revolution and French invasion. Perhaps he now thought, as he had in August, that a war would help speed unification. Like Haym and Duncker, however, his continued loyalty to Prussia was tinged with criticism. After all, the sort of unification that he wanted was not possible in the face of Prussian opposition, even though, in a letter to Justus Olshausen, he attributed the present crisis to "the insanity of Prussian diplomacy." In the same letter he explicitly blamed Prussia for dooming Germany to upheaval and invasion.[20] He no longer referred to Prussia's tradition of self-sacrifice.

It soon seemed that Droysen's worst fears were being realized. The truce was not popular, and the vote of 16 September made the deputies attractive targets in the streets of Frankfort. On 16 and 17 September, they were jeered, pelted, and threatened. Worse, on the eighteenth two conservative deputies, Prince Felix Lichnowsky and General Hans von Auerswald were attacked and killed by a mob. Even in quiet times, Droysen, Duncker, and Haym were alarmed at the idea of revolution. Now they thought they were in the middle of one, and Haym at one point found himself barricaded with sixty other deputies while the crowd outside smashed the windows and tried to break down the door.[21] It was only natural that in his next report to the voters in Mansfeld he asked for their unwavering support for the sternest measures to repress any new violence.[22] He had his physical security to think about, and he returned to the arguments that he had made in mid-June after the attack on the Berlin Arsenal. This time, they signaled a lasting movement rightward, and Duncker accordingly appealed to the conservative Georg von Vincke not to resign his seat in the wake of the September disorders. Duncker still disagreed with Vincke's belief that the constitution should be a contract between the states and the assembly, but he pleaded with him to stay because that collaboration between the center and the right were now more necessary.[23]

This was a sign of the difficult and essentially contradictory situation in which these men now found themselves. The acceptance of the armistice, although underscoring their dependence on Prussia, had left them disillusioned and skeptical about Prussian reliability. The September riots had then thrown them back on the old powers, Prussia in particular, as the only possible guarantors of law and order. Their political isolation was painfully evident. Both Droysen and Haym noted the anomaly of their position.[24] Their present circumstances were very different from those that had existed between May and mid-July, and would become worse as the success of counterrevolution in Austria and Prussia further circumscribed the small room for maneuver left to them. Of course, they were not alone in suffering under these constraints. A number of members of the *Casinopartei* seceded on the grounds that the party was too accommodationist toward Prussia and founded a rival right-center grouping at the Augsburger Hof. The remaining members at last found it necessary to draft a program, but could arrive at nothing clearer than a compromise formula that stated a continued desire for unification and argued against either further revolution or particularist reaction. It had nothing positive to offer in their places.[25]

Droysen, Duncker, and Haym were at a theoretical as well as a political impasse. Along with devising a new political strategy suited to their present helplessness, they also had to interpret history in order to understand what had gone wrong. Given their reliance on history for practical guidance, they could not attempt the former until they had completed the latter. This was what Duncker had in mind when, a year later, he described September 1848 as the "turning point" and when Droysen described it as a time of rigorous political education.[26] They did not arrive at definitive answers for some time, however, though Haym began to formulate one in his first letter to Hansemann since July. He could not report on affairs in Frankfort while ignoring the fact that matters had fundamentally changed in the intervening period. Haym now thought it necessary to reconsider his notion of historical progress. "A future historian," he urged, "will have to date from September of this year a new epoch in the entire movement: everything is so confused anew, new occurrences have so decisively intervened in what seemed to be so tractable a development of affairs (*Entwicklung der Dinge*)." He consequently believed that a "turning point in history" (*Wendepunkt der Geschichte*) had been passed and that new approaches to existing problems had to be discovered.[27] This was more than rhetorical complaint: because they approached politics from the perspective of foretelling history, day-to-day disappointments forced revision of their historical theory. Consequently, Haym's remarks now went well beyond the uncertainty that he expressed to his father on 28 August.[28] He was clear that something irreversible had occurred, even though he was not yet sure just what had happened or what to do, and he still evidently believed that historical analysis would yield reliable, if less reassuring, political guidance.

Droysen was of the same opinion, and advanced it with more brutal frankness. In a letter to Karl Josias von Bunsen in early October he argued that the settlement of the armistice question and its consequences had ended "all idyllic delusions and self-deceptions." Discouraged, he now confessed: "We believed the idea of unity to be stronger than it is; it is evident that interests, customs, disinclinations are far too discordant to be reconciled with the sovereignty of unity."[29] He now blamed himself (along with others, of course): he had misread the evidence, reached faulty conclusions, and, so, seen his warmest hopes disappointed. The experience of further disappointments that autumn forced them, at varying rates of speed, to consider the implications of these initial reactions. This consideration led first Droysen, and then Duncker and Haym, to revise their ideas in important ways in and after December.

In the nature of things, many of these unwelcome events were beyond their control, but in one instance, the so-called question to Austria (*Frage an Österreich*), Droysen himself precipitated the bad news. In framing this question, Droysen acted from a new sense of realism and his desire to learn the real state of affairs, however discouraging it might be. On 19 September—three days after the assembly's acceptance of the Malmö Truce and one day after the deaths of Lichnowsky and Auerswald—the Constitution Committee on which Droysen sat created a special subcommittee to draft the articles on the nation (*das Reich*) and the central power (*Reichsgewalt*). Droysen was a member of this subcommittee, along with Georg Beseler, Alexander von Soiron, Dahlmann, and K.J.A. Mittermaier. In the course of its first session, he took what turned out to a major step toward the final definition of the Prussian School.

He argued that it was time to determine Germany's actual territorial limits and, more specifically, to discover Austria's real intentions on inclusion in a unified Germany. It was obviously necessary to know how large the state would be and what dynastic interests might have to be accommodated, but Droysen was further convinced that if the assembly continued to work in ignorance of Austrian designs, the Habsburg monarchy would be in a position to sabotage its work. The result was the draft of articles 1, 2, and 3, which he and Dahlmann wrote together. The subcommittee discussed the proposed articles for several days and on 26 September sent them unamended to the Constitution Committee as a whole.[30] The committee studied them until 11 October and then sent them virtually unaltered to the plenary assembly, where, after heated debates lasting from 19 to 27 October, they were finally approved.[31]

Droysen and Dahlmann wrote the articles designed to elicit a clear Austrian response by posing national as well as historical requirements for admission. The first stipulated that member states would be those of the German Confederation. This was a historical standard. The second stated that no unit of the unified Germany might be connected with non-German lands. The third slightly qualified the second by allowing that, in cases where such a connection had existed previously, it might be maintained, but only in the form of personal union. These articles employed national criteria. They had potential bearing on several German territories, but Droysen was correct when on 19 September he termed them collectively the "Question to Austria." Tiny Limburg, for example, would be unaffected because it was, in any case, held by the Dutch crown only in personal union. From the German point of view, the same was true of Schleswig-Holstein; Germans had fought there to insist that the duchies were not parts of the Danish monarchy. Prussian Posen had never been in the German Confederation, and the majority of its inhabitants spoke Polish, but the assembly had long before declared it German, so it would not be lost. The Austrian Empire, however, would have to be partitioned in order for its German provinces to enter a unified Germany. Upper and Lower Austria, Styria, the Tyrol, and Bohemia could enter, but the rest of the empire could not. Droysen wished to force the Austrian government, still exiled from Vienna at Olmütz (Olomouc) in Moravia, to choose between entering the new Germany at the cost of territorial integrity and the preserving of that integrity at the cost of exclusion from German affairs.[32]

Droysen's motives are open to scrutiny. He was right that the assembly had to know what Austria intended, and purely diplomatic soundings might not have yielded the needed intelligence even had they been seriously attempted. These articles, however, were bound to force a crisis both between Austria and the assembly and between pro-Austrian and pro-Prussian deputies in the assembly. Droysen did not discuss these risks in public, although he may privately have reasoned that agreement based on a common desire to seek the unattainable was not worth preserving. It is also quite possible that he expected a negative answer from Austria as an offset to the disrepute into which the other great German power, Prussia, had fallen after the Malmö Truce. On two previous occasions he had noted that Austria's position in revolutionary northern Italy was parallel to that of Prussia in the war with Denmark, and it must have galled him that Austria had managed to maintain her prestige intact in Germany and Prussia had not.[33] Moreover, as he reported to Bunsen in early October, Berlin and Frankfort were at loggerheads, with neither able to bend the other to its will, and he feared an attempt to unify Germany without Prussia. Given those worries, a move that might force Austria to exclude herself from Germany would have the virtue of making Prussia seem indispensable.[34] It seems unlikely that he expected a positive response.[35] Of course, no one, not even Droysen, could have been entirely sure what the effect of these articles would be, and certainly the deputies who approved them were not, in their majority, bent on provoking Austria.[36]

Droysen was at least fairly certain that Austria's reply would be negative, that she would appear to be an enemy of national unification, and that this enmity would justify "Prussia and little Germany (*Kleindeutschland*) unifying the more integrally."[37] "Little Germany" still meant the smaller German states, as opposed to Austria and Prussia, although it was about to acquire its subsequent and more familiar meaning, namely, a Germany unified with Prussia but without Austria.[38] Despite his perennial distaste for Austria, however, this maneuver was not, strictly speaking, anti-Austrian. Droysen, like virtually all the deputies, wanted Austria's German provinces in the united Germany. In June that had been one of Droysen's reasons for accepting the election of Archduke Johann as National Administrator (a consideration that also helped bring Duncker and Haym to their senses after the *trias* plan was rejected).[39] They had based those hopes, however, on the belief that Austria was about to collapse and that the desired provinces could be had without unacceptable conditions. By late September it was clear that Austria had survived the shocks to which it had earlier been subjected.[40] In these changed circumstances, Droysen believed, Austria would resist entry into a tightly federated nation-state, and he did not want to loosen the terms of unification in Austria's interest. If, therefore, Austria in effect withdrew from Germany, this withdrawal would merely confirm a loss of territories already sustained. Germany would need Austria's military resources, but these could also be had through an alliance between two separate states.[41]

Droysen was prepared to surrender more than Austria's German provinces. He told Bunsen that if Austria did not enter the unified Germany, then Bunsen's proposal to divide Germany into national circles (*Kreiseinteilung*) would become unworkable.[42] The full details of Bunsen's scheme are besides the point here, but it required the dissolution of Prussia into smaller, component parts. That requirement had, of course, also been dear to Droysen, who had repeatedly insisted that it was a prerequisite to successful unification. By clear implication, Droysen was now willing to leave Prussia intact in a unified Germany. That was a major shift in his views because, given the disparity in size and resources between Prussia and the other states, this would amount to virtual Prussian hegemony. Presumably, he found unification even under that unsatisfactory condition preferable to any other foreseeable outcome.

Eventually, if not at first, Duncker and Haym reached substantially the same conclusions. Whatever their initial reactions to the "question to Austria," and they later voted for it in the plenary assembly, they were partly relieved when Prince Windischgrätz's army took Vienna on 31 October and ushered in a reaction virtually certain to answer the "question to Austria" in the negative. The triumph of counterrevolution saddened them, but they were happy that it occurred in Austria and not elsewhere.[43] This shows a clear readiness to think of Austria, though not Prussia, as dispensable for a unified Germany. They made their views even clearer when reports of the Kremsier Program, which was Austria's answer to articles 1, 2, and 3, reached Frankfort on 2 December. This program was drafted under the guidance of the new Austrian minister-president, Prince Felix zu Schwarzenberg, and published on 27 November. Its central thesis was that Austria's "continued existence as a political unity is a German as it is a European necessity." Under the terms of articles 2 and 3, this meant that Austria would not enter a unified Germany. To do so would have meant partitioning the German and non-German Habsburg territories. The program went on to explain that Austria would therefore hold herself apart until some later date, at which time both states, Germany and the Austrian Empire, would be rejuvenated and reformed and would determine the exact nature of their relationship to one another.[44] Droysen noted in his diary with grim satisfaction: "Now one knows what Austria wants."[45]

Similarly, Duncker and Haym believed that the Kremsier Program greatly simplified the question of who was to rule in Germany. They, too, now thought of unification in terms of the dominance of a great German power, and they were pleased that it would now be easier to secure Prussian leadership.[46] Consequently, they were delighted at the fall of the Schmerling government in Frankfort on 13 December, even though Schmerling had been a respected member of the *Casinopartei*, and strenuously resisted the efforts of those who, like the fallen minister, tried to restore the ties between Austria and Germany.[47]

Their support for the exclusion of Austria and their altered sense of Prussia's role in unification were not solely the effects of the September crisis. In the autumn the political situation in Prussia also underwent a profound change, and the events in Berlin strongly affected their sense of what could be expected from the Hohenzollern monarchy. A brief review of these events is necessary in order to understand the evolution of their views. The crisis in Prussia was the long-term result of the mutual distrust between the Prussian National Assembly on the one hand and Frederick William IV and successive Prussian governments on the other. This distrust arose from irreconcilable notions of the source and nature of legitimate authority and increased markedly in the late summer and early autumn. First, the Berlin assembly passed a resolution calling for a purge of reactionary officers. This was an irritant for two reasons. By tradition, the Prussian army was a royal army, and, so, the deputies seemed to be trespassing on the king's preserves. By passing the resolution, they implicitly claimed governmental as well as purely constitutive authority. The moderate ministry under Ernst von Pfuel, appointed in late September, was unable to silence the increasingly restive assembly through concessions. Open conflict became unavoidable in October, when the deputies voted to omit reference to the supposedly divine origins of the king's power from the new constitution. By so doing they directly challenged Frederick William's cherished sense of the nature of his office.[48]

King Frederick William responded by ordering a sizable increase in the number of troops stationed around Berlin and placed them under the unified command of General von Wrangel. When the king had capitulated to the revolution in the preceding March, he had ordered the army out of Berlin; he had not yet brought it back, but clearly he meant to do so if events required it. At the end of October, he let the Pfuel ministry resign and, on 1 November, announced a new government under Friedrich Wilhelm von Brandenburg, his nephew and a man of notoriously conservative views. The Berlin Assembly protested angrily, but without effect, while the new ministry prepared for action. On 9 November, citing disorders that had broken out in Berlin after two deputies had been too uncritical of the siege of Vienna, Brandenburg read a royal decree that adjourned the Prussian Assembly until the twenty-seventh and ordered it to reconvene at the provincial town of Brandenburg, where, allegedly, the assembly would find the calm needed for orderly proceedings. The deputies were outraged. On 15 November a majority of them contrived to meet privately (and illegally) to vote the withholding of taxes until such time as the Brandenburg ministry was dismissed from office and the recent decree rescinded.[49]

Inevitably, these events alarmed Droysen, Duncker, and Haym and, along with the problem of relations with Austria, dominated their political calculations throughout November. As it happened, Droysen was in Berlin to witness them. He had wanted to do all that he could to explain the "question to Austria" to the Berlin authorities and, if possible, to persuade them to share his views. On his own initiative he traveled to Berlin on 29 October, just after the National Assembly in Frankfort accepted articles 1, 2, and 3. When he learned that Windischgrätz had taken Vienna, he decided to prolong his stay and, so, was there when the crisis occurred.[50] Even so, he could not always be sure just what was happening and what it all meant because detailed and accurate information was nearly as hard to obtain in Berlin as in Frankfort.[51] Certain matters, however, seemed clear despite the prevailing confusion.

Given the pivotal position of Prussia in their political schemes, all major events there had national implications. They could not regard the crisis as just an internal Prussian affair. Furthermore, they were strongly inclined to side with the king and the Brandenburg ministry against the Prussian Assembly. There were several reasons for this predisposition. First, the assemblies in Frankfort and Berlin were jealous of each other and · often mutually antagonistic. Further, there were more democrats among the deputies in Berlin than in Frankfort. In consequence, the Berlin Assembly seemed to be a fomenter of democratic revolution in Prussia. After visiting one of its sessions on 2 November, Droysen described it as "childlike" and in a reference to the most radical phase of the French Revolution, "eager to play the Convention." When a crowd threatened one of his relatives, he was ready to conclude the worst: "The 'people' are extremely eager for murder, hanging, the sight of blood."[52]

Haym, too, accused the Berlin Assembly of a dangerous mixture of revolutionary zeal and infantile irresponsibility. He attributed the deputies' actions to ignorance and remarked characteristically that it was "as if they had never learned history or at least as if they had never learned anything from history." He feared that the tragedy of the French Revolution of 1789 was about to be replayed in Prussia and, presumably, in Germany as a whole.[53] Later, he was even less charitable. He claimed that the deputies had attacked their king and government "like children, others like mischievous youths" and described their motives as "ineptitude and confusion" on the one hand and "ambition and frivolity" on the other.[54] Duncker expressed these views even more forcefully. On 11 November he wrote to his electors at Halle that in Berlin "the rabble and their leaders" were plotting the seizure of power. If allowed to succeed in their design, he maintained, "Frederick William IV will climb the scaffold in about six months, and you will be lost along with the crown if you do not join in this step." After trying to frighten his constituents in this way, he urged them to action by comparing events in Berlin to a "rolling wagon" that had to be halted early in its career or not at all.[55]

This reaction was consistent with their repeated alarms at any seeming prospect of renewed revolution, and no doubt their recent brush with the September riots in Frankfort had heightened their sensitivities. They were, however, nearly as alarmed at the Prussian Assembly's seeming indifference to national questions in general and to the Frankfort Assembly's authority in particular. As recently as 23 October, the Berlin Assembly had angered them by voting a resolution that called into question the National Assembly's handling of Posen's status. They had thought that the final competence of their assembly had been settled once and for all by the passing of the Werner motion in June. As a result, they saw in the Prussian Assembly an alliance of the two forces that they feared and hated most, democracy and particularism.[56] This alliance seemed to compound previous disappointments by putting unification further at risk and evidently called for prompt action.

It was obviously necessary to defend the Prussian monarchy against its presumed attackers from within. For that reason, Duncker had written to his constituents at Halle to undercut any sympathy they might have felt for the deputies in Berlin. Haym was of the same mind.[57] On 12 November he wrote to his parents and explained that struggle in Prussia was not between despotism and constitutionalism but between "the crown and annihilation of the crown."[58] In one of his reports to the electors at Mansfeld he advised that support of the Prussian Assembly against the monarchy would open the way to "the onset of the republic and anarchy."[59] Defense of the monarchy was not by itself sufficient, however, because they also distrusted the monarch's motives, especially after Prussia's uncooperative behavior in the late summer and the conclusion of the Malmö Truce. For example, on 17 September, Haym had written to Hansemann of his fear that an attempt by the king and his ministers to reassert royal authority would provoke a violent and radical revolution.[60] He must have recalled this advice in November and in part blamed the monarchy's troubles on its own narrow-mindedness. Droysen was nearly as frightened of successful counterrevolution as of renewed revolution because he understood that the voice of Prussian particularism was as loud in "the detestable, hysterical nest at Potsdam" as in the Berlin assembly.[61]

Their fear of both revolution and of particularism bore on their reaction to rumors that the Brandenburg ministry might try to circumvent the Prussian National Assembly altogether by simply imposing a constitution by royal fiat. Droysen first heard speculation to that effect on 1 November, during his stay in Berlin.[62] They found this possibility alarming because they thought that the current Prussian government was composed of extreme reactionaries so that the issuance of a constitution could misfire in either of two ways. It might provoke the revolution that they feared or, alternately, it might succeed and lead to a particularist consolidation that would separate Prussia from the rest of Germany.[63] Their dependence on Prussia to carry out unification, however, was too great for them to be even-handed in their condemnation of the warring parties there, and eventually circumstances reconciled them to a royally decreed constitution.

At first, they joined hopefully in efforts to exploit the crisis in such a way as to bind Berlin to Frankfort. In that spirit, they voted against all measures proposed in the National Assembly at Frankfort that would have censured the king and his ministers and, instead, voted in favor of the resolution passed on 20 November that clearly acknowledged the justice of the Prussian government's position but urged upon it the need for moderation in the moment of its victory. That is, the resolution asked that the state of siege in Berlin be lifted and that the Prussian National Assembly be allowed to return from Brandenburg as soon as it was safe for it to do so. They followed this line because they hoped to curry favor with official Prussia while at the same time moderating its reactionary, and so probably particularist, tendencies. For that reason, they worried that the measure passed on 20 November might not be supportive enough to win Prussia's gratitude.[64]

Their belief in the imminent danger of revolution in Berlin suggested an extension of this tactic. Because they thought the threat to the Prussian throne was real, they hoped that Frankfort might be able to defend the king and his government in exchange for a relaxation of Prussia's hitherto uncompromising attitude towards the National Assembly and the provisional government. For that reason they warmly supported the dispatch to Berlin of a negotiating team led by Daniel Friedrich Bassermann, special National Commissars (*Reichskommissaren*) Eduard Simson and August Hergenhahn, and—unofficially but in fact on behalf of the whole assembly—Heinrich von Gagern.[65] At least in the beginning, Droysen seemed optimistic about the prospects for this approach. In a letter to Beseler on 2 November he remarked: "It is entirely certain to me that soon Frankfort will be . . . the only salvation for Prussia."[66] A day later he reported happily on the Prince of Prussia's supposed eagerness to win support in Frankfort.[67] It is at least possible that he hoped the crisis would continue long enough to extract maximum concessions from Prussia.[68]

This hopefulness actually masked an underlying desperation. On his return from Berlin on 8 November, Droysen urged that a delegation be sent as soon as possible, but when it actually departed on the twenty-third, he termed it the "last card" held by the National Assembly. His diary entries for the following days betray his hope for good news and his fear of further disappointments: he thought the situation might still be saved, but his painful memories of recent months told him that it was hardly a foregone conclusion that Prussia would take the opportunity that history offered her.[69] While he awaited reports from Berlin, he put all his energies into rapid completion of the constitution so that appropriate institutions would already exist if Frederick William, saved from revolution, at last agreed to be hereditary monarch of a unified Germany.[70]

These considerations help to explain the relief they felt when they learned about the Kremsier Program on 2 December. Austria's voluntary withdrawal from Germany seemed a favorable development inasmuch as it created a situation in which hereditary constitutional monarchy seemed the only practicable form of government and, equally good, one in which Prussia could assume national leadership without a contest with Austria and, given Germany's need for strength, largely on her own terms.[71] Probably for the same reason, Droysen was not bothered when he learned on 7 December that the Prussian king had decreed a new, and fairly liberal, constitution two days before.[72] The danger of Prussia consolidating itself apart from Germany seemed less now that Prussia could remain Prussia in a unified Germany ruled by a Hohenzollern monarch. Of course, in terms of their expectations in the spring and early summer, that would have been a very inferior sort of unification, but their historical outlook again counselled resigned acceptance of the inevitable. With Austria out of Germany, the possibility of merging Prussia completely into Germany was too slight to be an issue. At least the new constitution, despite their previous fears, was liberal enough to forestall revolution and showed that Prussia had not simply slid into reaction.[73] In an essay drafted on Christmas Day 1848, Droysen noted happily that the constitution had the added benefit of showing that Prussia was forward-looking, whereas recent events in Olmütz showed that Austria still wanted a return to the past.[74]

This is not to say that the events in Vienna and Berlin at the end of November and the beginning of December led them to return to their earlier optimism. They were merely relieved that not everything was lost and that a chance apparently still existed for national unification of some kind. Even to maintain that qualified hope they had to accept the loss of Austrian territories and the admission of Prussia on terms that would have appalled them a few months earlier. A less noticeable but equally important change in their outlook was their loss of confident certainty. They became increasingly interested in power as such and increasingly impressed with the role of moral will, of daringly pursuing one's goals when opportunity beckoned. Both developments fed on a growing belief in historical contingency. Once they had firm expectations; now they had only hopes. Because outcomes now seemed less certain, they wanted either to compel the changes they desired or at least to suppose that the degree of their desire made their success more likely. All three historians underwent these changes, and, with them as a basis, Droysen also began to revise his interpretation of Prussian and German history.

Droysen underwent this transformation somewhat earlier than Duncker and Haym, although he was slow to abandon his strongly providential view of history and, consequently, usually thought in terms of a narrowing of choices and of the difficulty of discovering what historical opportunities actually existed. The first evidence of change appears in a letter written to Wilhelm Arendt on 27 November 1848. His familiar views at first seem to be precariously intact, but subsequent statements show that he had already begun to alter them. When he was writing, the situation in Prussia was still unclear, and he was torn between fear of renewed revolution there and hope that the assembly in Frankfurt might yet be able to make a mutually advantageous deal with the Prussian monarchy. After describing the unruly mobs he had seen in Berlin a few weeks earlier, he exclaimed: "What times we live through! It is actually miraculous, if only one had no heart. In any case, history is at work (*Jedenfalls die Geschichte arbeitet*)." He acknowledged his anxiety in the present crisis, but expressed a continued belief, despite continual appearances to the contrary, that history was purposive and presumably beneficent. Thereafter his remarks betrayed a deeper uncertainty. He expressed continued trust in the Hohenzollern, but qualified this trust by saying "at least they are not ill-willed." Similarly, it was hardly a ringing statement of historical optimism to declare: "Prussia must advance if the least is to come out of this German mess (*deutsche Schweinerei*)." He claimed never to have been of "better courage," but concluded his remarks in the subjunctive: "Let it only happen (*Geschähe es nur*)."[75] He had conceded that the long-expected unification was by no means inevitable and now depended on the energy and willingness of the Hohenzollern.

This conclusion probably followed from his judgment that the assembly, after the events of the preceding ten weeks, lacked independent power. On 7 December he commented in his diary that the assembly was now "weak" because it had resisted anarchy at "Malmö, Vienna, and Berlin"; three days later he declared that it had only one option left, to declare for hereditary Hohenzollern rule over Germany and hope that Prussia would do what was asked.[76] The same argument appeared in a more elaborate and developed form in an essay drafted in incomplete form on Christmas Day 1848. The piece dealt with the main question then facing the deputies, namely, how to organize the permanent national executive, though it was really an opportunity for Droysen to organize his thoughts in a time of uncertainty. He censured the National Assembly of which he was a member for self-deception: it had failed to see that it was all-powerful "only to the extent" that it worked for "the possible, the necessary, the wholesome." In history as in physics, that is, "the law is not that which moves but rather the understanding of the movement."[77]

These comments, of course, were consistent with his long-held view that it was necessary to work with, not against, historical development, and in offering them he may have had a specific objective in mind. He faulted the deputies, himself among them, for having focused too narrowly on "the distinction between monarchy and republic," when, in fact, "particularism" was really the "common enemy."[78] This was a good ploy for attracting needed support from the left, and the same argument attracted nearly half the votes of the moderate leftist Westendhall Party into pro-Prussian ranks in the vote of 13 January.[79] He had more than tactical considerations in mind, however, and he meant to point out a fundamental error in his earlier thinking. The real mistake that he and others had made earlier in the year was to suppose that the "idea of national unity" was "so great, so convincing, so simple" that its victory was assured.[80] He now saw the future as far more uncertain and valued actual power far more highly.

In the essay, therefore, he argued to the conclusion that he had indicated earlier in his diary. The assembly had to concentrate on the only task that it might complete, namely, persuading the Hohenzollern to rule Germany: "Whatever the parliament has done of good and evil, it is certain that it has only One Decision left to make. And it will effect something great if it makes it with wisdom; if not, then it is quite irrelevant what it decides in this or any other question. History would desert the place where it was misunderstood."[81] In its weakness, the assembly no longer had a real choice, and, Droysen's seeming assurance that "wisdom" would bring success notwithstanding, even taking the right action offered no guarantee of a favorable result. History, that is, did not bring about outcomes; it only offered opportunities that fools and cowards might fail to seize. This is clear from his explanation of the way in which German history now had to be understood.

Much of his account parallels closely his argument in *Lectures on the Wars of Freedom* and other prerevolutionary writings, but some familiar themes and arguments are absent and some new ones have taken their place. Possibly as a means to save space, but more probably because of a change in focus, the world-historical character of his earlier discussions is lacking. He was now interested only in Germany and Prussia's mission there. In a clear reference to recent events, he contended that "particularism" had set the "basic tone" of German history until German unity became a mere "empty shell." This deplorable situation endured until the eighteenth century, when "spiritual developments" (*geistige Entwicklungen*) called forth a "German spirit" (*deutsche Geist*) for which the battle of Rossbach provided "the first day of its satisfaction." This preliminary success in the tug of war between particularism and the desire for unification was nearly undone in the "terrible times" of the late eighteenth and early nineteenth centuries, times that ended only in the "rising of Prussia and North Germany" which, in turn, left Germany caught in a "deep contradiction" because Prussia had engaged herself in the national interest but was also trapped in a set of obligations to Austria. This contradiction, he alleged, lasted until after 1830 with the result that all Germany suffered.[82] At first glance, this interpretation looks like the one Droysen offered before the revolution, but there is an important difference. He emphasized the war against Napoleon, but not the Prussian reforms and the refreshing foretaste of real freedom and he no longer portrayed the struggle as one between "powers" and "states."

There were other changes as well. Before March 1848, Droysen did not concern himself very much with Prussia's establishment, in the German north, of a Customs Union (*Zollverein*), but now this point seemed centrally important to him. It was a symptom of Prussia's dedication to German unity, just as Prussia's inability to extend it beyond North Germany showed that "unification even in material interests was not possible on the basis of the sovereignty principle of 1815, [and] people began to feel all the more painfully the necessity of new forms (*Nothwendigkeit neuer Formen*)." Two points need to be made here. First, Droysen was more interested than previously in outward manifestations of power, whether in the form of a successful war against the French Army or, in more pacific terms, the creation and thwarted extension of a customs union. Second, he now described in changed terms history as a process of "spirit" (*Geist*). It was no longer a matter of people's ideas logically moving toward the solution of a problem posed many centuries before but of their seeing more clearly the inadequacies and inequities in their actual circumstances.[83] No doubt his own recent disappointments helped lead him to this second insight. Just as his own painful experience of powerlessness showed him the importance of power, so it now helped him see how the inconveniences faced by others (say, in the conduct of commerce across a nation divided in tariffs, currencies, and weights and measures) might lead them to see the advantages of unification. This discovery must have been something of a consolation to him inasmuch as it was just one more instance of finding some hidden good in seeming bad.

These considerations led him to a further conclusion, odd though it seems in view of some of the harsh comments that he made about Prussian policies in the 1840s and in view of the degree to which Prussian actions had brought the assembly in Frankfort to its present impasse. He now discerned an increasingly national "direction" in Prussian policy after Frederick William IV's ascent in 1840 and claimed that the real possibility of "inner reconstruction" that it offered had been frustrated only by the stubborn particularism of the South German states, most notably Bavaria. It was, he now believed, their blocking of internal reform that had made the March revolution necessary.[84] Of course, he had never been fond of small states and had always distrusted the Catholic South, but this was new. He was well on the way to making Prussia not only the ultimate, but also the long-term and consistent champion of a unification that she would appear to be in his subsequent histories. In a way, these arguments were self-serving in the present conditions. They gave him a villain to blame for what had gone wrong, let him exonerate (and flatter) a Prussia whose services were still needed, and left intact at least his basic thesis that unification was necessary and that Prussia acted in its behalf. But they were more than convenient rationalizations. In Droysen's approach, one's understanding of the present informed one's study of the past just as knowledge of the past instructed actions in the present. The change in present circumstances, therefore, called for a reinterpretation of the past.

They also required some change in how he went about interpreting it. The first unmistakable evidence of this change appeared on 2 December in a letter to his close friend Justus Olshausen. "I have always sensed," Droysen reported, "how infinitely great the difference is between the merely well-meaning and the statesman-like." It was during the September crisis, he claimed, that he had learned "with horror" that

it is clearly easier and more comfortable to represent a principle and its consequences than to realize it; that in politics, *the science of the possible,* the best is ruinous and only the good, indeed the miserable has its value. It is certain, however, that we are going through a school here than which one more educational cannot be conceived; except that learning requires a strength, a self-denial, and an honesty that not everyone possesses. The most difficult task of all is to maintain a vision of the whole (*Blick für das Ganze*). The self-conquest that the armistice question cost me was only my first exercise in school! Happy are they who think that *fortiter velle* leads to the goal in political affairs [my emphasis].[85]

The letter managed to be both self-pitying and self-congratulatory at the same time. Droysen was more aware than he had been of the fallibility of human judgment in discerning historical tendencies and devising political strategies. That is, he was markedly more pessimistic about the possibility of drawing the correct conclusions from history. He did not doubt that history had a purpose; otherwise, he would not have complained that it was "difficult . . . to maintain a vision of the whole." He did acknowledge, however, that only those sternly disciplined enough not to misconstrue evidence as a result of fervent hope could practice politics as the "science of the possible."

He recurred to this argument in an essay, when he reflected that it had been German consciousness of the need for unification that had allowed the February revolution in France to spark the March risings in Germany that, in turn, led to convening the National Assembly to "give firm forms" to the "magical word of German unity." That consciousness, however, could not accomplish the "most difficult task of the political man," which Droysen defined as "recognizing the quietly forward-flowing movement that can alone endure in the midst of so great an upheaval whose nature it is to stir up all the passions and to release all possible demands, to confuse all ideas into a wild mixture of possibilities and impossibilities."[86] Droysen still insisted that there was a right course to follow, but it was just when one most needed to discover that course (in the middle of a revolution, for example) that it was most difficult to find and follow it. The obvious corrective was a patient study of the situation that would allow one to distinguish between what was possible and what was not. That entailed a careful consideration of contingency and a readiness, not shown by Droysen earlier in his career, to accommodate oneself to unpleasant consequences before they occurred.

If viewed from that perspective, his renewed and more energetic insistence on the centrality of particularism in German history was a hypothetical explanation of defeats yet to be suffered as well as those already encountered. Similarly, his insistence that Prussian politics had served the national interest throughout the 1840s was a means to showing that Prussia might yet do as she ought. Droysen searched carefully for any indication that the Hohenzollern monarchy would or could play the role he once was certain history had assigned to it. In conducting that search, he was chastened enough to attach the greatest importance to sheer power and to consider seriously that Prussia might not, after all, take the opportunity offered her.

Even so, he inclined to a cautious optimism. In a letter to August Kopisch on 3 January, he presented his central thesis, already implicitly present in his essay on the national executive: "A history like Prussia's cannot have been a mistake. Through the Great Elector, through the great Frederick, through the sly king of the Wars of Liberation [Frederick William III] Prussia has grown to the point of saving the interests of Germany from Austria which abused Germany for the sake of her foreign crown." The grand tendency of Prussian history, that is, had been to employ Prussian strength for the nation as a whole. This would be the organizing thesis of his sixteen-volume *History of Prussian Politics* (1855–86), the formative work of the Prussian School. For the present, however, Droysen wanted some assurance that victory was still possible, and he employed his thesis to show that it was in accord with earlier Prussian history that Frederick William IV had given all his lands to Germany, wishing to cease to be a European power (*Macht*) in order to become a German one." The terminology is interesting, because in earlier writings that shift was to create a "state" (*Staat*) in place of a mere "power." He also thought it a logical continuation of earlier Prussian history for Prussia to curb any further Austrian interference and to undertake command of a unified Germany.[87]

At the same time, he now found it entirely conceivable that Prussia would fail to fulfil her "German mission" (*deutscher Beruf*) and decide instead to "proceed in cooperation with Austria." If that happened, she would not merely revert to the "unhappy condition . . . in which she was the least of the great powers." On the contrary, she would "sink infinitely below" her prerevolutionary status because she would have "surrendered her mission" and become just a German state among German states like Saxony. Droysen therefore hoped, if only for reasons of her own self-interest, that Prussia would shun the latter course and energetically pursue the former by acting deliberately as "the German power." In so arguing, Droysen's improved sense of contingency led him to a heightened awareness of voluntarism in history, and he now wrote in terms of Prussia's need to "decide," "recognize," "acknowledge," "step forward," and "will."[88] This word choice made sense because Prussia's mission was now indicated, not required, by history.

In consequence, the main task remaining to the National Assembly was to persuade Prussia to continue to act in Germany's behalf. This persuasion was to take the form not of appeals to her better nature but to her needs and interests as a power. On 16 December, for example, in a letter to Arendt he reviewed the situation created by the Kremsier Program and the new Prussian constitution and claimed that a unified Germany and an independent Austria were historical complements. Austria would keep France out of northern Italy and prevent racial war in southeastern Europe while the Prusso-German state provided the needed barrier against Russia in the east and France in the west. He saw the need, therefore, to place "Prussia in such a position that she devotes herself wholly and gladly to this task." He once insisted on the need for Prussia's dissolution into a unified Germany; now he offered control over Germany as an inducement to cooperation: "I work ... for the hereditary hegemony of Prussia (*erbliche Hegemonie Preußens*)." Prussia had to know that Germany was hers for the taking so that she would link her "proud defensive system" to that of Germany as a whole.[89] This was not a stray thought, and he reiterated the case in a strongly worded letter to Olshausen on 7 January.[90]

As Droysen's analysis suggests, the possession or attainment of power, military power, now seemed the true measure of political success. He had always rated it highly, and the same experience of the assembly's inability to control events that informed his increased awareness of historical contingency also made him see more clearly the advantages of being able to dictate outcomes. His statements, however, show that he now treated power as an end in itself as well as means to higher ends. As early as 3 December he wrote to Kopisch that his primary "goal" was to increase the "*power* of Germany" and further declared: "Power is salvation (*Die Macht ist Rettung*)."[91] He was equally explicit in his Christmas essay on the formation of the national executive: "The practical English understand better than we the old Greek saying: 'Gold is the man.' And by the same token: 'Power is the state' seems to be more regretted than comprehended by us. All our constitutional forms and basic rights are nothing if we do not know how to raise our nation (*Reich*) to a power (*Macht*). Indeed, it is so much a matter of power and only of power that even freedom is worthless in its absence."[92] Here, again, he now used "power" as a term of praise rather than opprobrium. His basic argument was that Germans were too good to understand that they had to be strong, though Droysen surely hoped that they would soon learn this important lesson. Of course, he did not actually say that power was more important than freedom, merely that freedom was "worthless" without it. Certainly he did not mean that Germany had to be strong rather than free, and in his 2 December letter to Olshausen he took pains not be misunderstood on that point by explaining that he wanted "to strengthen and maintain the external framework of Germany *on the way to constitution and reform* [my emphasis]." He assured Olshausen that "freedom will not elude us as soon as we attain a tolerable position on the route to unification."[93] Nevertheless, his statement shows a major shift in priority. He had formerly thought that freedom was the precondition for power; now he thought exactly the opposite to be the case.

During December, Duncker's thinking underwent parallel changes that appear in the "Report of the Commission of the Casino Society on the

Central Executive." This report, issued just before Christmas 1848, was supposedly the work of a four-man committee, but it was really Duncker's doing. He called for the committee, dominated its sessions, and did the actual writing.[94] The document's purpose was to give the *Casinopartei* much needed guidance in deciding on the shape of the nation's executive. This topic seemed especially urgent once it was clear that Austria had withdrawn and, in any case, the relevant articles of the draft constitution would soon be discussed by the assembly.[95] In presenting his views on this question, Duncker also revealed the changed contours of his historical and political thinking, and for this reason his reflections deserve close study.

He made the command of effective force the supreme criterion for judging executive arrangements by assessing each possibility in terms of the strength that it would offer or deny to Germany. Thus, he rejected either the "renewal or reformation" of the old German Confederation not on the grounds that history had bypassed it or that it was illegitimate but because, if its delegates had first to confer with their governments, "any quick and strong (*rasch und kräftig*) administration would be impossible." By the same token, he opposed any scheme in which the old delegations would be replaced by a senate elected by the states. The result, he alleged, would be a sort of "republic" that would contradict the constitutional arrangements in the states and, so, disorganize and weaken the nation as a whole. German strength depended on a "strictly introduced conformity . . . between the parts and the whole." He also objected to the *Turnus* idea in which the executive position would rotate among monarchs. Habsburg and Hohenzollern rulers would work to thwart each other, he warned, and dynasts from the lesser states would command insufficient respect. In all cases, national strength would suffer. Unsurprisingly, given his record in June during discussions of the provisional executive, he was faintly more sympathetic to the idea of a *Trias* and conceded that joint executive tenure by a Habsburg, Hohenzollern, and Wittelsbach would have something to offer by way of "permanence and stability," and he was pleased that it did not threaten the monarchic principle, but he nonetheless noted that the proposal had two irremediable flaws.[96]

First, Duncker plausibly claimed that three men would have difficulty reaching prompt decisions. Further, and more serious, a *Trias* would not command sufficient respect in Germany. In a statement that shows the bitterness that he felt about the events of the preceding several months, he commented:

The provisional condition in which we now find ourselves has sufficiently shown how weak a central government is, especially in its dealings with the larger states, especially when it does not have decisive power (*entscheidende Macht*) directly at its disposal which, even through its moral weight, through the fear that a word can provoke, prevents any thought of resistance from arising. If, however, the central power was impotent at a time when the upsurge of the whole nation, when the vitally and strongly driving idea of unification stood by helpfully and supportively, how will it be when, in the necessary course of history (*notwendiger Gang der Geschichte*) decline, retreat, and the backlash of particularism follow rising, progress, and the drive to unity? Both moments, the drive towards unification and the familiarity with separate existence, the sense for the whole and the traditions of the history of the tribe (*Stamm*) interpenetrate and oppose one another in the past and present of Germany and in the breast of every individual.[97]

The measure of suitability, then, was strength, especially the strength to compel respect and obedience within Germany. Duncker thought this strength to be necessary because he now was far more aware of the continued hold of particularism and now thought that historical necessity was on the side of division as well as of unification. In other words, his insistence on the need for power was a result of his altered historical diagnosis of Germany's situation.

Predictably, Duncker also opposed the scheme for an elective constitutional monarchy. His opposition resulted from two considerations. First, he plausibly argued that German history showed it to have one major disadvantage: "Elective monarchy tore apart our unity and our people (*unsere Einheit, unser Volk ausgerissen*)." It had, in fact, been the "basic source of everything wrong with the nation," and he believed that there was no reason to expect happier results from a second attempt. Now, as under the Holy Roman Empire, candidates for the office would be forced to make damaging concessions in order to be elected so that national strength would erode with each succession. Second, he believed that elective monarchy would tempt rulers to exploit their position for selfish interests because, in an elective monarchy, "the dignity is only temporarily conveyed to a prince." He might, therefore, regard his office as an "affair of honor," but it was unlikely to "claim his interest and strength to the full extent." Here, too, "previous German history provides sufficient warning examples." Rather than endanger his hereditary holdings at the cost of his posterity, the ruler would tend to exploit the rest of the nation in his dynastic interest. Quite simply, an elective monarch would not have enough of a stake in the long-term welfare of Germany as a whole.[98]

The conclusion was obvious. Only a hereditary monarch could assure "the necessary firmness and steadiness in the constitution and the government," could preside over "the organic growth of the new formation of affairs in Germany," and could provide the "indispensable external power and position of Germany." These were what Duncker really wanted for Germany, but to attain them it was not enough that the office be hereditary. Its incumbent had also to possess an independent power based on his state of origin. For that reason, the monarch would have to be either a Habsburg or a Hohenzollern. Duncker preferred the latter in any case, and in explaining this he sought to show, in case anyone had misunderstood the significance of the Kremsier Program, that Austrian and German interests diverged and that the Habsburgs were basically unsuited to rule Germany. Multinationality, he contended, was the essential historical principle of Austria. That meant that investing a Habsburg with German monarchy would be bad for Germany because its king would have at heart interests irrelevant and at times opposed to those of Germany proper. It might also be bad for Austria and Europe; if the German parliament forced the king to act strictly in the German interest, Eastern Europe might be thrown into chaos. He was therefore strongly opposed to a simple merger between the German states and the whole Austrian Empire, and he was scarcely more sympathetic to the idea of admitting only the German provinces of Austria into a German federation (*Bundesstaat*) while Germany and Austria combined as the two units of a confederation (*Staatenbund*).

It was, he maintained, historically necessary for Austria to exist independent of, though closely aligned with, a unified Germany: "Austrian politics have consistently worked toward that conclusion since 1815, not to go back any farther: she has retreated from Germany step by step in order to round out and consolidate the Austrian monarchy as a whole." In recent years, he argued, Austria had ignored German politics except when she intervened to repress "political innovations" and had, in effect, "abandoned the rest of Germany to Prussian hegemony under the name of the *Zollverein*." Viewed in that light, the Kremsier Program was the "keystone" of a long-standing and powerful historical development that had to be accepted and respected.[99]

Under those circumstances, Duncker reasoned, Germany really had no choice: she had to choose a Hohenzollern as hereditary constitutional monarch. He acknowledged the danger of Prussian hegemony, but he believed, or professed to believe, that this danger could be averted by timely action. "If we for our part grasp this situation quickly and in a statesmanlike manner," he argued, "it will be possible to abolish every contradiction between dynastic power and the power of the nation in the executive to be created for this federal state." As long as the deputies were swift and decisive in offering the crown to the Hohenzollern, the result would be not "the feared hegemony of Prussia, but, on the contrary, Germany's conquest of Prussia" and her "immediate and unconditional control of the great powers of this state." In order to support this claim, Duncker pointed out that the Hohenzollern, if given power over Germany as a whole, would be unable to distinguish Prussian from German interests. The dynasty would therefore think and act in national terms, though he admitted that the South German Catholic states would have to be protected with specific guarantees and reminded that Austria would be able to intervene diplomatically on their behalf.[100]

Duncker was not being altogether candid. He clearly wanted a German constitutional monarchy with the Hohenzollern as hereditary rulers, and he undoubtedly wanted Prussia's power for the unified state, but some of his other recommendations did not reflect his real thinking. He insisted on the need for speed, but in a letter to his wife written on or about 20 December, only a few days before publication of his report, he criticized Heinrich von Gagern for seeking a "rapid decision." It was first necessary, he argued, that "the people get used to the idea of excluding Austria which is too new and huge for them." He no doubt hoped that his report with its temperate explanation of why Germany and Austria had to move in different directions would help to accustom them to this novel prospect. Furthermore, his private statements about Austria show that his personal estimation of her was less generous than that which appeared in the report. For example, he also told his wife that Germany faced a stark alternative: "With Austria, no unity; without Austria, the remainder will form a strong state."[101] He was even harsher in another letter, written on New Year's Day, 1849.[102] National unity and strength were what really interested him, and he probably dismissed in the report the danger of Prussian hegemony more as a means to reassure worried readers than out of genuine conviction, for he was prepared to accept unification on any available terms. At least, in a nearly contemporaneous letter to his wife he was unabashed in describing a unified Germany as a "Prussian empire."[103]

Such an attitude was consistent with his general appraisal of the situation. On the one hand, he believed that the program that he recommended in his report was the correct one.[104] On the other, he no longer took its fulfillment as inevitable. Unification had become for him a moral, rather than a historical, necessity, something hopefully to attempt rather than something confidently to await. He thought that his cause had finally reached its time of crisis, and wrote to his wife: "The ship is really cracking at all her joints and the billows are rising high." He therefore counselled her, also in inflated language, to "raise high the banner of hope" and claimed that his side would conquer because it "had to conquer."[105] That is, it should conquer because it was right and because good people wanted it to succeed. The future now seemed more contingent than it had, and his remarks seem desperate and determined rather than confident and optimistic.

Haym's analysis of the situation, despite some distinctive emphases, was close to Duncker's. He agreed fully with Duncker's report, and began to express his own views openly and forcefully in January 1849.[106] He heavily emphasized the primacy of power. On 4 January, for example, he addressed the assembly for the first and last time to speak against a motion to censure the Prussian government for both its actions against the Prussian National Assembly in November and its proclamation of a constitution in December. In November he had conceded the formal illegality of Prussian actions but had defended them as justifiable measures of self-defense in the face of imminent revolution. He now broadened this argument into an apology for power. He contended that questions of legality were irrelevant in the present instance because Prussia had acted out of political necessity. The assembly had to do the same.[107] He urged his listeners to view matters "in a *practical* sense" and to employ "a viewpoint turned not *backwards* but *forwards*." This led him to stress two points. First, elections were due in Prussia, and Haym advised the assembly to act in such a way that Prussian voters would trust their government and thus lend it the strength needed for its role in national unification. Second, he pointed out that the matter under discussion was "less a question of *freedom* than a question of *power*."[108]

He, too, now gave power primacy over freedom. Haym saw the matter as a "question of power" in several senses. On the simplest level, the assembly's power was "only moral" so that the assembly would be defeated in a contest with Berlin. He also thought that the assembly could increase its meager strength by winning the "applause of one of the greatest peoples of the Fatherland (*eines der größten Stämme des Vaterlandes*)."[109] That is, it should try to win Prussia to its side by placating the Prussian government. He thought that power was at issue in yet a third sense: "It is not merely a matter of the power of this assembly, for the service of power (*Dienst der Macht*) is mutual." By this he meant that the assembly should use this chance "to strengthen the *power of the Prussian state (Macht des preußischen Staates)*" in the expectation that Prussia would make a decent return on the favor.[110] It was in Germany's interest to increase the power it would soon need when the national constitution was ready to implement. In that attitude, he had argued two days earlier in a letter to Hansemann that Germany needed a "Prussian imperial crown" and would point out in a report to the electors at Mansfeld on 22 January, the German "people" (*Volk*) deserved to belong to "a state that was unitary in itself, externally strong, and, to say it all, a state among the states of Europe." He therefore advised the deputies to cease debating the motion of censure and to return to the business of the day.[111]

His pronounced admiration for physical power and his admonition that the assembly's power was "only moral," however, did not mean that he had entirely abandoned his prerevolutionary belief in the necessity and efficacy of moral power. Haym now expressed this belief with the term "revolutionary idealism," a concept that he first invoked in a letter to Hansemann on 2 January and then elaborated in subsequent letters. He wrote to defend himself and like-minded deputies against Hansemann's irritating charge that they were impractical and more interested in ideas than in reality. Haym conceded that there was some justice in Hansemann's reproaches: Some of his colleagues were indeed "ideological" and, so, might create a "fiasco" while trying to pursue their "bold politics." He also wanted Hansemann to understand that the other party in Germany was not composed of "practical men" like himself but of men who countered the "perhaps very ideologically conceived program" of the right center in Frankfurt with ideas "still more chimerical, still more insane." Haym had in mind both those who wanted a return to prerevolutionary conditions and those who desired a German republic. In his view, the majority of deputies who wished the exclusion of Austria and unification under the Hohenzollern were realistic by contrast because their "revolutionary idealism" was essentially "historical."[112]

This defense of his own program and approach seems almost to damn both through faint praise, because Haym did not claim to be practical, only to be less impractical than those he opposed. In his next letter to Hansemann, he was rather more forceful, but he lacked confidence and the tone remained apologetic. He wrote to report on the effects of the Austrian note of 4 February, which, despite the latitude for national unification seemingly granted in the Kremsier Program, strongly protested the mooted creation of a unified Germany under the Hohenzollern. Haym claimed that the note had awakened and enlivened the assembly rather than demoralizing it as, he believed, the Austrians had intended. He attributed this to the assembly's "idealism," and he defined this "idealism" as "the higher ascending politics of the National Assembly, the revolution, in other words, the ideal opinion (*ideelle Meinung*) deposited in the Church of St. Paul's [where the assembly met] after the flood waters of riot had run their course."[113] The ideas that he put to use in this argument drew on those in his statements before the revolution and during its earlier course. He drew on his prerevolutionary theory of "real identities," according to which will preceded act and ideas preceded will, and on his springtime view that although "riot" and revolution had to be suppressed, the fact of the March revolution established its historical legitimacy and thus legitimated the National Assembly and its efforts.

He changed the terms of the argument, however, when he gave Hansemann a closer look at the nature and importance of the assembly's "idealism":

This idealism—which, by the way, is not an abstract but a historical idealism—may in many ways appear abandoned and impractical to a practical man, and we received his teachings with scrupulous attentiveness. Because the power of our faith and courage are about to be tested and, we do not doubt, to carry the day, I feel forced to . . . explain again to you that this idealism, present the whole time in our dispositions, is a 'reality' just as powerful and just as deserving of attention . . . as the particularist strivings of the dynasties and the threatening aspect of foreign lands. Our ideal politics is to your practical political artfulness as Alexander was to Diogenes. We would choose to be Diogenes—if we were not Alexander![114]

Haym's allusion to Plutarch's account of Alexander the Great's encounter with Diogenes of Sinope is a little precious and may have been lost on Hansemann, but it is helpful in understanding what Haym meant. Unlike other philosophers, Diogenes did not seek out Alexander, so Alexander went to him. He found him lying in the sun and asked if he wanted anything. Diogenes told him to stand so as to shade him from the sun, and, on leaving, Alexander remarked that, if he were not Alexander, he would like to be Diogenes. Haym used the story to illustrate his chief contention. With it, he compared "practical" men such as Hansemann to philosophers such as Diogenes and idealists such as himself to Alexander.

In Plutarch's account, after all, both protagonists are admirable, Diogenes for his detachment and Alexander for his prowess. Haym was ready to compliment Hansemann for his clear-sighted appreciation of political reality but enjoyed the irony of pointing out that he and others like him had real power because they and their ideals were facts, just as Alexander's victories over the Greeks had been. They were, however, only facts among facts. Like Duncker, Haym was now aware of historical contingency. His idealism was a "reality" to take account of—just as he knew Hansemann took account of "the particularist strivings of the dynasties." In other words, he was again defending his position by showing that it was at least as good as that occupied by his opponents, though he now defined its goodness in terms of moral force. Moreover, and again like Duncker, he was predicting victory less in terms of historical inevitability, although he did note the " historical" rather than "abstract" character of his "idealism," than of "faith and courage."[115] He rated power as supreme, but ranked moral will as a special kind of power. Possibly for rhetorical reasons, the letter of 11 February exuded a declared confidence that his side would win against all odds, but his letters to Hansemann over the next three weeks contained admissions that things might go wrong, that, for example, the Hohenzollern might refuse the crown when it was offered to them.[116]

Haym carried these ideas to their logical conclusion in another letter to Hansemann on 6 March. Hansemann had suggested that the *Trias* plan be revived, and Haym heatedly replied that the "form" of the unified German state was "no longer in question." The real question was "whether something new was to be created at all." Haym readily acknowledged that Germany might simply return to its unhappy prerevolutionary condition, but he insisted that, if unification did occur, it would take the form of a "hereditary imperium" (*Erbkaiserthum*) of the Hohenzollern. He thought that historical tendencies inclined in that direction, but understood that the result was by no means a foregone conclusion. Success really depended on the moral strength of the dynasty in question and its people. Victory was still possible if "even a spark of the spirit of the conqueror of Silesia [Frederick the Great] remained among his successors." Failing that, he suggested that "the mind of the great Frederick, if not present on the throne, must surely be alive in his people." "If," he argued, "the government does not push forward along the track upon which the destiny of the Prussian state should fulfil itself in accordance with its historical determination, then the chambers should drive the government onwards." He still thought that history had a logic, but it was logic easily defied or ignored. Given the recent record of the Prussian government, chambers, and people, he cannot have been too hopeful. His persistence in the face of continual, discouraging reports is to be explained by an important admission that he made to Hansemann: "One does not surrender at a low price an idea followed for months, even if the conviction of its correctness and inner necessity did not permeate all of us."[117] His shift from historical determinism to a moral voluntarism aligned with history was complete.

These revisions and modifications brought their ideas into line with those that Sybel had published the preceding spring in his pamphlet "On the National Constitution of the Seventeen Trustees." There he had argued against hereditary constitutional monarchy for Germany on the grounds that most Germans were too deeply particularist to follow a dynasty other than their own. Events since midsummer seemed to have confirmed his analysis. In his pamphlet, Sybel had also argued for an "aristocratic college" as national executive unless, as had now happened, Austria withdrew from Germany and consolidated itself as a separate state. In that case, Germany would have to "place at its head the man who will show the greatest power and will in the German cause," namely, the king of Prussia. That prospect had depressed Sybel, not out of a disregard for Prussia or the Hohenzollern, but because then it would be a matter of saving "whatever can be saved," of substituting a "field commander" for a "constitution." Sybel also admitted, however, that such a development would have some compensating features, if only because the national monarch and the unity he provided would be greeted as a "firm anchor of salvation . . . in the midst of such misfortune."[118]

Now, in late 1848 and early 1849, events had met his conditions for favoring hereditary Hohenzollern over Germany. What he had urged as a hypothesis then, was observable reality now, and Droysen, Duncker, and Haym were recommending the Hohenzollern for reasons about which he had speculated in the spring. The record of Sybel's actions and ideas in the summer and autumn of 1848 is too incomplete to reconstruct how his views evolved during this period. He was at a distance from the center of action as a deputy to the provincial assembly at Cassell, and the surviving fragments of his correspondence are few and uninformative. By January he strongly supported unification with the Hohenzollern as hereditary constitutional monarchs, possibly as the best solution possible in the circumstances or, possibly, as a result of changed perspective, as something good in itself. If Eduard Zeller, a friend who boarded at the Sybel house in Marburg for most of 1849 is to be believed, Sybel was now an enthusiastic and consistent advocate of Hohenzollern rule, even at the price of Austria's exclusion.[119] It is at least clear that he was well enough apprised of who did what at Frankfort to know to write, on 10 January, to Droysen, as member of and record-keeper for the assembly's Constitution Committee (*Verfassungsausschuß*) to request documents that he thought might be useful in drafting a constitution for Hesse. He seems never to have been in contact with Droysen before, but he evidently knew that they agreed on basic matters: while soliciting further information on Droysen's views, he congratulated him on being "thoroughly Prussian and imperial in the present crisis." Sybel emphasized his own strong support for hereditary rule by the Hohenzollern in Germany.[120] It was the beginning of their political association. Droysen at once sent back a warmly appreciative reply and soon wrote Sybel again to urge him to agitate in Cassell for the Hohenzollern candidacy.[121] They continued their association into later years. In a number of respects, it was a natural alliance, and not only because circumstances now forced Sybel, even if he was not otherwise inclined, to support the Hohenzollern candidacy. Circumstances had also forced Droysen—and Duncker and Haym—to take a view of history and its implications for present politics that came more easily to Sybel. Before the revolution and during its first months, after all, they had held fast to a belief that history was ineluctably progressive and interpretable in a way that allowed fairly certain prediction. The idea that it might nearly defy interpretation and had therefore to be thought of as filled with dangerous contingencies, such that one had to try to strike the best bargain possible, was at first alien to them. It took successive defeats and disappointments to make it an integral part of their outlook. Sybel, by contrast, had taken a more open-ended view of progress. He was a

Ranke student, largely uninstructed in the mysteries of Hegel's philosophy of history. He believed that there was such a thing as progress and he believed that the outlines of the future could be discerned vaguely, but he had always inclined to take affairs on a day-to-day basis, to hope for the best, and to define the best as the best possible under the circumstances.

That was very different from supposing that if something happened, it happened for the best. The latter belief was easy enough to sustain as long as one lacked even seeming power, and it could be maintained for a while when Germany's reconstruction seemed to be proceeding, despite occasional frustrations. Unexpected disappointments might, after all, be explained away as unforeseen paths to the ultimate good. But Droysen, Duncker, and Haym took empiricism seriously. The accumulation of evidence eventually told against their initial optimism and made self-conscious realists of them. Where once they had looked forward to the moral regeneration of humanity, or at least of Europe, through Germany's achievement of freedom, they now hoped at least that Germany might be unified. Where once they had seen the urge for freedom as the cause for unification, they now looked on freedom as, at best, a byproduct of national unity and strength. Nor were the changes limited to alterations in political program. History had seemed, in Droysen's metaphor, a "stream" whose destination could be discerned. Now it appeared to be a torrent that was navigable only with difficulty and considerable risk. They knew where they wanted to go, but now felt that they were navigating without a reliable map.

What had happened to them was, in one way, not very remarkable. They were just men with ideas who tried their ideas against realities and found out that their ideas were defective. They might have simply given up on politics. Instead, following the logic of their faith in history, they attempted an accommodation. As tamed ideologues, they would throw away what they had to and keep what they could. At least they could spare themselves excessive self-reproach. It was not as if they had been really in charge of events. They had never been in a position to remake Germany. This meant that they could blame others, as well as themselves for what went wrong and try to instruct the nation in how avoid the mistakes just made. Certainly, the change did not unmake them as historians. The experience led Droysen to untenable conclusions in his *History of Prussian Politics*, but it vividly informed his lectures on the philosophy and methods of history, the *Historik* for which (along with *Alexander the Great* and *The History of Hellenism*) he is still celebrated. Duncker's and Haym's major works still lay ahead, and so did Sybel's. His were tendentious, but the tendencies in part antedated the failure of the revolution. Actually, the fact that they continued as active historians is what makes their experience important: they taught their students to regard historical results as legitimate and as not subject to any external standard but success. With the map gone, that assumption was bound to result in a mixture of cynicism and voluntarism. It took them a few years, however, to sort out and think through the lessons just learned.

7

Toward the Prussian School

The disappointing spring of 1849 forced Droysen and his colleagues to modify further their historical and political thinking. The result was the historical outlook called the Prussian School, an outlook still optimistic about the Prusso-German future but now more self-consciously realist and more focused on military force and moral will. It is worth noting that this change occurred while they were still fairly young. They had long careers ahead of them in which to follow the implications of the ideas they devised. Droysen, the eldest, was forty-one in 1849. Duncker was thirty-eight, Sybel thirty-two, and Haym a youthful twenty-eight. This continued shift in their thinking did not occur all at once, of course, because at first they could not be fully clear about what had happened.

On 3 April, Frederick William of Prussia had refused to accept the German crown from the National Assembly. It was clear what he would not do, but it was not yet clear what he would do. This also made it clear to Droysen and the others what could not happen, namely, national unification by a Prussia that would cease to be Prussian in the process. Nonetheless, it was not evident to them what would happen instead—complete defeat or compromised victory. The result was a strategic uncertainty that led to a tactical unsureness. They were forced to think, to modify and to reorder their ideas. Until the conclusion of the Punctation of Olmütz (Olomouc) between Prussia and Austria in November 1850 (an event that deeply shocked and angered them), it seemed at least possible that Prussia would unify northern Germany in the Erfurt Union, which briefly had its own parliament. In the short term, the four had to estimate this union's value and decide whether to work for its realization. The answers to these tactical questions depended on their strategic estimates of actual Prussian policy and, more important, their new sense of what historians could and could not achieve in politics. Once Prussian capitulation to Austria was manifest in 1850, they faced the essentially different strategic problems of deciding what could yet be attained by the strategy of motivating Prussia to move in the possibly distant future. Their solutions dictated a tactical decision about the kind of history to write under the changed circumstances.

In order to establish the context for their decisions both before and after Olmütz, it is advisable to survey briefly Prussian policies in and after March 1849. The architect of those policies was the remarkable Catholic conservative Joseph Maria von Radowitz, a descendant of Magyar nobles who had moved to northern Germany, a soldier in Napoleon's army, French educated, Prussian only since 1823, and a trusted friend and adviser of King Frederick William. Radowitz was one of those conservatives in the generation after Metternich who rejected the latter's pessimistic immobilism in favor of cautious reform that would conserve what was essential in the old order.[1] As a member of the assembly at Frankfort, therefore, he had favored the limited, *kleindeutsch* variety of unification sought by Droysen and the others. Like Droysen's ideal Prussian statesman, he thought this to be in Prussia's real interest, as well as in the interest of social stability. Frederick William's refusal of the proferred crown in April 1849 did not change Radowitz's mind, and he persuaded the Prussian king to try to unify Germany on his own. At first, circumstances helped Radowitz make his case, in Prussia and in some of the other German states. Austria was tied down in fighting revolt in Hungary and could not do much to oppose Prussia. Moreover, social revolution, furthered by economic woes and regional differences, had rekindled in the German Southwest after the Prussian refusal of March 1849. It required the Prussian army to quell these, and the suppression was complete only with the fall of Rastatt in July. Obviously, this made the princes dependent on Prussia, and even Württemberg and Bavaria fell in with Prussian proposals for union as long as the rebels were threateningly active within their frontiers. When they did feel bold enough to turn Prussia down in late May, they still did not dare actively oppose the Three Kings' Federation (*Dreikönigsbund*) of Prussia, Hannover, and Saxony. The states issued a constitution (*Unionsverfassung*) on 28 May 1849 that excluded Austria, made the Prussian king the chief executive, and provided for a parliament elected on indirect suffrage with voting by classes instead of the more democratic franchise of the Frankfort constitution. All the German states other than Austria were invited to join this union.[2] In consequence, 150 liberals—Duncker among them—from the former assembly in Frankfort gathered at Gotha to give their blessings to the union.[3] (Some of these same liberals, including Duncker and Sybel, also sat in the union's Parliament at Erfurt.[4]

It is easy to see the attraction of Radowitz's experiment for some liberals, although others, like Droysen, never held much hope for it. It is certainly fascinating to speculate about what might have become of this earlier, gentler version of what Bismarck later brought about by force, namely, partial unification of Germany in the form of extended Prussian domination over the other German states. In the event, the prospects of the union dimmed perceptibly after August 1849, when Austria, with Russian help, defeated the revolt in Hungary. Austria's Prince Schwarzenberg naturally opposed a scheme that would exclude Austria from leadership in German affairs and instead preferred a German federation led by Austria. The defeat of the Magyar revolt, combined with Russian diplomatic support, gave Schwarzenberg a free hand. For a time he waited. Then, in the summer of 1850, the Prussian-led Erfurt Union threatened intervention in the member state Electoral Hesse, where the prince-elector was about to abrogate his own constitution. Austria, backed by Russia, sided with the Prince-Elector, and German civil war seemed to be in the offing. After some light skirmishing, the Prussian king was prevailed on to give way by the many Prussian conservatives who looked on Austria and Russia as friends, distrusted the liberals who supported the Union, and had opposed Radowitz's scheme all along. So, in October 1850 at Olmütz (Olomouc) in Moravia, Prussia agreed to let the union lapse. As Schwarzenberg's federal scheme was also unworkable, Germany reverted, in national constitutional terms, to the old German Confederation that had supposedly ended in March of 1848.[5]

The school resulted from their twofold response to this disappointment. First, they made important changes in historical analysis. Droysen and the others, in order to take account of what had and had not happened, revised their views on the course of German history and their evaluation of the forces that made history happen, in Germany and elsewhere. Second, they changed their strategy by continually abandoning direct political action in favor of political instruction. In doing so, they did not simply return to prerevolutionary practice. Too much had changed for that to happen: the lessons that they now taught were different, and so was the nature and objective of their instruction. They exchanged confident prediction for urgent reminders of what Prussia had been (and could be again) and hoped that those who would be in power would read their works and return to the fray inspired and informed, ready and able to advance Prussia's deeply German interests. The first mature work of this sort, a book whose publication is the starting point of the Prussian School of history, was Droysen's *Life of Field Marshall Count York von Wartenberg* (2 vols., 1851–54). In its pages, Droysen meticulously recorded, but also celebrated and recommended, the decisions and doings of the Prussian general who in 1812, seeing Prussia's main chance in Napoleon's disaster at Moscow, single-handedly and cleverly detached Prussia from the French alliance and led her into an alliance with the other powers in the liberating struggle against Napoleon. Droysen was recommending—and Duncker, Haym, and Sybel applauded him for this—clear-sighted recognition of specific Prussian interests in German unity, energy in pursuing these interests, and unblinkered appreciation of military force and political calculation.

This was a book Droysen could not have written earlier in his life. It simply would not have made sense to do so as long his chief objective was to prepare Germans for citizenship, rather than to goad Prussian officials to action. Nor would it have made sense to do so as long as Droysen and his colleagues were hopeful about the future. *York,* and the many other, later works of the Prussian School, were emplotted so as also to show what had gone so badly wrong in 1848 and 1849. That is, the virtues and genius of a Field Marshal York (or of any successful Prussian leader) always appear to be those that the hapless deputies at Frankfort lacked: realism, dynamism, state egoism, and the possession of, and readiness to employ, adequate military force. In contrast to such prerevolutionary works as Droysen's *Lectures on the Wars of Freedom* (2 vols., 1846–48), these newer works seem refreshingly commonsensical in not equating the future Germany with God's kingdom on earth. They are much less pleasant to read, however, because of the recurrent note in them of self-abasement. Not squeamish about military force before the revolution, these historians now saw force as the real source of legitimacy and were deeply embarrassed ever to have thought that mere parliamentary decrees would effect what only an army could accomplish.

None of this is to say that they simply turned their backs on their previous careers. Most of their postrevolutionary ideas had prerevolutionary precedents. They thought, with considerable justice, that they had corrected theory and practice in the light of the lessons learned during the successive disappointments encountered between late summer 1848 and spring 1849. This new realism, however, was bound to have something brutal and opportunistic about it because of their pronounced tendency to accept the results of history as by definition good. Recent history seemed to show the triumph of force and interest over ideals, and they revised their ideas accordingly. This recompounding of their ideas, however, is not fully intelligible without at least a brief look at their work after 3 April 1849, because the two parts of their response were really answers to two very large questions they had not had to pose until after Frederick William's refusal: What was there left to hope for now? And what should they do in the present circumstances? These questions were urgent because, first, Prussia had not acted as they had expected and, second, they now had no obvious political role to play even though their commitment to unification under Prussia remained unbroken.

After the disappointment at Frankfort in April 1849, they agreed about what should happen next: Prussia should energetically lead Germany to unification, by military means if necessary, while defending and extend-

ing moderate constitutionalism. For a time, however, they did not agree
about the tactics that they should employ to encourage this outcome. This
disagreement, though basically friendly, was most pronounced between
Droysen and Duncker. Sybel's initial ideas on this subject are not in evidence, although his practice followed the lines laid down by Duncker, and
Haym, now as earlier, was guided in all political matters by Duncker. The
disagreement was over the utility of parliamentary politics in the present
circumstances. It first arose with respect to the status and tasks of the National Assembly after Frederick William's refusal. Droysen concluded,
with harsh realism, that the assembly's work was finished and that the
deputies should surrender their mandates and go home. After a brief
intelligence-gathering mission to Berlin in May, he did just that and went
back to Kiel, which, in acknowledgment of the political retreat that this implied, he referred to as his "Patmos."[6] At least for the moment, he was really quite sure that the old party of the right center had no national role as
an organization. Affairs were in the hands of the princes and their governments, especially Frederick William's. In letters to Duncker, he therefore criticized the meeting at Gotha in late June 1849 to reconstitute the
right center as a party and, despite Duncker's insistent urgings, refused to
attend the gathering.[7]

Duncker saw matters differently. He believed that a reorganization of
"our firm, our party" would provide much needed "moral support" for
those in Berlin still set on a national course.[8] Even before this, he hung on
at Frankfort for weeks after Droysen thought it useless, because he believed that the right center could at least bear moral witness against the extremes of revolution and reaction.[9] Moreover, he did not know what else
to do with his time. It was, as Haym discovered, hard simply to leave politics and return to the study.[10] Droysen, after all, was still associated with
the provisional government in Schleswig-Holstein; in returning to Kiel, he
was returning to what seemed to be a major theater of the national struggle. Droysen could not actually do much there, but at least he had an out-
let for his political energy. That seemed enviable at the time. His friends,
Duncker prominent among them, repeatedly wrote to him in the next two
years for reports on activities there, and Duncker even briefly considered
following Heinrich von Gagern's lead and enlisting in the German volun-
teer army in Schleswig-Holstein for a final, heroic stand against the Danes
and, perhaps, the Russians.[11]

This disagreement, however, was over tactics, not strategy. In his later
biography of Duncker, Haym emphasized the remarkably close friendship
that Droysen and Duncker forged in the final days of the assembly, and especially noted the frequency and respect with which they corresponded
about politics in order to discover the best means to common ends.[12] The

surviving correspondence between the two, and Duncker's own memoir on Droysen, bear this out.[13] They were obviously very close friends—at least until February 1851, when Duncker, rightly or wrongly, accused Droysen of reneging on an agreement to publish his biography of York with his father's firm—and they agreed more often than they disagreed.[14] Furthermore, their respective preferences for different tactics were relative rather than absolute. Each paid some respect to the other's preference.

If Droysen considered it foolish to linger at Frankfort and thought that the Gotha meeting was useless and ill-advised, he did not suppose that it did actual harm or object to Duncker's continuing references to "our party" (by which he meant those of the right center who had favored hereditary constitutional monarchy under the Hohenzollern). In addition, he consistently gave the party, through Duncker and, more sparingly, Haym, as much constructive advice as he could. In other words, he evidently wished that Duncker were right, but ill-humoredly doubted that he was. Thus, Droysen was delighted that Duncker was elected to the Prussian Parliament in June 1849, obviously thought of him as representing a sort of national party, and advised him on tactics. He suggested, for example, that, in deference to Prussian opinion, he make as little of his Frankfort connections as possible and that he lead his colleagues in a responsible opposition with its own program and with a demonstrable readiness to guide the conduct of Prussian policy when necessary.[15] Similarly, he agreed with Duncker that the Berlin-based *Konstitutionelle-Zeitung*, originally Hansemann's paper, which Duncker, after great efforts, arranged for Haym to edit, was a necessity for Prussia and Germany because their cause needed a daily paper.[16] Thereafter, he frequently advised Haym on its tone and contents and was a frequent contributor.[17] These instances show that, disillusioned with parliamentary practice as he was, Droysen had not yet lost all hope that something might come out of Duncker's strivings.

He did not believe, however, that such actions could have much effect on events, whereas Duncker and his "friends" (including Haym, whom he more or less forced to edit the *Konstitutionelle Zeitung*) still thought that a dignified, public exposition of their ideas might move the Prussian authorities in the right direction.[18] This was really a difference of opinion over how much influence a certain kind of pressure could exert, for they all agreed on the direction in which Prussia needed to move and that only moral pressure, sooner or later, could occasion that movement. For his part, Duncker returned to parliamentary politics with some reluctance, and even before Olmütz seriously considered the sort of retirement that Droysen had recommended.[19] That was logical, because Duncker also agreed with Droysen that Prussian military power now held the key to national developments and that, in the last analysis, the Prussian king and his ministers had to decide whether and when to turn that key. This was not a conclusion drawn from cynicism or militarism. Rather, it was a finding based on their hopes and experiences. They wanted unification without revolution, and Prussia had refused the compromise that the assembly had offered. Obviously, the princes would have to be forced to go where they would not be led, and Prussia was the obvious candidate for forcing them because history had selected her for national leadership by making her the only major German state with an interest in and ability for such leadership.

With that as his outlook, Duncker visited Berlin in late May, conferred with Princess Augusta and Prince William, and recorded his words to them in an unpublished essay. He spoke and wrote of the need for Prussia to conquer Germany, not only morally by proclaiming national and liberal goals, but also militarily by overawing Germany with its army and forcing the other states either to follow its lead or, in Austria's case, to stand aside while Prussia unified the rest of the nation: "One must see batallions and hear trumpets everywhere."[20] Droysen was of much the same opinion, and his word choice shows clearly his heightened appreciation of force in the making of history. On 6 June 1849, he complained to his old friend Wilhelm Arendt that Prussia had erred in not accepting power from the assembly and now had no sensible recourse but to obtain it by force: "Now purely Prussian (*Jetzt nur stockpreußisch*)! There will be another national power (*Reichsmacht*) if this Prussia obstinately seeks its position by its own will and according to Germany's demonstrated necessity. Power is the best legitimacy (*Macht ist die beste Legitimität*)."[21] Not only is this the language of force. It is also the language of moral voluntarism, which also became a major element in his postrevolutionary historiography. Prussia had to act "obstinately" and "by its own will." Stubborn wanting had replaced the freely dawning consciousness of Droysen's prerevolutionary analysis of history. The real question between Droysen and Duncker, then, was how to get Prussia to decide to use the power she possessed.

Duncker's answer, and it seemed tenable to him until the Prussian government discredited itself at Olmütz, was moral persuasion. He wanted there to be an active and identifiable center party throughout Germany to tell Germans in general and the Prussian government in particular what ought to be done and to offer a clear alternative to the timid and reactionary policies that he found too much in evidence at Berlin. For that reason, Duncker defended to the skeptical Droysen the Gotha meeting of liberals bent on supporting Prussia's Union Constitution, and he worked hard to find a suitable editor (Haym finally agreed after several other candidates, including Droysen, refused) for the daily *Konstitutionelle Zeitung*.[22] His lobbying with Prussian officials and with Augusta and William in May

1849 was another form of persuasion. He also believed in the continued need for parliamentary work, uncongenial though he found it. He therefore allowed his followers at Halle to nominate him for a seat in the Prussian lower house to which, despite the introduction of the notorious three-class electoral system and a growing distrust of the left with which, unfairly, many now associated him, he was elected by a solid majority in July 1849.[23] In January 1850, he also agreed to run for a seat in the Erfurt Parliament.[24]

In one respect, continued parliamentary activity was an extension of his efforts to persuade. Duncker was not fond of speaking, but a seat provided a forum from which to spread his views. He also wanted some opportunity to influence policy. In Berlin, he worked to prevent reactionary revisions of the Prussian constitution (he became a member of the Constitutional Committee) and to keep Prussian foreign policy firm in the defense of Schleswig-Holstein and in the pursuit of national unification.[25] Similarly, at Erfurt—where Sybel also sat as a deputy—Duncker worked energetically and effectively to secure the presidency for the liberal Eduard Simson.[26] Even Droysen, who came to Erfurt as a spectator, saw this as a major accomplishment, though he did not single out Duncker for praise.[27]

It is hard to say how much Duncker expected to come of these efforts, but his stated hopes were modest enough. In a remark specifically intended to persuade Droysen to attend the June 1849 gathering at Gotha but that has wider relevance for his view of his activities, he said simply: "We two cannot do much, but we can do something."[28] Of course, he would not have put himself to the trouble of attending if he had thought that any effort would fail. One suspects that his hopes were higher than his statement suggests, if only because he became so angry when Prussia did not follow the advice that he and his colleagues offered.

At one point in July 1849, he felt almost ready "to prefer the democratic hoggishness (*Schweinerei*) to the princely"—a remarkable confession for Duncker.[29] Haym later recalled Duncker's view of the Erfurt Parliament as a battle to be won if, but only if, the party of unification could display massive powers of endurance.[30] It is also worth noting that Duncker was furious after what he considered the faked battle between Prussia and Austria at Bronzell in October 1850 and the consequent abandonment of Prussian plans for national unification at Olmütz. He was enraged because he felt deceived. After some hesitation, he decided to serve out his term in the Prussian Parliament, though he now felt that its work was useless. Duncker now shifted, quite naturally, to what he did best: advancing political arguments through historical writing. This strategy was not entirely new to him, of course. Before 1848 he had used historical lectures to prepare educated Germans for moral citizenship, and since the revolution he had written two historical works with strong political implications, namely, his *History of the German National Assembly at Frankfort* (1849) and his *Heinrich von Gagern* (1850).[31] Those were reflective works that told German liberals what they had done right and what wrong. He now put his main effort into researching the slender volumes of contemporary history, *Four Weeks of Foreign Policy* and, later, *Four Months of Foreign Policy*. Both were carefully researched exposés of what he portrayed as treacherous and cowardly Prussian subservience to Austria and, behind her, Russia. These were polemical histories about what official Prussia had done wrong. This criticism was no doubt a consequence of pent up disappointment at many Prussian failures, but it also reveals the same kind of moral voluntarism noted in Droysen's statements in 1849. Prussia had acted badly because she had not willed to act rightly. This was very different from Duncker's earlier confident belief in historical process. The immediate result, it must be added, was an unsuccessful official prosecution of Duncker and his publisher Veit. Interestingly and suspiciously, he published both works with Veit in Berlin, and his earlier book on Gagern with Costenlohe and Remmelmann in Leipzig. All his other works to date, including his politically more matter-of-fact *History of the German National Assembly*, were published by his family firm Duncker and Humblot. Perhaps he expected to be prosecuted.[32]

Droysen, by contrast, returned to historical instruction immediately after he left Frankfort in 1849 because he was more pessimistic about the chances for progress in the near future. He therefore chose to await its eventual resumption while writing histories of Prussian politics that identified sound and unsound tendencies in Prussian history in order to remind Prussian statesmen both to pursue the former and to shun the latter. To that extent, his intention was didactic. He proposed more than simple moralizing, however, inasmuch as he identified sound policies with Prussian interests and Prussian interests with German unification and the concomitant benefits of national strength and the reconciliation of freedom with authority. He was still in the business of prediction, though his predictions now dealt with the future play of state interests more than with the triumph of moral ideals. Again, this was a response to political failure, and in this response Droysen changed not only his strategy but also the analysis on which that strategy rested. Droysen had taught those lessons before, but now he wanted to remind rulers of their duties rather than to prepare Germans for citizenship. Prussia's disappointing performance to date had heightened his appreciation of moral will as a factor in history.

In addition, though the distinction may at first seem tenuous, Droysen had earlier treated Prussian self-interest as a means to the end of statehood. He now treated it as an end as well as a means. In addition, his earlier predictions were cosmopolitan because he considered national unification a solution to a universal problem of freedom. It would primarily benefit Germany, but it would also bless the whole world by resolving the world historical problem of freedom discussed in early chapters. Now Droysen wrote only about the good unification would do for Prussia and Germany. In the process, he stopped referring to God in his writings. This does not mean that Droysen lost his faith. Indeed, his resignation no doubt followed at least in part from a certainty that God would at last provide a way that he, Droysen, could not discover. But Droysen now directed his analysis so closely to objective self-interest that it no doubt seemed beside the point to invoke Providence. He continued to think of history as purposive and self-justifying, but power—and the will to use it—now seemed the mechanism that made history move. The assembly had possessed the will but lacked the power, Prussia the power but not the will. Droysen wanted to be sure that the next time, and he believed that there would be a next time, the two, will and power, would come together. In any case, a confident Augustinian sense of where history is going is inherently unstable, because by definition human beings cannot truly understand what God has in mind. Droysen stopped talking about God because bad times showed that the ways of Providence were less intelligible than they once had seemed.

This outlook had the further advantage of assuring Droysen that what had gone wrong was not his fault. He told Duncker in a letter of 13 June 1849 to remember: "Now we are only private people."[33] There was, at least, some satisfaction in being right when so many others were wrong. He felt betrayed by the princes and, worse, by the German people, but at least his own conscience was clear.[34] If history was somehow providential, there was no possibility of simply condemning its outcome. Moreover, Droysen was actually optimistic, if only in terms of a peculiar logic distantly derived from Hegel. He reasoned that things had become so bad that they had to become better. Because he believed that it was in Prussia's interest to unify Germany, and because he saw Prussia now following the opposite course with predictably unhappy effects, he concluded that circumstances alone would soon force Prussia onto the right path.[35]

Droysen's new historical writings, accordingly, had the added advantage of reassuring him about the future. Granted, he could not always maintain such equanimity. Right after Olmütz, for example, he wrote to his old friend Gruner in some anxiety, but at nearly the same time he assured Duncker that everything would have come right within ten years.[36] In general terms, and for similar reasons, he reasoned as, a little later, Marxists waiting for revolution would reason: the worse, the better. Of

course, they also were working with the implications of Hegelian dialectic: What went wrong now, because it irritated and energized, made later
success all the more certain. More specifically, Droysen took comfort in
precedents in Prussian history: periods of defeat and seeming decline, the
Seven Years' War or the Napoleonic conquest, had always given way to reform and new advances, the League of Princes (*Fürstenbund*) or the reforms under Stein.[37] Of course, this was not an entirely new component in
his thinking, because long before the revolution he had envisioned Germany's modern history as an instance of the last becoming the first. Now,
however, a somewhat revised interpretation of the logic of Prussian history sustained him in these comforting thoughts.

The best known of Droysen's contributions to the literature of the
Prussian School is his massive yet incomplete *History of Prussian Politics.*
The first volume appeared in 1855, and he published sixteen volumes of it
before his death in 1886. Despite his own longevity, Droysen's life ran out
faster than Prussia's diplomatic and military history; when he died, his
narration had not come within a century of the present. This immense
book was the logical product of this postrevolutionary musings. In a lead
article for the *Konstitutionelle Zeitung,* written in part to help the always im-
portunate Haym, who had otherwise to fill the front page as well as proof-
read copy and see it to the printer, he wrote on 10 October 1850: "Someone must finally decide to write an *histoire de la diplomatie prussienne;* that
will be very instructive."[38] He also wrote to his brother Karl in May 1851
about the need for such a work.[39] This work, however, was still a distant
prospect; it would require, obviously, extended research, and the relevant
archives were not yet open to Droysen. For the present, his seminal contribution was the work mentioned above, his *Life of Field Marshall Count
York von Wartenburg.*[40] This portrait of the great Field Marshal is important
because, through meticulous scholarship, it admiringly shows him exem-
plifying the traits that Droysen, in his *History of Prussian Politics,* would associate with the sweep of the Prussian past.

To be sure, the work was also meant to instill a sentimental Prussian
patriotism. In a defensive but basically honest answer to Theodor von
Schön, to whom he frequently wrote for material on York and who demanded that he emphasize the "specific Prussianness" (*spezifischen Preuß-
enthums*) of York, Droysen sentimentally recalled seeing "old Blücher" on
his horse in front of his father's house in 1813 and claimed always, even in
1848, to have worked in Prussia's interest because those were Germany's
and, as in 1813, Prussia could again raise herself to greatness by identifying her history with Germany's.[41] He wanted his biography to have just
that effect. Nor did he suppose that only he could or should write to such
an effect. For example, in a letter dated 15 January 1851, written to Field

Marshall Karl Count von Müffling (who had been quartermaster-general of Prussia's Silesian army in the 1813 campaign) to solicit further information about General York, Droysen suggested that Müffling himself write a memoir to inspire the present generation with past Prussian greatness, even—or especially—if he brought the story "only to 1815."[42]

His larger purpose remained instruction of responsible Prussian officials in such historical verities as would suit them for the kind of principled opportunism he admired in the field marshal. In this respect, *York* was a summing up as well as an anticipation. Its characteristic assumptions had already appeared in Droysen's important essay, dated 7 August 1849 and printed by Duncker and Humblot, entitled "Prussia and the System of the Great Powers: Opinions of a Schleswig-Holsteiner."[43] That work deserves careful consideration. Apart from having the claim of chronological priority, it has three other noteworthy features. First, Droysen himself thought highly of it. He often referred to it in his correspondence, and, in a lead article written anonymously for the *Konstitutionelle Zeitung* in 1850, he coyly recommended it as a genial and persuasive work.[44] Far from being a merely incidental piece, it was an authoritative statement of his postrevolutionary views and a preliminary statement of ideas that he would soon treat at much greater length. Second, it is wonderfully comprehensive in its treatment of Prussia's past, especially its recent past, and its future prospects. Its brevity, and the purely illustrative use of evidence permitted this since it enforced trenchant generalization. Detail and scholarly caution make *York* a more tentative statement of the same themes. Third, and important as evidence of Droysen's conscious effort to revise his prerevolutionary views in light of revolutionary and postrevolutionary experience, he put an old insight to new uses.

The old insight was his thesis that the 1815 settlement condemned Prussia for geographical and demographic reasons to be the least of the five "great powers" (England, France, Russia, and Austria were the others) on terms that ultimately would force Prussia to unify Germany, if only as a means to augment its own power.[45] This thesis had first appeared in full form in his article "The Political Position of Prussia," written in 1845, with Duncker's agreement, for the *Halle'sche Allgemeine Literatur-Zeitung*, and thereafter was a commonplace in Droysen's political reckonings. This basic thesis, however, now received several new elaborations and emphases that became characteristic of the Prussian School. The first of these was his claim that Prussian history consisted in a series of "great crises" in which the monarchy found itself called on to decide its future and, consequently, the future of Germany. In other words, crises like the present one were common, and they could be mastered if only the requisite moral will was present in Prussia's rulers. Prussia had not always made the right decisions in the past (for example, it had not in 1815), but it often had. He hoped that it would do so now, and he was sure that, eventually, it would.[46] Of course, this was a case in point of the new importance that he attached to will and decisive action as factors in history. Those who ruled Prussia had to learn, presumably in part through studying works like this, to act resolutely in the Prussian and German interest. Relatedly, he also placed much greater emphasis than previously on the importance of self-interest. He had always supposed that Providence worked through self-interested historical agents, but he had not previously held up the ruthless pursuit of self-interest as a sufficient as well as necessary cause of change. For example, after demonstrating the anti-German tendency of Austria's pursuit of her own interests, he asked rhetorically whether Prussia did not also follow "only its own interest," only to reply: "God grant, that it fully, ruthlessly, quite boldly follow its interest; because it embraces not only a third of the nation but—thanks to the artificial politics of 1815—its *disjecta membra* are spread from the extreme northeast to the southwest of the Fatherland." Any state so placed, he believed, would find it "convenient" that its contours fit those of the larger nation and that it could profit from their incorporation.[47] His argument, one that he repeated in his correspondence, was that Prussia had only to pursue remorselessly its own selfish interests and Germany would be unified.[48]

This celebration of will and selfishness as the agents of history's making derived, in turn, from an avowedly realistic acknowledgment of the centrality of force. When he turned to the events of 1848, he tried to distinguish reality from appearance. "The March Revolution," he explained, "appeared at last to have put the nation's destiny into its own hands. 'German Unity' was the magic word that promised to free us from all evil." Of course, that had not been the case. He had always been skeptical about legal formalities, but now he was openly contemptuous: "It is an empty verbal debate, whether the parliament could decree through the power of national sovereignty, or whether it had only the mandate to contract. It had [the] right insofar as it had power (*Es hatte Recht, so weit es Macht hatte*); and that ended at just the point where it had to be most effective." The historical moral seemed clear: "Realities began to triumph over ideals, interests over abstractions."[49] This attitude, which in 1853 Ludwig August von Rochau enduringly christened *Realpolitik,* was less cynical than at first it seems. Droysen did not mean that "ideals" and "abstractions" counted for nothing; he did mean that they should be counted on to the extent, and only to the extent, that they were backed by adequate force. In a sense, that is both a truism and an exaggeration, but it mattered to Droysen less as a moral proposition than as an assurance that unity and freedom were eventually inevitable because Prussia had an interest in them and had the power to achieve them—if only she possessed the requisite will.

To achieve that will, she had only to compare her interests to those of her great historical rival, Austria. Here was another, though more specific, change in his thinking, this one dating back to his posing of the "question to Austria" the previous autumn. He now no longer expected to gain Austria's German provinces for Germany and therefore had less reason to conceal his opinions about Austrian statecraft. Moreover, he rightly saw in Schwarzenberg's government in Vienna a resourceful opponent of national unification. Even so, given his new appreciation, he reluctantly admired Austria for its historical successes: "Who fails to note the glorious past of this proud Habsburg monarchy? While we other Germans declined and our name became shameful, Austria had its victories over the Turks, its dominion over Hungary and Italy, its European politics. But it lived from the decline of Germany; its greatness was conditioned by our impotence. The policy of Austria was and is not to let Germany act for itself."[50]

Droysen had become "little German" (*kleindeutsch*), in the updated meaning of the term and with a passion. Germany should be "small" in the sense that Austria would not be part of it. Austria's exclusion from a unified Germany was no longer the regrettable but necessary result of the impossibility of having two masters in the same house. She had to be excluded because her interests were, in historical tendency, inimical to those of the larger Germany.

Prussian interests, by happy contrast, corresponded exactly with those of Germany as a whole. Droysen was at pains to rebut the common charge that Prussia had been the ruin of the Holy Roman Empire. He insisted instead that "out of the dividedness, out of the rottenness of the empire" Prussia had arisen as the only power capable of "national development."[51] This, of course, was the governing thesis of the sixteen volumes of the *History of Prussian Politics*. In the present work, Droysen chose for reasons of space to limit his examples to the policies of Frederick the Great, Stein, and the founding of the customs union (*Zollverein*), which he singled out for special praise. These were instances of his larger claim that Prussian rulers always, when they really pursued their own interests, simultaneously advanced those of Germany.

That finding, of course, had powerful and immediate bearing on present politics: "Now more than ever Prussia must seek its calling and its strength in German development." This meant, first, recognizing that the German Confederation was not only not in Prussia's interest but had actually been founded contrary to that interest.[52] Never a respecter of legal niceties, especially in international law, Droysen now implicitly invoked his older conception of the "right of history" to justify a radical Prussian revision of the German political system:

The affair of the nation is now in Prussia's hands (*Die Sache der Nation ist jetzt bei Preußen*). And Prussia can save it and itself in no other way than by making a deeper historical right (*tiefere historische Recht*) of a great national development current against the dead rules, used only as a pretext, whose inability to confine it [national development] any further is factually proven. Prussia must henceforth take upon itself alone the position in Germany that it was supposed to share with Austria. . . . Prussia must be ready to break the apex of the system of 1815, this deathbed of the middle of Europe, because not to be able to do so means its doom.[53]

This was a pretty brutal view of affairs. When, in earlier years, Droysen invoked the "right of history," he had done so defensively in order to refute the immobilism of the doctrine of "historical rights" to which he, as a moderate, felt nonetheless drawn. Now he was so mastered by his love for the idea of a unified nation that he was calling for Prussia to defy the existing treaty system, surely by force, for the sake of unification and national power.

He was quite explicit about this. Droysen employed phrases that anticipate Bismarck's famous "blood and iron" speech of 1862. (That is not surprising; according to Droysen's student Alfred Dove, Bismarck read and greatly admired Droysen's essay.) For example, Droysen concluded the work by arguing: "Not from freedom, not from national declarations was the unity of Germany to be achieved. It required a power against the other powers, to break their resistance, to defend us against their selfishness."[54] This was, of course, more than just a promise, or threat, of war. It was also a complete break with the latent cosmopolitanism of his prerevolutionary theories. He more or less assumed the hostility, because of adversarial interests, of all the other powers, though in later writings he speculated about the possibility of an alliance with England.[55]

This view of national prospects explains Droysen's disinclination to attend further party meetings or to conduct further parliamentary business. That is, by arguing in these terms he left matters to the Prussian king, his government, and his army. His actions were consistent with his convictions, and in later years he made it a practice to intervene in day-to-day politics only on issues affecting higher education.[56] But it was really not in his nature to stand aside. The Prussian School, again, was a response to failure in two ways. It was a response inasmuch as it was a revision of a prior analysis of history, and the contents of "Prussia and the System of the Great Powers" show clearly the effects of that revision. It was also a response in strategy, and Droysen's withdrawal from practical politics was merely the negative side of that response. Publishing works like this was its positive aspect. Droysen thought that telling the truth would help history follow its proper course.

Droysen plainly thought that this literature was an area in which he himself could make a signal contribution through his publications. Indeed, in these years his career became bifurcated. At least after he left Kiel, where because of his political past he was no longer welcome as a state servant on the faculty, he no longer made political instruction the central focus of his teaching. He did teach recent history at Jena, but his lectures also dealt with historical methodology and in his seminar he led students to a variety of topics, many of them far afield from modern, and modern German, history.[57] Actually, that made a good deal of sense, given his new definition of purpose: He no longer needed to direct his political lessons at the general, even the general academic, public, though he did need to produce books for Prussia's present and future rulers. Over the longer term, his sense of this need led him to project and then, to the extent that time permitted, to complete his *History of Prussian Politics.*

He certainly tried to achieve it. His introduction to the work accurately stated the moral that the thousand succeeding pages were to document. His first paragraph, obviously composed with a view to the present, read: "Never has a state raised itself more quickly and proudly than Prussia after the days of Jena." Droysen conceded that events elsewhere contributed to national liberation, but he insisted that "the essential point" was that Prussia "picked itself up," that men "crowded to create new goals and form for the old strength and loyalty of Prussianness." His stated purpose was to write a "remembrance" (*Gedächtniß*) for one of the men "from that circle."[58] A *Gedächtniß*, of course, is a memorial piece, invariably a work of praise, usually uncritical praise. Droysen wanted to praise York because by withdrawing the Prussian contingent from the French *grande armée* and allying it with the now advancing Russians, he had liberated Prussia and helped overthrow Napoleon. In his present exultation of force and will, however, Droysen admired York's ruthlessness to the point of antagonizing Schön, who cut off relations with him after the book appeared.[59] Droysen's purpose, transparently and avowedly, was to present a figure for imitation and admiration, and in this he succeeded. The work was long for a biography, though not unduly so, and it was generally quite readable. Nevertheless, Sybel's criticism that Droysen was too "laconic" in his analyses is well founded.[60]

At least, the York biography was more influential than his *History of Prussian Politics*, for obvious reasons. First, it was more accessible. Even a long biography, with a "laconic" interpretive voice, is easier to handle than a history that begins in the fourteenth century and promises to proceed, volume after long volume, through the years until death of author or the conclusion of Prussian history stops it. Droysen promised a lot in his introduction to the *History*, but any discerning reader knew that it would take him many years to keep that promise. Second, the biography appeared at the right time. Its first volume was published in 1851, when those who wanted to believe in Prussia's mission most needed encouragement, and when Georg Heinrich Pertz's four-volume biography of Stein was still literary news. Pertz's work aroused interest in the lives of the Prussian reformers without satisfying it and seemed long, diffuse, and too unsympathetic to its subject. Droysen's work shone in contrast. Moreover, it had the advantage that biography has over history in the matter of didacticism: it showed virtues in action, exercised by a single agent for his own reasons but also for the general good. In his foreword to the *History*, Droysen promised the same benefits by claiming that he was interested in the present and its needs and that his book would meet those needs by "understanding through research (*forschend zu verstehen*)."[61] *York*, by contrast, offered this benefit through the inspection of a single, active life and was correspondingly influential.

The reactions of his historical and political colleagues to *York* must have gratified Droysen. Certainly these reactions show the essential affinities among their views. Sybel, for example, was delighted with its contents and its thesis. Droysen and he had been in friendly correspondence at least since January 1849, though they briefly lost contact the following year and in October 1850 Droysen asked Sybel's brother-in-law about him.[62] In June 1851 Sybel wrote to Droysen in reply to the latter's solicitation of an article for a scholarly monthly that Droysen planned to publish, though nothing came of the plans. Sybel liked the book for reasons that Droysen appreciated. Sybel had been writing critical letters to the *Braunschweige Reichszeitung* in order to refute their thesis that Prussian "regeneration" was "hopeless" and that only "Prussia's defeat" could bring "our political salvation." Sybel, of course, disagreed and was distressed at how these views were dividing the "party" to which he and Droysen adhered. He said that he welcomed *York* because it made it easier to refute these views by showing, as Droysen intended, the latent strength that Prussia possessed even in moments of weakness and defeat.[63] He noted and appreciated Droysen's intended parallelism between York's age and his own. For the present, however, Sybel did not imitate Droysen's example. He had too much else to do. At the time he wrote to Droysen, he was investigating earlier examples of the Roman influence on early German kingship that he first wrote about, controversially, in 1844. In addition, he was about to begin research for his magisterial *History of the Revolutionary Age*, which he first projected in the spring of 1848 with the contemporary Hessian revolution in mind. This work reflected far deeper interest in social forces than Droysen showed.[64] By late summer he was already consulting the archives in Paris, and the first volume appeared in 1853. Sybel turned to sustained research in Prussian history only later, at first in minor works, such as his published lecture "On the Development of Absolute Monarchy in Prussia," given at Bonn in August 1863 and then, more massively, in 1886, when he began to publish his six-volume *Founding of the German Empire by William I*. This, of course, was after unification and after the relevant source materials were present.[65] In a sense, however, he was resuming a task he began in a small way in 1851.

Certainly Droysen saw in Sybel a historiographic as well as political ally. He was delighted at Sybel's praise of *York*, despite Sybel's accompanying, and warranted, criticism of his prose style. That was more than an instance of gratified vanity; Droysen was pleased because Sybel approved the book's political utility.[66] This pleasure seems to have informed the next stage in his correspondence with Sybel. On 9 September 1851, he wrote to inform Sybel that, for political reasons, he was leaving Kiel for a chair at Jena and invited him to fill the vacancy. He did so with the approval of the university authorities, but his insistent and repeated efforts at persuasion show that he really wanted Sybel to exchange Marburg for Kiel, presumably so that Sybel could continue Droysen's political orientation there.[67] In the event, after the reimposition of Danish authority, it was hard to win official approval. The delay annoyed Sybel, and he withdrew his application.[68] Droysen would not have involved himself so deeply in recruiting Sybel unless he thought that he represented the same political and historical approach. He was really not that tolerant a person. For that reason, Droysen repaid Sybel's earlier compliments when the first volume of *The History of the Revolutionary Age* appeared. He thought it much the best book on the subject and found it politically instructive. It taught contemporaries what not to do. His only criticism, and here too he was repaying Sybel, was stylistic. He thought that Sybel was too much influenced by Ranke and thus too prone to include detail. This made it hard to find the forest because of the trees. Droysen simply assumed, correctly, that Sybel agreed with him that "our science is one of those that, above everything, should make a person better; its best strength is of an ethical nature (*den Menschen auch besser machen sollen; ihre beste Kraft ist ethischer Art*)."[69]

Haym was also deeply impressed by Droysen's *York*. Haym was bound to approve the political and moral tenor of York because it was the same as his own. During his tenure as editor of the *Konstitutionelle Zeitung*, Haym gladly published lead articles submitted in 1850 by Droysen, most of which in one way or another drew on his interpretation of Prussian history, not just because he was harried and overworked but because he agreed with them.[70] Droysen's *York*, however, was important for Haym in a more special sense. It helped give him a sense of vocation, professional and political, when he most needed it. In order to see how this was so, it is necessary briefly to review some pertinent facts in Haym's professional biography. When Haym entered politics in 1848, he had completed his inaugural dissertation but not his *Habilitationsschrift*, the second, more demanding dissertation. He was in the unenviable, though not unusual, situation of possessing the title "doctor" while lacking an academic career. He could not teach in a university, and that was what he wanted to do. When he left Frankfort in 1849, therefore, his first intention was to remedy this situation through prompt habilitation before the Prussian authorities took unfavorable note of his recent political activities. To this end, he submitted his prerevolutionary article "Philosophy" and successfully defended it while maintaining secrecy about his simultaneous editorship of the *Konstitutionelle Zeitung*.[71]

This gave him the standing he desired, but little else. After his ejection from Berlin in the wake of an article that he wrote and published about the Punctation of Olmütz, he periodically gave the unpaid lectures that he was now entitled to give at the University of Halle, but he could not find a paying position. Inevitably, he ran out of money and decided to support himself while he looked for an appointment by writing works that would convey major intellectual truths to a literate lay readership.[72] That decision posed a major problem beyond the obvious one of how to support himself with publications of that sort. The problem followed from his simultaneous determination to write works that were politically instructive. Now as before, he earnestly wanted national unification under Prussia, but he was still haunted by the difficulty that he experienced before 1848: he wanted to argue from history but he still had no real historical training. Droysen's *York* made this difficulty more acute. Between 1849 and 1851 Georg Heinrich Pertz's four volumes on the life of Stein appeared. Then, in 1851, *York* was published and Haym read and liked it. Droysen's book, and the previous examples of Dahlmann's prerevolutionary histories of the English and French revolutions, at first suggested to Haym the possibility of mining Pertz's book for materials for a short and readable life of Stein. He abandoned this idea, however, because of his unfamiliarity with administrative techniques and because it was obviously dubious simply to rewrite someone else's work and publish the results under one's own name.[73]

Haym could not, however, abandon the idea of writing some kind of history. He was too impressed with the effect of Droysen's work, even though he also thought that it was too demanding for a large public to read.[74] He thought that biography, because of the possibility of establishing an elective affinity between the reader and the character read about, was an excellent means for political and moral instruction. He probably felt that sort of attraction to individual lives himself. This much, at least, is clear: in both his autobiography and his life of Duncker, he recalls the excitement aroused by Droysen's book and also recalls that it was much discussed in meetings at Gotha, sponsored by Duke Ernst of Coburg, the brother of Victoria's Prince Albert, held to consider literary alternatives to practical politics during the current period of reaction. He also mentions that in these meetings the instructional use of biography was a favorite topic.[75] In the same period, 1851–52, he finally abandoned his alternate plan of writing a synthetic intellectual history of Germany from Kant to the present in favor of writing intellectual biographies of leading German thinkers. He had already, as a stopgap to earn some money, written on Friedrich Gentz; he now began to write such works as a matter of course, beginning with his biography of Wilhelm von Humboldt.[76] Droysen's work, though by no means the sole cause, had contributed heavily to Haym's discovery of a way in which he could write politically instructive history.

In the same period, Duncker also turned to political historiography as the best means for remedying Germany's present political ills. He had, again, employed it as a secondary strategy before Olmütz with his history of the National Assembly and his brief biography of Heinrich von Gagern. He used it for moral and political indictment just after Olmütz, when he published, first, "Four Weeks of Foreign Policy" and, then, "Four Months of Foreign Policy" in order to show what he took to be the cowardice and deceit of Prussia's government in the face of Austrian and Russian opposition. These were detailed and convincing works that showed a remarkable ability to infer the details and nuances of Prussian foreign policy. As Haym rightly remarked, they were unsurpassed in detail and accuracy until Sybel, with the archives opened to him by now friendly Prussian authorities, published his *Foundation of the German Empire*.[77] These works showed his talent and inclination for the political use of history, but he also wrote each for specific purposes. The history of the assembly began as a report to his electors that he decided to share with the larger public to explain what had gone wrong, and his work on Gagern was written at the request of a publisher planning a larger anthology of short biographies.[78] As previously explained, his two works on Prussian foreign policy were results of his anger, the effect of his belief that he had to do something.

In the wake of Olmütz, however, Duncker decided that a more consistent and ambitious historiographic strategy was necessary, although in the event he did little himself to carry it into effect, because he had long ago committed himself to write his *History of Antiquity* and was just then writing the first volume.[79] His own writings on Prussian history came only later, mainly after 1867, when he was appointed director of the

Prussian State Archives, and took the form of detailed monographs on particular subjects. That is not surprising because, by then, Droysen already was producing the synthetic account that Duncker thought the present circumstances required. Duncker's actual output is less important here than the convergence of his views with those of Droysen on the need for historical works that would show the prior tendency of Prussian history and teach Prussia's leaders how to behave in the future. He certainly had a lot planned, before the demands of his existing obligations overwhelmed his new projects. He was very excited by the meetings at Gotha in 1853 held to coordinate literary and historical efforts in behalf of unification, the same meetings that Haym attended in which Droysen's *York* was held up as an example of what could be accomplished.[80] Despite their tiff about Droysen's choice of publishers for *York*, Duncker awaited its appearance impatiently.[81]

In the aftermath of the Gotha meeting in 1853, that book, and the larger genre of instructive biographies, was very much on Duncker's mind. He wrote to Droysen on 11 December 1853 in the friendliest terms. Those at the session had instructed him to ask Droysen for advice about whether it would be fair to the publisher Riemer for him to write a short biography of Stein based entirely on Pertz's recent work and to find out if, as Georg Wilhelm Nitsch claimed, Droysen was himself working on a book on the reaction in Prussia. He asked only for "suggestions and advice," though Droysen thought that he wanted to write a popular condensation of his own *York*—permission for which he readily gave. Droysen may have read carelessly, or perhaps he read very carefully between the lines, because a popularization of Droysen was a major item of discussion at the meetings. Certainly, he understood the kind of work that Duncker had in mind. As Duncker stated in the letter, he was already rewriting Pertz's *Stein* and was seriously considering writing biographies of the Prussian military reformer Scharnhorst and of Wilhelm von Humboldt (as Haym, also at the meetings, eventually did for the latter).[82] A nearly contemporary letter from Droysen to Gustav Freytag, who was also at Gotha and wrote independently to Droysen, shows that Droysen thought that the great need was for work in the unexplored areas of Prussian social and agrarian history, but he also welcomed Duncker's plans to do what he had done with York's life with his and other lives and in a popular form.[83]

In fact, Duncker's letter shows his final adherence to the strategy that Droysen had advised since the end of the National Assembly, namely, the use of historiography to prepare for a renewed effort at national unification under Prussia. It also shows a partial renewal of Duncker's optimism. He responded to recent complaints by Droysen about "materialism" by claiming also to see "germs of something better": "I see these above all in the direction that our literature on history, on recent history and Prussian history, is taking and in the public's participation in these matters. We have to support this tendency against the materialism of natural science and to put the real idealism of history (*realen Idealismus der Historie*) in the place of the fantastical idealism of philosophy (*phantastischen Idealismus der Philosophie*) that filled and blew around in the heads of youth before 1848."[84]

Before 1848, in his *Crisis of the Reformation,* Duncker had drawn a contrast between "philosophical" and "historical" idealism in order to distinguish between two ways of viewing and acting in the world. Now he used analogous terms to distinguish between two genres of moral instruction. This was, of course, an acknowledgment that Droysen had been right, both in his strategy and in his earlier optimism. It was also a compliment paid to Droysen's recent work, completed and in process, which was plainly central in the literature to which Duncker pointed. Duncker now saw Droysen's postrevolutionary histories as the logical outcome of the saving movement toward empiricism to which he had pointed even before the revolution. Droysen understood this to be a letter of agreement, and wished that it were possible for the two to meet. In his letter of reply he scored two major points. First, for the present any political efforts that went beyond literary politics were "in part in vain, in part dubious," and, second, such efforts could and should affect Prussian policy: "Without the German orientation Prussia . . . is not to be saved."[85] Those two points are a good, compact statement of what had become, and thereafter remained, the attitude of the Prussian School.

Notes

Introduction

1. This distinction is very nicely discussed, with reference to the present age, in Francis Fukuyama, *The End of History and the Last Man* (New York, 1992), xiv–xxii.

2. David Blackbourn and Geoff Eley, *The Peculiarities of German History: Bourgeois Society and German Politics in Nineteenth Century Germany* (Oxford, 1984), passim.

3. Leonard Krieger, *The German Idea of Freedom. History of a Political Tradition* (Boston, 1957), passim and esp. 3–7.

1. Droysen and the Problem of Freedom

1. Johann Gustav Droysen, *Briefwechsel*, ed. Rudolf Hübner (Berlin, 1929), 1:33–34; Paul Achatius Pfizer, *Briefwechsel zweier Deutscher. Ziel und Aufgabe des deutschen Liberalismus*, ed. Georg Küntzel (Berlin, 1911), 164–65.

2. Otto Hintze, "Johann Gustav Droysen," in *Soziologie und Geschichte. Gesammelte Abhandlungen zur Soziologie, Politik und Geschichte*, ed. Gerhard Oestreich, 2d ed. (Göttingen, 1964), 455–57.

3. Johann Gustav Droysen, *Johann Gustav Droysen. Erster Theil. Bis zum Beginn der Frankfurter Tätigkeit* (Leipzip, 1910), 42–43.

4. Johann Gustav Droysen, *Des Aischylos Werke* (Berlin, 1832); idem, *Geschichte Alexanders des Grossen* (Düsseldorf, 1966); idem, *Geschichte des Hellenismus. I. Teil. Geschichte der Nachfolger Alexanders* (Hamburg, 1836).

5. Droysen, *Droysen*, 46–47.

6. Benedetto Bravo, *Philosophie, Historie, Philosophie de l'Histoire. tude sur J.G. Droysen Historien de l'Antiquité* (Wroclaw, 1968), 78–126; George Peabody Gooch, *History and Historians in the Nineteenth Century*, rev. ed. (London, 1952), 24–28; Peter Hünerman, *Der Durchbruch geschichtlichen Denkens im 19. Jahrhundert. Johann Gustav Droysen, Wilhelm Dilthey, Graf Paul von Wartenburg—Ihr Weg und ihre Weisung für die Theologie* (Freiburg, 1967), 63–68; Rudolf Pfeiffer, *History of Classical Scholarship from 1300 to 1850* (Oxford, 1976), 2:173–80, 188–89; Heinrich Ritter von Srbik, *Geist und Geschichte des deutschen Humanismus* (Munich, 1951), 1:197–213, 239–46.

7. Max Hoffman, *August Boeckh. Lebensbeschreibung und Auswahl aus seinem wissenschaftlichen Briefwechsel* (Leipzig, 1901), 472.

8. Johann Gustav Droysen, "Theologie der Geschichte. Vorwort zur *Geschichte des Hellenismus II*, in idem, *Historik. Vorlesungen über Enzyklopädie und Methodologie der Geschichte*, ed. Rudolf Hübner, 5th ed. (Darmstadt, 1967), 374–76.

9. Droysen, *Droysen*, 49–50; Hintze, "Johann Gustav Droysen," 463; Felix Gilbert, *Johann Gustav Droysen und die preussisch-deutsche Frage* (Berlin, 1931), 39–46; Hermann Heller, *Hegel und der nationale Staatsgedanke* (Leipzig, 1921), 176; Jörn Rüsen, *Begriffene Geschichte. Genesis und Begründung der Geschichtstheorie J.G. Droysens* (Paderborn, 1969), 16–21; Erich Rothacker, *Einleitung in die Geschichtswissenschaften* (Tübingen, 1920), 8–16, 167–72; Kuno Fischer, *Hegels Leben, Werke und Lehre*, 2 pts. (Heidelberg, 1901), 1:209.

10. Droysen, *Briefwechsel* 1:33.

11. See Shlomo Avineri, *Hegel's Theory of the Modern State* (New York, 1974), 118–22, 161.

12. Ibid. 1:103–4.

13. Georg Wilhelm Friedrich Hegel, *Grundlinien der Philosophie des Rechts, oder Naturrecht und Staatswissenschaft im Grundrisse* (Stuttgart, 1964), 33.

14. Avineri, *Hegel's Theory*, 126 n. 31.

15. Hegel, *Vorlesungen üben die Philosophie der Geschichte* (Stuttgart, 1961), 39.

16. Ibid., 47.

17. Ibid., 49.

18. Hegel, *Philosophie des Rechts*, 36.

19. Cf. Avineri, *Hegel's Theory*, 128–29.

20. Ronald A. Knox, *Enthusiasm: A Chapter in the History of Religion with Special Reference to the Seventeenth and Eighteenth Centuries* (New York, 1961), 1.

21. Giovanni Filorama, *A History of Gnosticism* (Oxford, 1990), xv, 10–11.

22. Droysen, *Briefwechsel*, 1:34.

23. Cf. Avineri, *Hegel's Theory*, 161–75; Walter Kaufmann, ed., *Hegel's Political Philosophy* (New York, 1970), 73, 83–85.

24. Droysen, *Briefwechsel*, 1:39–40.

25. Ibid.

26. Ibid.

27. Ibid.

28. Ibid. 1:34.

29. Ibid.

30. Ibid.

31. Ibid. 1:39.

32. Ibid. 1:40.

33. Extensively quoted in Werner Friedrich Kümmel, *Geschichte und Musikgeschichte. Die Musik der Neuzeit in Geschichtsschreibung und Geschichtsauffassung bis zu J.G. Droysen und Jakob Burckhardt* (Cassell, 1967), 243–44.

34. Droysen, *Briefwechsel* 1:38.

35. Droysen, *Aischylos Werke* 1:162. See also ibid. 2:282–83.

36. Ibid. 1:163–64. See also ibid. 2:278; idem, *Hellenismus* 1:1.

37. Cf. Michael Neumüller, *Liberalismus und Revolution. Das Problem der Revolution in der deutschen Geschichtsschreibung des 19. Jahrhunderts* (Düsseldorf, 1973), 76–78.

38. Droysen, *Aischylos Werke* 2:275–77.

39. Walter Kaufmann, *Hegel: A Reinterpretation* (Garden City, 1965), 153–62.

40. Droysen, *Aischylos Werke,* 2:283–85.

41. Ibid. 2:285. See also ibid. 1:173–75; Droysen, *Des Aristophanes Werke* (Berlin: Veit, 1835–37), 1:3–4.

42. Droysen, *Aischylos Werke,* 2:287. See also idem, "Zur griechischen Literatur," in *Kleine Schriften zur alten Geschichte* (Leipzig: Veit, 1893), 2:66–67.

43. Droysen, "Zur griechischen Literatur," 2:65–66.

44. Hegel, *Philosophie der Geschichte,* 59–60.

45. Droysen, *Geschichte des Hellenismus* 1:vii.

46. Ibid. 1:4.

47. Droysen, *Geschichte Alexanders des Grossen,* 1.

48. Ibid., 286.

49. Idem, *Hellenismus* 1:4.

50. Idem, *Alexanders des Grossen,* 287.

51. Ibid., 288–89.

52. Arnaldo Momigliano, "J.G. Droysen between Greeks and Jews," in *Essays in Ancient and Modern Historiography* (Middletown, Conn.: 1977), 307–24.

53. Droysen, *Hellenismus* 1:1.

54. Ibid. 1:60.

55. Idem, *Aischylos Werke* 1:163; *Alexanders des Grossen,* 1; idem, "Zur griechischen Literatur" 2:72–74.

56. Droysen, "Zur griechischen Literatur" 2:73–74.

57. Droysen, *Briefwechsel* 1:16.

58. Ibid. 1:40–41.

59. Droysen, *Aischylos Werke* 1:179.

60. Droysen, *Briefwechsel* 1:104.

61. Ibid. 1:18–19.

62. Ibid. 1:33.

63. Ibid. 1:103–4.

64. Ibid. 1:118.

65. Ibid. 1:118–19.

66. For this section I am greatly indebted to Charles Norris Cochrane, *Christianity and Classical Culture* (Oxford, 1972), 456–516; R.A. Markus, *Saeculum: History and Society in the Theology of St. Augustine* (Cambridge, 1970); Robert A. Nisbet, *Social Change and History; Aspects of the Western Theory of Development* (Oxford, 1969) 3–11, 62–103.

67. Boethius, *Philosophiae Consolationis,* bk. 5, sec. vi, ll. 109-175.

68. Cf. J.G.A. Pocock, *The Machiavellian Moment. Florentine Political Thought and the Atlantic Republican Tradition* (Princeton, N.J., 1975), 33–44.

2. Droysen: Interpretation and Prediction

1. Droysen, *Briefwechsel* 1:230–31.

2. Droysen, *Vorlesungen über die Freiheitskriege,* 2 vols. (Kiel, 1846–48).

3. Ibid. 1:150–51.

4. Ibid.

5. Droysen, "Theologie der Geschichte," 380–82.

6. Ibid., 382.

7. Ibid., 383.

8. Ibid., 371.

9. Droysen, *Freiheitskriege* 1:5.

10. Droysen, "Theologie der Geschichte," 378.

11. Droysen, "Zur griechischen Literatur," 1:62–64.

12. Droysen, "Theologie der Geschichte," 385. See also idem, *Politische Schriften*, ed. Felix Gilbert (Berlin, 1933), 11.

13. See the extended quotation in Kümmel, *Geschichte und Musikgeschichte*, 243–44.

14. Droysen, "Theologie der Geschichte," 375.

15. Droysen, *Hellenismus* 1:6.

16. Droysen, "Theologie der Geschichte," 376.

17. Droysen, "Rede zur tausendjährigen Gedächtnisfeier des Vertrags zu Verdun," in *Deutsche Akademiereden*, ed. Fritz Strich (Munich, 1934), 95–96. See also idem, *Freiheitskriege* 1:78.

18. Droysen, "Verdunrede," 94–96.

19. Cf. Avineri, *Hegel's Theory*, 111–12.

20. Droysen, *Politische Schriften*, 27.

21. Ibid.

22. Cf. Krieger, *German Idea of Freedom*, x–x, 358–64.

23. Droysen, *Politische Schriften*, 13, 16.

24. Ibid. 1:8–9, also 1:185–87.

25. Ibid. 2:361–62.

26. Ibid.

27. Cf. Michael Neumüller, *Liberalismus und Revolution. Das Problem der Revolution in der deutschen liberalen Geschichtsschreibung des 19. Jahrhunderts* (Düsseldorf, 1973), 49–50, 62–66, 72–76.

28. Droysen, *Freiheitskriege* 1:270–74, also 284–85.

29. Ibid. 2:5; see also Droysen, *Politische Schriften*, 16.

30. Droysen, *Freiheitskriege* 1:25–53.

31. Ibid. 2:3–20; Droysen, *Politische Schriften*, 6, 48, 59.

32. Droysen, *Freiheitskriege* 1:57–61.

33. Cf. Droysen, *Geschichte Alexanders des Grossens*, 1–2.

34. Droysen, "Schreiben an den Herausgeber, die 'Geschichte Deutschlands von 1806–1830' von Prof. Friedrich Bülau, Hamb. 1842 betreffend," in *Zeitschrift für Geschichtswissenschaft* 1:490–91.

35. Droysen, *Freiheitskriege* 2:404–5.

36. Ibid. 2:410–11.

37. Droysen, "Verdunrede," 96.

38. Ibid. 2:410–11.

39. Ibid. 2:411; also, ibid. 2:406–7, and Droysen, *Politische Schriften*, 40.

40. Droysen, "Schreiben an den Herausgeber," 1:510.

41. Ibid. 1:511; also, idem, "Verdunrede," 100.

42. Droysen, *Politische Schriften*, 10–11; also, idem, "Verdunrede," 100.

43. Droysen, *Politische Schriften*, 56.

44. Ibid., 72–76; cf. Friedrich Meinecke, *Weltbürgertum und Nationalstaat*, ed. Hans Herzfeld (Munich, 1962), 281–300.

45. Droysen, *Politische Schriften*, 60–61; also, Droysen, *Briefwechsel* 1:288–89.

46. Droysen, *Politische Schriften*, 62–63.

47. Ibid., 60–61.

48. Ibid., 22.

49. Droysen, "Schreiben an den Herausgeber," 1:483.

50. Droysen, "Verdunrede," 96.

51. Droysen, "Gelehrtenschulwesen," (Kiel, 1846), 7–8.

52. Ibid., 16–17.

53. Ibid., 6–7.

54. Ibid., 4.

55. Ibid.

56. Ibid., 6–7.

57. Ibid., 16.

58. Rochus Freiherr von Liliencron, *Frohe Jugendtage. Lebenserinnerungen Kinder und Enkeln erzählt* (Berlin, 1902), 106.

59. Droysen, "Theologie der Geschichte," 375–76.

60. W. Carr, *Schleswig-Holstein 1815–1848: A Study in National Conflict* (Manchester, 1963), 61–96.

61. Ibid., 22.

62. Ibid., 194–95.

63. Anni Meetz, *Johann Gustav Droysen politische Tätigkeit in der schleswig-holsteinischen Frage* (Erlangen, 1930), 15–16.

64. Droysen, *Briefwechsel* 1:302.

65. Ibid. 1:301

66. Ibid. 1:288–89; see also 1:295.

67. Ibid. 1:323.

68. Ibid. 1:337.

69. Ibid. 1:337, 341–42.

70. Ibid, 232–44; Droysen, *Briefwechsel* 1:299, 301.

71. Carr, *Schleswig-Holstein 1815–1848*, 249–52.

72. N. Falck, M. Tönsen, E. Hermann, Joh, Christiansen, Georg Waitz, J.C. Ravit, L. Stein, Joh. Gus. Droysen, *Staats- und Erbrecht des Herzogthums Schleswig. Kritik des Kommissionsbedenken* (Hamburg, 1846); see Meetz, *Johann Gustav Droysens politische Tätigkeit*, 13–14.

73. Droysen, *Briefwechsel*, 1:336–37, 341–42.

74. Ibid. 1:342–43.

75. Ibid. 1:382–83, 387–90; cf. Meetz, *Johann Gustav Droysens politische Tätigkeit*, 33–34.

76. Droysen, *Politische Schriften*, 106.

77. Droysen, *Briefwechsel*, 1:349, 354.

78. Ibid. 1:359–60.

79. Droysen, *Politische Schriften*, 69.

80. Ibid.

81. Ibid., 96.

82. Ibid., 84-85.

83. Droysen, "Verdunrede," 102–3.

84. Ibid., 104.

85. Droysen, *Politische Schriften*, 72.

86. Ibid., 73–74.
87. Ibid., 75.
88. Cf. Gilbert, *Johann Gustav Droysen*, 70–72.
89. Droysen, *Politische Schriften*, 83–84.
90. Ibid., 114.
91. Ibid., 103–4.
92. Ibid., 109–10.
93. Ibid., 111.
94. Ibid., 106.
95. Ibid., 112.
96. Ibid., 107–8.
97. Ibid., 116.

3. Parallel Careers: Duncker, Haym, Sybel

1. Rudolf Haym, *Das Leben Max Duncker* (Berlin, 1891), 6, 13–14. For a highly sentimental impression of Duncker's childhood home, see Dora Duncker, *Das Haus Duncker. Ein Buchhändlerroman aus der Biedermeierzeit*, 3d ed. (Berlin, 1918).

2. Maximilian Wolfgang Duncker, *Origines Germanicae. Commentatio Prima* (Berlin, 1840); Haym, *Max Duncker*, 23.

3. Haym, *Max Duncker*, 12.

4. Ibid., 6, 12–16; Konrad Varrentrapp, "Rankes Historisch-Politische Zeitschrift und das Berliner Politische Wochenblatt," in *Historische Zeitschrift* 99 (1907): 104–5 n. 3.

5. Haym, *Max Duncker*, 6–12; Heinrich von Sybel, "Drei Bonner Historiker. Rede beim Antritt des Rektorats, 18. Oktober, 1867," reprinted in *Vorträge und Aufsätze* (Berlin: Hofman, 1874), 289–91; idem, "Vorwort," in *Gregor von Tours und seine Zeit, vornehmlich aus seinen Werken geschildert. Ein Beitrag zur Geschichte der Entstehung und ersten Entwicklung romanisch-germanischen Verhältnisse*, ed. Johann Wilhelm Loebell, 2d ed. (Leipzig, 1869), vii–viii.

6. Max Duncker, "Vorrede," in Karl Friedrich Becker, *Weltgeschichte*, 7th ed., 12 vols., ed. Johann Wilhelm Loebell (Berlin, 1836), 4:viii.

7. Ibid. 4:ix–x.

8. Ibid. 4:vi.

9. Ibid. 4:vii.

10. Haym, *Ausgewählter Briefwechsel*, ed. Hans Rosenberg (Berlin and Leipzig, 1930), 23; idem, *Aus meinem Leben. Erinnerungen aus dem Nachlaß gegeben* (Berlin, 1901), 166–67; idem, *Max Duncker*, 59–61. Cf. Hans Rosenberg, *Rudolf Haym und die Anfänge des klassischen Liberalismus* (Munich and Berlin, 1933), 41, 51–52.

11. Droysen, *Briefwechsel* 1:306, 308.

12. Duncker, *Die Krisis der Reformation. Ein Vortrag in der Versammlung der protestantischen Freunde zu Halle am 6. August gehalten* (Leipzig, 1845), vii–viii.

13. Duncker, *Krisis*, x–xi.

14. Ibid., viii.

15. Ibid., xii.

16. Ibid.

17. Ibid.

18. Ibid.

19. Ibid., xiv.

20. Haym, *Max Duncker*, 58–60. In so arguing, Haym had access to Duncker's lectures, which now cannot be located.

21. Duncker, *Krisis*, 12.

22. Haym, *Max Duncker*, 10–11.

23. James J. Sheehan, *German History 1770–1866* (Oxford, 1989), 625–26.

24. Droysen, *Briefwechsel* 1:306–8.

25. [Duncker], "Politische Predigten der Gegenwart," in *Halle'sche Allgemeine Literatur-Zeitung*, nos. 238, 239 (Sept. 1844): esp. col. 568; Droysen, *Briefwechsel* 1:358–60.

26. Duncker, *Krisis*, 10; cf. Haym, *Max Duncker*, 10–11.

27. Duncker, *Krisis*, 18–19.

28. Droysen, *Briefwechsel* 1:303–304.

29. Duncker, *Krisis*, 6.

30. Ibid., 50.

31. Ibid., 10, 20–21, 40–42.

32. Ibid., 50.

33. Ibid.

34. [Duncker], "Ueber die Hindernisse einer gesetzmäßigen Entwickelung des öffentlichen Geistes in Deutschland," in *Halle'sche Allgemeine Literatur-Zeitung* 1, nos. 93–96 (1844); 2, nos. 266–70; Haym, *Max Duncker*, 61–64.

35. Duncker, *Krisis*, xii.

36. Haym, *Max Duncker*, 74.

37. Ibid., 59–60.

38. Ibid., 77–78.

39. Droysen, *Briefwechsel* 1:359–60.

40. Ibid. 1:295.

41. Ibid. 1:282.

42. Haym, *Aus meinem Leben*, 166–67.

43. Haym, *Max Duncker*, 76.

44. [Duncker], "Von der Saale," in *Deutsche Zeitung*, no. 42 (2 Feb. 1848): 332.

45. Duncker, *Zur Geschichte der deutschen Reichsversammlung zu Frankfurt* (Berlin, 1849), 18.

46. Droysen, *Briefwechsel* 1:369.

47. Haym, *Max Duncker*, 78.

48. Ibid., 79.

49. Droysen, *Briefwechsel* 1:358.

50. Ibid. 1:359–60.

51. Haym, *Max Duncker*, 60

52. Ibid., 78–79.

53. Droysen, *Briefwechsel* 1:369–71.

54. Haym, *Ausgewählter Briefwechsel*, 22–25, 90–91.

55. Haym, *Max Duncker*, 19–21, 32–36, 60–61; Rosenberg, *Rudolf Haym*, 85–88.

56. Haym, *Max Duncker*, 32–36.

57. Max Lenz, *Geschichte der Königlichen Friedrich-Wilhelms-Universität zu Berlin*, 4 vols. (Halle a. S., 1910–18), 2:103–4; Conrad Varrentrapp, *Johannes Schulze und das höhere preußische Unterrichtswesen in seiner Zeit* (Leipzig, 1889), 546–47.

58. Haym, *Max Duncker*, 58–59.

59. Haym, *Aus meinem Leben*, 1–2, 75.

60. Ibid., 167–69.

61. Haym, "Besprechung von Leopold Ranke, 'Deutsche Geschichte im Zeitalter der Reformation' " and "Besprechung von Gothardt Viktor, 'Geschichte des englischen Deismus,' " in *Halle'sche Allgemeine Literatur Zeitung*, no 65 (1842): col. 59 and no. 158, cols. 41–44.

62. Haym, *Aus meinem Leben*, 3–4.

63. Ibid., 131–32; idem, *Gesenius: Eine Erinnerung für seine Freunde*, (Berlin, 1842), 38–39.

64. Haym, *Gesenius*, 18, 22–23.

65. Droysen, *Briefwechsel* 1:254–55.

66. Haym, *Aus meinem Leben*, 131.

67. Ibid., 166–67; idem, *Ausgewählter Briefwechsel*, 23; cf. Rosenberg, *Rudolf Haym*, 41, 51–52.

68. Haym, *Hegel und seine Zeit. Vorlesungen über Entstehung und Entwicklung, Wesen und Werth der Hegel'schen Philosophie* (Berlin, 1857), 4.

69. Haym, "Philosophie," in *Allgemeine Encyklopädie der Wissenschaften und Künste*, ed. J.S. Ersch and J.G. Gruber, 26 vols. (Leipzig, 1846–48), 24:183.

70. Ibid. 24:183–84.

71. Ibid. 24:195–97.

72. Ibid. 24:183–84.

73. Ibid. 24:197.

74. Haym, *Die Autorität, welche fällt und die, welche bleibt: Ein populärphilosophischer Aufsatz* (Halle a. S., 1846), 27.

75. Haym, *Ausgewählter Briefwechsel*, 25.

76. Ibid.; idem, *Feuerbach und die Philosophie. Zur Kritik Beider* (Halle a. S., 1847), 30–31; idem, "Philosophie," 156–57.

77. Haym, *Ausgewählter Briefwechsel*, 25; idem, "Philosophie," 224–26.

78. Haym, *Autorität*, 7–10, 27.

79. Ibid., 10.

80. Ibid., 30.

81. Ibid. 24:229–31; idem, *Ausgewählter Briefwechsel*, 27; idem, *Feuerbach*, 76–77.

82. Haym, "Philosophie," 24:184, 225–27, 230–31.

83. Ibid. 24:229–30.

84. Ibid. 24:153, 161, 227–28.

85. Ibid. 24:176–78.

86. Ibid.

87. Haym, *Autorität*, 26; idem, "Philosophie," 24:196.

88. Haym, "Philosophie," 24:75–76.

89. Haym, *Aus meinem Leben*, 167, 175, 184–85.

90. Ibid., 166–67.

91. Ibid., 159; Rosenberg, *Rudolf Haym*, 108–10.

92. Haym, *Aus meinem Leben*, 167–70; idem, *Ausgewählter Briefwechsel*, 32.

93. Haym, *Reden und Redner*, i.

94. Ibid., iii.

95. Ibid., ii; Droysen, *Politische Schriften*, 70.

96. Friedrich Ludwig Karl von Sybel, *Nachrichten über die Soester Familie Sybel* (Munich, 1890), iii–v; Conrad Varrentrapp, "Biographische Einleitung," in *Vorträge und Abhandlungen*, ed. Heinrich von Sybel (Munich and Berlin, 1897), 4–6, 8.

97. Varrentrapp, "Rankes Historisch-politische Zeitschrift," 103–4 n. 3.

98. Lenz, *Geschichte der Königlichen Friedrich-Wilhelms-Universität* 3:255–59; Paul Egon Hübinger, *Das historische Seminar der Rheinischen Friedrichs-Wilhelms-Universiät zu Bonn. Vorläufer—Gründung—Entwicklung. Ein Wegstück deutscher Universitätsgeschichte* (Bonn, 1963), 40–41.

99. Varrentrapp, "Biographische Einleitung," 12.

100. Ibid., 28.

101. Ibid., 13–14.

102. Sybel, *De fontibus Libri Jordanis de Origine Actuque Getarum* (Berlin: Diss, 1838), 45.

103. Varrentrapp, "Biographische Einleitung," 13.

104. Sybel, *Geschichte des ersten Kreuzzugs* (Düsseldorf, 1841); idem, *Entstehung des deutschen Königthums* (Frankfort, 1844); Varrentrapp, "Biographische Einleitung," 22–26.

105. Varrentrapp, "Biographische Einleitung," 29.

106. Varrentrapp, "Briefe an Ranke von einigen seiner Schüler: Sybel, Carlsen, Hermann, Pauli und Noorden," in *Historische Zeitschrift* (1911), 107:45.

107. Sybel, "Ueber die heutigen Tories. Rede geh. zur academischen Feier des Geburtstags Seiner Königlichen Hoheit des Kurfürsten am 28. Juli 1846" (Marburg: Universitätsbuchhandlung, 1846), 5.

108. Sybel, *De fontibus*, 45.

109. Sybel, "Ueber die heutigen Tories," 11–12.

110. "Ueber das Verhältniß unserer Universitäten zum öffentlichen Leben. Rede gehalten zur academischen Feier des Geburtstags seiner Königlichen Hoheits des Kurfürsten am 28. Juli 1847" (Marburg, 1847), 7.

111. Ibid.

112. Sybel and J. Gildemeister, *Der heilige Rock zu Trier und die zwanzig andere Heiligen Ungenähten Röcke. Eine historische Untersuchung* (Düsseldorf, 1844), esp. v–x; cf. Varrentrapp, "Briefe an Ranke," 44–45.

113. Sybel, "E.M. Arndt über die Autonomen," *Kölnische Zeitung*, no. 32 (1 Feb. 1845); "Konservative Gesinnung und die Luxemburg Zeitung," *KZ*, no. 48 (17 Feb. 1845). See also, Karl Buchheim, "Heinrich von Sybel und die Staatsgedanke. Publizistische Dokumente aus der Kölnischen Zeitung 1844," in *Historische Vierteljahrschrift* (1831) 26:98–99.

114. Sybel, *Die politische Parteien im Rheinland in ihrem Verhältnis zur preuß ischen Verfassung geschildert* (Düsseldorf, 1847), 10.

115. Sybel, "Edmund Burke und Irland," in *Allgemeine Zeitschrift für Geschichtswissenschaft* (1848) 8:489.

116. Sybel, "Edmund Burke und die französische Revolution," in *Allgemeine Zeitschrift für Geschichtswissenschaft* (1847) 7:1–2, 4–5, 12.

117. Sybel, "Edmund Burke und Irland," 8:489; "Edmund Burke und die französische Revolution," 7:19–20.

118. Sybel, "Universitäten," 4–5.

119. Sybel, *Politische Parteien*, 8.

120. Sybel, "Universitäten," 6–7.

121. Ibid.

122. Sybel, "Edmund Burke und die französische Revolution," 7:19–20.

123. Sybel, *Politische Parteien*, 44–45.

124. Sybel, "Universitäten," 7–8.

125. Sybel, "Edmund Burke und die französische Revolution," 7:22; "Universitäten," 16–17.

126. Sybel, "Universitäten," 9–10.

127. Sybel, *Politische Parteien*, 58–59.

128. Ibid., 9–10.

129. Ibid., 59–60.

130. Ibid., 73–74.

131. Ibid., 34–38.

132. Ibid., 59–60.

133. Ibid., 65.

134. Ibid., 44.

135. Ibid., 66–72.

136. Ibid., 66; also, idem, "Edmund Burke und die französische Revolution," 7:16–17.

137. Sybel, *Politische Parteien*, 63.

138. Ibid., 66–72.

139. Ibid., iii–v.

4. Expectation and Action: March to May 1848

1. Haym, *Ausgewählter Briefwechsel*, 35–36.

2. Johann Gustav Droysen, *Aktenstücke und Aufzeichnungen zur Geschichte der Frankfurter Nationalversammlung*, ed. Rudolf Hübner (Berlin and Leipzig, 1924), 1–20; Walter Fenske, *Johann Gustav Droysen und das deutsche Nationalstaatsproblem. Ein Beitrag zur Geschichte der Frankfurter Nationalversammlung 1848–1849* (Erlangen, 1930), 65–93; Hintze, "Johann Gustav Droysen," 470–72; Meetz, *Johann Gustav Droysens politische Tätigkeit*, 47–68.

3. Droysen, *Aktenstücke und Aufzeichnungen*, 12–19, 793; Rudolf Hübner, "Der Verfassungentwurf der siebzehn Vertrauensmänner," in *Festschrift für Eduard Rosenthal zum siebzigsten Geburtstag* (Jena, 1923), 117–22.

4. Droysen, *Briefwechsel* 1:416–20.

5. Max Duncker, *Geschichte des Alterthums*, 7 vols. (Berlin, 1855–57).

6. Haym, *Max Duncker*, 83–85.

7. Haym, *Aus meinem Leben*, 183.

8. Ibid.; idem, *Max Duncker*, 85; Max Duncker, *Politischer Briefwechsel aus seinem Nachlaß*, ed. Johannes Schulze (Stuttgart and Berlin, 1923), 2.

9. Haym, *Ausgewählter Briefwechsel*, 35; idem, *Aus meinem Leben*, 179–80.

10. Haym, *Aus meinem Leben*, 181–83; Rosenberg, *Rudolf Haym*, 118–22.

11. Varrentrapp, "Biographische Einleitung," 51–56; "Höhe Ständeversammlung!," 26 April 1848, Marburg Universitätsbibliothek Flugschriften, no. 72.

12. Varrentrapp, "Biographische Einleitung," 51–56, 73–79.

13. Duncker, *Reichsversammlung*, 1.

14. Droysen, *Briefwechsel* 1:399.

15. Ibid. 1:400–401.

16. Haym, *Aus meinem Leben*, 184–85.

17. Haym, *Ausgewählter Briefwechsel*, 37–38.

18. Haym, *Aus meinem Leben*, 185.

19. Haym, *Ausgewählter Briefwechsel*, 45.

20. [Sybel,] "Entwurf zu einem Programm des Vaterlandsverein," Marburg, 28 April 1848, Marburg Universitätsbibliothek Flugschriften, nos. 76, 76a.

21. Varrentrapp, "Biographische Einleitung," 52.

22. Sybel, "Pariser Studien," in *Vorträge und Abhandlungen*, 362–63.

23. Sybel, *Geschichte der Revolutionszeit vom 1789–1795*, 5 vols. (Düsseldorf, 1853–79).

24. Duncker, *Reichsversammlung*, 1–6.

25. Ernst Rudolf Huber, ed., *Dokumente zur deutschen Verfassungsgeschichte*, 3 vols. (Stuttgart, 1961–66), 1:284–90; Hübner, "Verfassungsentwurf der siebzehn Vertrauensmänner," 43–44, 117–22.

26. Cf. Meinecke, *Weltbürgerthum und Nationalstaat*, 303.

27. Droysen, *Briefwechsel* 1:401.

28. Ibid. 1:417.

29. Ibid. 1:416.

30. Ibid. 1:418.

31. Ibid.

32. Droysen, *Aktenstücke und Aufzeichnungen*, 797, 799, 803.

33. Ibid., 803–4.

34. Droysen, *Politische Schriften*, 121–24.

35. Ibid., 133–34.

36. Ibid., 135.

37. Ibid., 135–36.

38. Extensively quoted in Gilbert, *Johann Gustav Droysen*, 83.

39. Droysen, *Briefwechsel* 1:407–9; idem, *Politische Schriften*, 135 n. 3.

40. Droysen, *Politische Schriften*, 135–36.

41. Ibid.

42. Cf. Gilbert, *Johann Gustav Droysen*, 85–86; Meinecke, *Weltbürgerthum und Nationalstaat*, 307–14.

43. Duncker, *Reichsversammlung*, 1–6.

44. Haym, *Aus meinem Leben*, 184–85.

45. Haym, *Ausgewählter Briefwechsel*, 37–38.

46. Ibid.

47. Duncker, *Reichsversammlung*, 1–6.

48. Ibid., 36–38.

49. Sybel, "Ueber das Reichsgrundgesetz der XVII Vertrauensmänner," (Marburg, 1848), 3.

50. Ibid., 5.

51. Ibid. 6.

52. Ibid., 7–8.

53. Ibid.

54. Ibid., 12–13.

55. Ibid., 11–12.

56. Varrentrapp, "Biographische Einleitung," 52–53.

57. Sybel, "Reichsgrundgesetz," 12.

58. Ibid., 14.

59. [Sybel et al.], "An die Bewohner der Provinz Oberhessen," Marburg, 17 May 1848, Marburg Universitätsbibliothek Flugschriften no. 84.

60. Sybel, "Reichsgrundgesetz," 14.

5. In the National Assembly: May to August

1. Droysen, *Aktenstücke und Aufzeichnungen*, 810; Rudolf Haym, *Die deutsche Nationalversammlung*, 3 vols. (Frankfort, 1848 for vol. 1; Berlin: Gärtner, 1849–50 for vols. 2 and 3), 1:9–10; cf. Frank Eyck, *The Frankfort Parliament 1848–1849* (New York, 1968), 103–4.

2. Droysen, *Briefwechsel* 1:422.

3. Droysen, *Aktenstücke und Aufzeichnungen*, 811.

4. Droysen, *Briefwechsel* 1:424, 428.

5. Haym, *Ausgewählter Briefwechsel*, 41; idem, *Aus meinem Leben*, 186–87.

6. Haym, *Max Duncker*, 85–86; Duncker, *Reichsversammlung*, 2.

7. Haym, *Max Duncker*, 86–87.

8. Haym, *Aus meinem Leben*, 189; idem, *Deutsche Nationalversammlung* 1:i–iii.

9. Haym, *Ausgewählter Briefwechsel*, 50–51.

10. Heinrich Laube, *Das erste deutsche Parlament*, 3 vols. (Leipzig, 1849), 2:35.

11. Droysen, *Briefwechsel* 1:441.

12. Ibid. 1:416.

13. Cf. Ernst Rudolf Huber, *Deutsche Verfassungsgeschichte seit 1789*, 4 vols. (Stuttgart, 1960–68), 2:619–21; Andreas Frahm, "Paulskirche und Volkssouveränität," in *Historische Zeitschrift* (1924), 130:222–27.

14. Veit Valentin, *Geschichte der deutschen Revolution von 1848–1849*, 2 vols. (Berlin, 1931), 1:528–30.

15. Droysen, *Aktenstücke und Aufzeichnungen*, 807.

16. Droysen, *Politische Schriften*, 138–39.

17. Ibid., 141.

18. Ibid., 138–39, 145–48, 150–51, 155–56.

19. Ibid. 138–41.

20. Duncker, *Reichsversammlung*, 9; Haym, *Deutsche Nationalversammlung* 1:8–9.

21. [Sybel et al.], "Kurfürstliches Staatsministerium!," Marburg, 13 May 1848, Marburg Universitätsbibliothek Flugschriften, nos. 85, 86.

22. Droysen, *Aktenstücke und Aufzeichnungen*, 809.

23. *Stenographischer Bericht über die Verhandlungen der deutschen constituierenden Nationalversammlung zu Frankfurt am Main*, ed. Franz Wigard (Frankfurt, 1848), 1:17.

24. Haym, *Ausgewählter Briefwechsel*, 4, 52–54.

25. Ludwig Bergsträsser, *Geschichte der politischen Parteien in Deutschland*, ed. Wilhelm Mommsen, 11th ed. (Munich and Vienna, 1965), 80–81; Eyck, *Frankfurt Parliament*, 149; Helmut Kramer, *Fraktionsbindungen in den deutschen Volksvertretungen 1819–1849* (Berlin, 1968), 78–80, 284.

26. Kramer, *Fraktionsbindungen*, 78–80.

27. Ibid., 92–98, 141–43; Bergsträsser, *Politischen Parteien*, 80–81.

28. Droysen, *Aktenstücke und Aufzeichnungen*, 808, 810, 812, 815; Haym, *Ausgewählter Briefwechsel*, 42, 50; Kramer, *Fraktionsbindungen*, 78–82, 277–78.

29. Kramer, *Fraktionsbindungen*, 77–78.

30. Droysen, *Aktenstücke und Aufzeichnungen*, 810–13, 815, 817–19; Haym, *Ausgewählter Briefwechsel*, 49–50; idem, *Aus meinem Leben*, 193–94.

31. Droysen, *Aktenstücke und Aufzeichnungen*, 812, 815; Haym, *Ausgewählter Briefwechsel*, 50.

32. Haym, *Aus meinem Leben*, 192–93; idem, *Max Duncker*, 90.

33. *Verzeichniss derjenigen Abgeordneten, die sich bis zum 11. August 1848 zur Theilnahme an der Reichsversammlung angemeldet und legitimirt haben* (Frankfort, 1848).

34. Droysen, *Aktenstücke und Aufzeichnungen*, 810–11; Duncker, *Heinrich von Gagern* (Leipzig, 1850), passim; Haym, *Ausgewählter Briefwechsel*, 40–41; Haym, *Deutsche Nationalversammlung* 2:168–69; cf. Eyck, *Frankfort Parliament*, 102–13.

35. Droysen, *Briefwechsel* 1:424–25; Haym, *Ausgewählter Briefwechsel*, 40. See also, Haym, *Deutsche Nationalversammlung* 1:8–10.

36. Droysen, ed., *Die Verhandlungen des Verfassungsausschußes der deutschen Nationalversammlung* (Leipzig, 1849), pt. 1, 15–17; cf. Fenske, *Johann Gustav Droysen*, 130.

37. Droysen, *Aktenstücke und Aufzeichnungen*, 817.

38. Ibid., 818; idem, *Verhandlungen*, 3, 33; Duncker, *Reichsversammlung*, 36–37; Haym, *Deutsche Nationalversammlung* 1:47–67.

39. *Stenographischer Bericht* 1:18; Eyck, *Frankfort Parliament*, 113–33; Huber, *Deutsche Verfassungsgeschichte* 2:622; Valentin, *Deutsche Revolution* 2:16–18.

40. Droysen, *Aktenstücke und Aufzeichnungen*, 811.

41. *Stenographischer Bericht* 1:62.

42. Eyck, *Frankfort Parliament*, 121–25; Valentin, *Deutsche Revolution* 2:19–20.

43. *Stenographischer Bericht* 1:114.

44. Ibid. 1:125.

45. Ibid. 1:115–16; Droysen, *Politische Schriften*, 146; Duncker, *Reichsversammlung*, 15–16; Haym, *Deutsche Nationalversammlung* 1:15.

46. Haym, *Deutsche Nationalversammlung* 2:17.

47. Ibid. 1:15.

48. Haym, *Ausgewählter Briefwechsel*, 39.

49. Droysen, *Briefwechsel*, 428.

50. Haym, *Deutsche Nationalversammlung* 1:16.

51. Droysen, *Briefwechsel*, 428–29.

52. Haym, *Ausgewählter Briefwechsel*, 40–41.

53. *Stenographischer Bericht* 1:201.

54. Cf. Eyck, *Frankfort Parliament*, 164–69, 185.

55. Bergsträsser, *Politischen Parteien*, 79–81; Haym, *Aus meinem Leben*, 193–94; Haym, *Deutsche Nationalversammlung* 1:39–46; Kramer, *Fraktionsbindungen*, 74–80; Laube, *Deutsche Parlament* 1:241–43.

56. *Stenographischer Bericht* 1:385; Duncker, *Reichsversammlung*, 9; Haym, *Ausgewählter Briefwechsel*, 42; Haym, *Deutsche Nationalversammlung* 1:19–20.

57. Droysen, *Politische Schriften*, 156; Haym, *Ausgewählter Briefwechsel*, 43.

58. *Stenographischer Bericht* 1:356–59.

59. *Stenographischer Bericht* 1:384–85.

60. Ibid.

61. Haym, *Ausgewählter Briefwechsel*, 27, 42, 44; idem, *Deutsche Nationalversammlung* 1:22.

62. Droysen, *Briefwechsel*, 429.

63. Droysen, *Aktenstücke und Aufzeichnungen*, 815.

64. Droysen, *Briefwechsel*, 429.

65. *Stenographsicher Bericht* 1:397–98.

66. Duncker, *Reichsversammlung*, 11–12.

67. Droysen, *Briefwechsel*, 441–43, 459–60; Duncker, *Reichsversammlung*, 11–12; Haym, *Max Duncker*, 89.

68. Haym, *Ausgewählter Briefwechsel*, 48–49.

69. *Stenographischer Bericht* 1:521–22, 593–95, 598–601; Eyck, *Frankfurt Parliament*, 189–92.

70. Droysen, *Briefwechsel* 1:489; idem, *Politische Schriften*, 148; Haym, *Ausgewählter Briefwechsel*, 48.

71. *Stenographischer Bericht* 1:576–81.

72. Duncker, *Reichsversammlung*, 11–12.

73. Droysen, *Aktenstücke und Aufzeichnungen*, 816.

74. *Stenographischer Bericht* 1:581–84.

75. Droysen, *Aktenstücke und Aufzeichnungen*, 816.

76. Haym, *Max Duncker*, 87–88; Duncker, *Reichsversammlung*, 9–12.

77. Haym, *Ausgewählter Briefwechsel*, 51.

78. Droysen, *Aktenstücke und Aufzeichnungen*, 818.

79. Droysen, *Briefwechsel*, 440–41.

80. Haym, *Deutsche Nationalversammlung* 1:95–96.

81. Droysen, *Politische Schriften*, 147.

82. Haym, *Ausgewählter Briefwechsel*, 55–56.

83. Rudolf Stadelmann, *Soziale und politische Geschichte der Revolution von 1848* (Darmstadt, 1962), 122–23; Valentin, *Deutsche Revolution* 2:73–74.

84. Cf. Duncker, *Reichsversammlung*, 17–18; Haym, *Deutsche Nationalversammlung* 1:95–98.

85. Droysen, *Aktenstücke und Aufzeichnungen*, 817–20; Droysen, *Briefwechsel*, 445–46, 457.

86. Eyck, *Frankfort Parliament*, 204–5; Huber, *Deutsche Verfassungsgeschichte* 2:651–55.

87. Droysen, *Aktenstücke und Aufzeichnungen*, 204–5; Haym, *Max Duncker*, 88–89.

88. Veit Valentin, *Fürst Karl Leiningen und das deutsche Einheitsproblem* (Stuttgart, 1910), 107–9.

89. Droysen, *Aktenstücke und Aufzeichnungen*, 823.

90. Droysen, *Briefwechsel*, 442–43. See also, ibid., 438–39.

91. Ibid., 443–45.

92. *Stenographischer Bericht* 2:817–29; Droysen, *Aktenstücke und Aufzeichnungen*, 819–20.

93. Droysen, *Briefwechsel*, 451–52.

94. Ibid., 449–51.

95. Droysen, *Verhandlungen*, 66; cf. Fenske, *Johann Gustav Droysen*, 134–35.

96. Droysen, *Aktenstücke und Aufzeichnungen*, 820.

97. Unsigned, "Die deutsche Zentralgewalt und die preußische Armee. Geschrieben am 23. Juli 1848" (Berlin: Decker, 1848). I have been unable to locate an extant copy of this work. There is, however, a detailed summary in the prewar work: Paul Wentzcke, *Kritische Bibliographie der Flugschriften zur deutschenerfassungsfrage 1848–1851*, repro. ed (Hildesheim, 1967) no. 364, 104.

98. Droysen, *Aktenstücke und Aufzeichnungen*, 821–22; Haym, *Deutsche Nationalversammlung* 1:95; idem, *Max Duncker*, 88–89.

99. Droysen, *Aktenstücke und Aufzeichnungen*, 818–22.

100. Haym, *Ausgewählter Briefwechsel*, 51–57.

101. Droysen, *Politische Schriften*, 166.

102. Ibid., 166–67.

103. Ibid.

104. Droysen, *Aktenstücke und Aufzeichnungen*, 823.

105. Ibid.

106. Droysen, *Briefwechsel*, 460.

107. Ibid., 468–69, 478.

108. Haym, *Max Duncker*, 88–89.

109. Duncker, *Politischer Briefwechsel*, 2–3; Droysen, *Aktenstücke und Aufzeichnungen*, 822–23; Haym, *Aus meinem Leben*, 188; Haym, *Deutsche Nationalversammlung* 1:99–104.

110. Haym, "Bericht an seinen Wähler," 12 August 1848, extensively quoted in Rosenberg, *Rudolf Haym*, 136–37.

111. Haym, *Ausgewählter Briefwechsel*, 57.

6. Crisis and Reconstruction

1. Duncker, *Reichsversammlung*, 33–34; Haym, *Deutsche Nationalversammlung* 1:105–11; Meetz, *Johann Gustav Droysens Thätigkeit politische*, 13–44.

2. *Stenographischer Bericht* 1:299–305; cf. Haym, *Nationalversammlung* 1:105.

3. Droysen, *Politische Schriften*, 163, 165–66, 168–71.

4. Duncker, *Reichsversammlung*, 34; Haym, *Nationalversammlung* 1:115–16. For Duncker's parliamentary speech on the subject, see *Stenographischer Bericht* 2:817.

5. Droysen, *Briefwechsel* 1:430–31, 457; Duncker, *Reichsversammlung*, 33; Haym, *Deutsche Nationalversammlung* 1:106–11.

6. Otto Brandt, *Geschichte Schleswig-Holsteins. Ein Grundriß*, 4th ed. (Kiel, 1949), 176–78; Carr, *Schleswig-Holstein 1815–1848*, 291–94; Eyck, *Frankfurt Parliament*, 288–311; Huber, *Deutsche Verfassungsgeschichte* 2:673–81; Volker Weimar, *Der Malmöer Waffenstillstand von 1848* (Neumünster, 1959, 46–50.

7. *Stenographischer Bericht* 2:817.

8. Droysen, *Briefwechsel*, 463; idem, *Aktenstücke und Aufzeichnungen*, 826; Haym, *Ausgewählter Briefwechsel*, 58–59; Rosenberg, *Rudolf Haym*, 140–41.

9. Eyck, *Frankfort Parliament*, 294–95.

10. *Stenographischer Bericht* 3; 1915; Duncker, *Reichsversammlung*, 34; Haym, *Deutsche Nationalversammlung* 1:114–17.

11. Droysen, *Briefwechsel* 1:464.

12. Ibid. 1:468–69.

13. *Stenographischer Bericht* 3; 2149–54.

14. Droysen, *Briefwechsel* 1:468–69; Haym, *Ausgewählter Briefwechsel*, 59.

15. Haym, *Max Duncker* (Berlin: Gärtner, 1891), 91.

16. Duncker, *Reichsversammlung*, 34.

17. Haym, *Ausgewählter Briefwechsel*, 59.

18. Droysen, *Briefwechsel*, 463–64.

19. Ibid. 1:467.

20. Ibid., 468–69.

21. Haym, *Ausgewählter Briefwechsel*, 59–60. Cf. idem, *Deutsche Nationalversammlung* 1:139–40; idem, *Aus meinem Leben*, 139–40; Duncker, *Reichsversammlung*, 35–36.

22. No longer extant, the report is quoted extensively in Rosenberg, *Rudolf Haym*, 141–43.

23. Duncker, *Politischer Briefwechsel*, 4; Haym, *Deutsche Nationalversammlung* 1:157–59.

24. Droysen, *Aktenstücke und Aufzeichnungen*, 835; Haym, *Ausgewählter Briefwechsel*, 57–59.

25. Haym, *Deutsche Nationalversammlung* 1:153–56. The text of the program may also be found in Felix Solomon, *Die deutsche Parteiprogramme*, Heft I (Leipzig and Berlin, 1907), 26.

26. Duncker, *Reichsversammlung*, 14; Droysen, *Briefwechsel* 1:483.

27. Haym, *Ausgewählter Briefwechsel*, 57.

28. Ibid.

29. Droysen, *Briefwechsel* 1:468–69.

30. Fenske, *Johann Gustav Droysen*, 141–42; Anton Springer, *Friedrich Christoph Dahlmann*, 2 vols. (Leipzig, 1872), 2:306–10.

31. *Stenographischer Bericht* 4:2918–23, 2933–36.

32. Droysen, *Verhandlungen*, 312–13; idem, *Briefwechsel* 1:495; Haym, *Deutsche Nationalversammlung* 2:59.

33. Droysen, *Politische Schriften*, 169–71; idem, *Briefwechsel* 1:443.

34. Droysen, *Briefwechsel* 1:468–69; idem, *Politische Schriften*, 173–74.

35. Cf. Heinrich Ritter von Srbik, *Deutsche Einheit. Idee und Wirklichkeit vom Heiligen Reich bis Königgrätz*, repro. of 1933 ed., 4 vols. (Darmstadt, 1963), 1:369–71.

36. Laube, *Deutsche Parlament* 3:50–51.

37. Droysen, *Briefwechsel* 1:469.

38. Heidrun von Möller, *Großdeutsch und Kleindeutsch. Die Entstehung der Wörter in den Jahre 1848–1849* (Berlin, 1937), 18–24, 49–50.

39. Droysen, *Briefwechsel* 1:439, 441–44; idem, *Politische Schriften*, 147; Haym, *Deutsche Nationalversammlung* 2:112–14; Duncker, *Reichsversammlung*, 71.

40. Haym, *Deutsche Nationalversammlung* 2:51–55. Cf. Rudolf Kiszling, *Die Revolution in Kaisertum Österreich 1848–1849*, 2 vols. (Vienna, 1948), 1:220–35.

41. Droysen, *Politische Schriften*, 173–76; idem, *Briefwechsel* 1:495–97.

42. Droysen, *Briefwechsel* 1:469; Walther Ulbricht, *Bunsen und die deutsche Einheitsbewegung* (Leipzig, 1910), 66–69.

43. Haym, *Deutsche Nationalversammlung* 2:51–54.

44. Rudolf Kiszling, *Fürst Felix zu Schwarzenberg. Der politische Lehrmeister Franz Josephs* (Graz and Cologne, 1952), 55–58; idem, *Revolution in Kaisertum Österreich* 1:306–7; Srbik, *Deutsche Einheit* 1:389.

45. Droysen, *Aktenstücke und Aufzeichnungen*, 834.

46. Duncker, *Reichsversammlung*, 71; Haym, *Deutsche Nationalversammlung* 2:113–14.

47. Duncker, *Politischer Briefwechsel*, 6–8; Haym, *Deutsche Nationalversammlung* 2:141–43.

48. Valentin, *Deutschen Revolution* 2:229–60; Friedrich Frahm, "Entstehungs- und Entwicklungsgeschichte der preußischen Verfassung," in *Forschungen zur Brandenburgischen und Preußischen Geschichte* (1928), 41:264–71.

49. Valentin, *Deutsche Revolution* 2:263–73.

50. Droysen, *Aktenstücke und Aufzeichnungen*, 826–31; *Briefwechsel* 1:477.

51. Droysen, *Aktenstücke und Aufzeichnungen*, 829; Haym, *Deutsche Nationalversammlung* 2:24.

52. Droysen, *Aktenstücke und Aufzeichnungen*, 828.

53. Haym, *Ausgewählter Briefwechsel*, 60.

54. Haym, *Deutsche Nationalversammlung* 2:17.

55. Haym, *Max Duncker*, 93–94; cf. Duncker, *Reichsversammlung*, 15.

56. Droysen, *Briefwechsel* 1:477–78; Duncker, *Reichsversammlung*, 15–16; Haym, *Deutsche Nationalversammlung* 2:18–19.

57. Haym, *Max Duncker*, 93–94.

58. Haym, *Ausgewählter Briefwechsel*, 60.

59. Quoted from: Rosenberg, *Rudolf Haym*, 149; cf. idem, "Bassermanns Bericht und die Abgesandten aus der Berliner Nationalversammlung," in *Extrablatt zu den Flugblättern aus der deutschen Nationalversammlung*, no. 12, Frankfort, Wednesday, 30 November 1848; Haym, *Deutsche Nationalversammlung* 2:16.

60. Haym, *Ausgewählter Briefwechsel*, 58.

61. Droysen, *Aktenstücke und Aufzeichnungen*, 831; idem, *Briefwechsel* 1:475–76.

62. Droysen, *Briefwechsel* 1:472.

63. Ibid. 1:474–75; idem, *Aktenstücke und Aufzeichnungen*, 828; Duncker, *Reichsversammlung*, 17; Haym, *Deutsche Nationalversammlung* 2:19–20.

64. *Stenographischer Bericht* 5:3303, 3308, 3313, 3316; Droysen, *Briefwechsel* 1:482; Duncker, *Reichsversammlung*, 16; Haym, *Deutsche Nationalversammlung* 2:21–26, 38.

65. Daniel Friedrich Bassermann, *Denkwürdigkeiten. 1811–1851* (Frankfort: Frankfurter Verlags-Anstalt, 1926), 258–80; Frahm, "Entstehungs- und Entwicklungsgeschichte," 276–79; Gilbert, *Johann Gustav Droysen*, 108–12; Meinecke, *Weltbürgerthum und Nationalstaat*, 331–48.

66. Droysen, *Briefwechsel* 1:474.

67. Ibid. 1:476.

68. Gilbert, *Johann Gustav Droysen*, 111.

69. Droysen, *Aktenstücke und Aufzeichungnen*, 830–34.

70. Droysen, *Briefwechsel* 1:477–78.

71. Duncker, "Bericht der von der Gesellschaft im Casino zur Betrachtung der Oberhauptsfrage niedergesetzten Commission," reprinted in Droysen, *Aktenstücke und Aufzeichnungen*, 727–35.

72. Ibid., 835.

73. Ibid.; Droysen, *Briefwechsel* 1:504; idem, *Politische Schriften*, 103, 186; Duncker, *Reichsversammlung*, 72; Haym, *Deutsche Nationalversammlung* 2:228; *Stenographischer Bericht* 6:4437.

74. Droysen, *Politische Schriften*, 183.

75. Droysen, *Briefwechsel* 1:482.

76. Droysen, *Aktenstücke und Aufzeichnungen*, 835, 837.

77. Droysen, *Politische Schriften*, 181.

78. Ibid.

79. Eyck, *Frankfurt Parliament*, 358–59.

80. Droysen, *Politische Schriften*, 181.

81. Ibid., 183.

82. Ibid., 178–79.

83. Ibid., 179–81.

84. Ibid., 180–81.

85. Droysen, *Briefwechsel* 1:483.

86. Droysen, *Politische Schriften*, 180–81.

87. Droysen, *Briefwechsel* 1:505.

88. Ibid.

89. Ibid. 1:496–97.

90. Ibid. 1:508.

91. Ibid. 1:489.

92. Droysen, *Politische Schriften*, 184.

93. Droysen, *Briefwechsel* 1:483.

94. Haym, *Max Duncker*, 98–100.

95. Haym, *Deutsche Nationalversammlung* 2:140–43.

96. Duncker, "Bericht," in Droysen, *Aktenstücke und Aufzeichnungen*, 727–29.

97. Ibid., 729.

98. Ibid., 731.

99. Ibid., 732–34.

100. Ibid., 734–35.

101. Duncker, *Politischer Briefwechsel*, 7.

102. Ibid., 8–9.

103. Ibid., 7.

104. Duncker, *Reichsversammlung*, 73–74.

105. Duncker, *Politischer Briefwechsel*, 7.

106. Haym, *Max Duncker*, 98–100; idem, *Deutsche Nationalversammlung* 2:217–29.

107. *Stenographischer Bericht* 6:4436.

108. Ibid. 6:4437–38.

109. Ibid. 6:4438.

110. Ibid.

111. Haym, *Ausgewählter Briefwechsel*, 61; idem, "Bericht an seinen Wähler," 167.

112. Haym, *Ausgewählter Briefwechsel*, 61–62.

113. Ibid., 64.

114. Ibid.

115. Ibid.

116. Ibid., 67–68, 71–73.

117. Ibid., 78.

118. Sybel, "Reichsgrundgesetz," 14.

119. Varrentrapp, "Biographische Eineitung," 73–79.

120. Droysen, *Briefwechsel* 1:510.

121. Ibid. 1:510–11, 516.

7. Toward the Prussian School

1. The standard work on Radowitz remains Friedrich Meinecke's classic *Radowitz und die deutsche Revolution* (Berlin, 1913), passim and esp. chap. 1.

2. Fritz Hartung, *Deutsche Verfassungsgeschichte vom 15. Jahrhundert bis zur Gegenwart*, 8th ed. (Stuttgart, 1950), 215; Huber, *Deutsche Verfassungsgeschichte* 2:885ff; Sheehan, *German History 1770–1866*, 712.

3. Manfred Botzenhart, *Deutscher Parlamentarismus in der Revolutionszeit, 1849–49* (Düsseldorf, 1977), 723; Haym, *Max Dunckers*, 118–19.

4. Haym, *Max Duncker*, 117.

5. Sheehan, *German History*, 714–17.

6. Droysen, *Briefwechsel* 1:541, 557.

7. Ibid. 1:544–45, 547–48.

8. Ibid. 1:547–48.

9. Haym, *Max Duncker*, 101.

10. Haym, *Aus meinem Leben*, 198.

11. Ibid., 122, 125–27; Droysen, *Briefwechsel* 1:653, 672–73, 687.

12. Haym, *Max Duncker*, 107–9.

13. Droysen, *Briefwechsel* 1:542–43, 546–49, 550–57, 559–61; Max Duncker, "Johann Gustav Droysen," in *Abhandlungen aus der neueren Geschichte* (Leipzig, 1887), 376–77.

14. Droysen, *Briefwechsel* 1:714.

15. Ibid. 1:553, 556.

16. Ibid. 1:561.

17. Ibid. 1:658–60, 662–63, 670, 678.

18. Haym, *Ausgewählter Briefwechsel*, 81, 85; *Aus meinem Leben*, 203–10; *Max Duncker*, 108, 118.

19. Haym, *Max Duncker*, 115, 127.

20. Ibid., 105.

21. Droysen, *Briefwechsel* 1:545–46.

22. Droysen, *Briefwechsel* 1:547–49; Haym, *Ausgewählter Briefwechsel*, 22; idem, *Max Duncker*, 118–19.

23. Haym, *Max Duncker*, 109–10.

24. Ibid., 116–17.

25. Droysen, *Briefwechsel* 1:554; Haym, *Max Duncker*, 110f.

26. Haym, *Max Duncker*, 117.

27. Droysen, *Briefwechsel* 1:626.

28. Ibid. 1:548; also quoted in Haym, *Max Duncker*, 108.

29. Droysen, *Briefwechsel* 1:554, 647–48; Duncker, *Politischer Briefwechsel*, 16; Haym, *Max Duncker*, 119.

30. Haym, *Max Duncker*, 117.

31. Duncker, *Reichsversammlung*; idem, *Heinrich von Gagern*.

32. Ibid., 136–44; Duncker, *Vier Wochen auswärtiger Politik* (Berlin, 1851) and *Vier Monaten auswärtiger Politik* (Berlin, 1851).

33. Droysen, *Briefwechsel* 1:547.

34. Ibid. 1:650; Haym, *Max Duncker*, 122.

35. Ibid. 1:563–64, 640, 648, 668, 690–91.

36. Ibid. 1:678, 682.

37. Ibid. 1:615–16, 668, 690–91.

38. Droysen, *Politische Schriften*, 287.

39. Ibid. 1:738.

40. Droysen, *Geschichte der preußischen Politik*, 16 vols. (Berlin, 1855–86); idem, *Das Leben des Feldmarschall Grafen York von Wartenburg*, vol. 1 (Berlin, 1851), vols. 1 and 2, rev. eds. (Berlin: Veit, 1854).

41. Ibid. 1:615–16.

42. Droysen, *Briefwechsel* 1:697. Droysen was too late; Müffling had just died: ibid. 1:699.

43. Droysen, "Preußen und das System der Großmächte. Gutachten eines Schleswig-Holsteiners" (Berlin, 1849). The piece was reprinted, with some revi-

sions in idem, *Zur neueren Geschichte* (Leipzig, 1876) and in its original form, with later changes noted in idem, *Politische Schriften.*

44. Droysen, *Briefwechsel* 1:556, 564, 572, 574, 583, 616; idem, *Politische Schriften,* 285.

45. Droysen, *Politische Schriften,* 216.

46. Ibid., 212.

47. Ibid. 224–25.

48. Droysen, *Briefwechsel* 1:545–46, 552, 556.

49. Droysen, *Politische Schriften,* 222.

50. Ibid., 213.

51. Ibid., 214.

52. Ibid., 218.

53. Ibid., 227.

54. Ibid., 229; for the Dove claim, see Droysen, *Briefwechsel* 1:556 n. 2.

55. Droysen, *Politische Schriften,* 320.

56. Duncker, "Johann Gustav Droysen," 390.

57. Duncker, "Johann Gustav Droysen," 379–80, 389–91.

58. Duncker, *York von Wartenburg* 1:1.

59. Hintze, "Johann Gustav Droysen," 480–81.

60. Droysen, *Briefwechsel* 1:754.

61. Droysen, *Geschichte der preußischen Politik* 1:iii.

62. Droysen, *Briefwechsel* 1:668.

63. Ibid. 1:754.

64. Cf. Georg Iggers, *The German Conception of History* (Middletown, Ct. 1968), 114–15.

65. Sybel, *Die Begründung des deutschen Reiches durch Wilhelm I,* 4th ed., 6 vols. (Munich and Berlin, 1901), 1:ix–xi; "Ueber die Entwicklung der absoluten Monarchie in Preußen," in idem, *Kleine historische Schriften* (Stuttgart, 1880), 517–57.

66. Droysen, *Briefwechsel* 1:755.

67. Ibid. 1:775–76, 782–84.

68. Ibid. 2:9–10, 13.

69. Ibid. 2:168–69.

70. Haym, *Aus meinem Leben,* 204, 206–8; idem, *Das Leben Max Duncker,* 118–19.

71. Haym, *Aus meinem Leben,* 202.

72. Ibid., 212–16.

73. Ibid., 216–17.

74. Haym, *Max Duncker,* 152.

75. Haym, *Aus meinem Leben,* 223–24; ibid., 150–52.

76. Haym, *Aus meinem Leben,* p 217, 225.

77. Haym, *Max Duncker,* 142–43.

78. Ibid., 113–14, 120.

79. Duncker, *Geschichte des Alterthums;* Haym, *Max Duncker,* 146.

80. Haym, *Max Duncker,* 150–52.

81. Droysen, *Briefwechsel* 1:714.

82. Ibid. 2:201, 207.

83. Ibid. 2:203–6.

84. Ibid. 2:201.

85. Ibid. 2:207.

Suggested Readings

The following is a selective list of secondary literature for further exploration of major topics in the preceding discussion. It is not intended to be a complete bibliography. I have tried to suggest titles that are gateways to further study of particular topics. Most of these works provide bibliography for study in depth. Many of these titles do not appear in my citations, because I used those to acknowledge specific debts. Conversely, I have not listed here all secondary literature cited above. Primary texts appear below only when they also serve as secondary texts.

Historians of the Prussian School

Interesting, insightful, and synthetic, but limited to 1848 and its preparation, is Wolfgang Hock, *Liberales Denken im Zeitalter der Paulskirche* (Münster, 1957). Those who are interested in Droysen's mature historical theory, the eventual product of the development traced above, should go directly to his *Historik. Vorlesungen über Enzyklopädie und Methodologie der Geschichte,* ed. R. Hübner, 5th ed. (Darmstadt, 1967). These are the lectures he gave at Berlin until the 1880s and continuously revised; hence, they show where he came out, not where he entered, as a theorist. The *Grundriß* portion has been published in English as *Outlines of the Principles of History* (Boston, 1893). His son, Gustav Droysen—himself a historian of some note—wrote the first half of a good biography of his father, *Johann Gustav Droysen. Bis zu Beginn der Frankfurter Tätigkeit* (Leipzig and Berlin, 1910). Droysen's career as a whole is described, in necessary brevity, in his student Otto Hintze's biographic essay "Johann Gustav Droysen" in *Soziologie und Geschichte. Gesammelte Abhandlungen zur Soziologie, Politik und Theorie der Geschichte,* ed. Gerhard Oestreich (Göttingen, 1964). Reading the entirety of the massive Droysen *Briefwechsel* (2 vols., ed. Rudolf Hübner [Berlin, 1929]) provides the equivalent of biography.

The best work on Droysen's political theory, though I think it suffers from its ahistorical organization, is Günther Birtsch, *Die Nation als sittliche Begriff. Der Nationalstaatsbegriff in Geschichtsschreibung und politischer Gedankenwelt Johann Gustav Droysens* (Cologne and Graz, 1964). Still commanding, fifty years later, as an explanation of Droysen's Prussian politics is Felix Gilbert's *Johann Gustav Droysen und die preußisch-deutsche Frage* (Berlin, 1933). Part of it has been translated and reprinted in Gilbert, *History: Choice and Commitment* (Cambridge, Mass., 1977), 17–38. Gilbert is famous in this country for his work in Renaissance and diplomatic history. Before he emigrated from Nazi Germany, he worked on Droysen—friend and tutor of his ancestor Felix Mendelssohn.

The politics of Schleswig-Holstein are terribly complicated. Anni Meetz tried to explain what Droysen was doing there in *Johann Gustav Droysens politische Tätigkeit in der Schleswig-Holsteinischen Frage* (Erlangen, 1931). It would be well to supplement Meetz with W. Carr, *Schleswig-Holstein 1815–1848. A Study in National Conflict* (Manchester, 1963). Carr, who became interested in the duchies while in military service there at the end of the war, continually mentions Droysen. Because Carr writes as one who at first understood nothing, he is wonderfully clear in his explanations. See also R. S. Elkar, *Junges Deutschland in polemischen Zeitalter: Das schleswig-holsteinische Bildungsbürgertum in der ersten hälfte des 19. Jahrhunderts* (Düsseldorf, 1979).

Droysen's historical theory is ably discussed in terms of its continued relevance in Jörn Rüsen, *Begriffene Geschichte. Genesis und Begründung der Geschichtstheorie J. G. Droysens* (Paderborn, 1969). Rüsen also discusses Droysen's political thought in "Politisches Denken und Geschichtswissenschaft bei J. G. Droysen" in *Politische Ideologie und nationalstaatliche Ordnung. Studien zur Geschichte des 19. Jahrhunderts. Festschrift für Theodor Schieder*, ed. K. Kluxen and W. Mommsen (Munich and Berlin, 1968). I discuss Droysen's theological views in "Theology in Droysen's Political Historiography: Free Will, Necessity, and the Historian" in *History and Theory* 3 (1979): 378–96. On Droysen's puzzling silence about Judaism as a source for Christianity, see Arnaldo Momigliano, "J.G. Droysen between Greeks and Jews," in *Essays in Ancient and Modern Historiography* (Middletown, Conn., 1977), 307–25. Momigliano explains that Droysen's wife (like Max Duncker's) was a sincere convert to Christianity who remained interested in Judaism. Droysen's background in philology is discussed in detail in Benedetto Bravo, *Philosophie, histoire, philosophie de l'histoire. Etude sur J. G. Droysen historien de l'antiquité* (Wroclaw, 1968). These works, of course, will refer the reader to yet more literature on Droysen.

His colleagues, unfortunately, are less written about. For Duncker there is Haym's engaging but, of course, uncritical *Das Leben Max Duncker* (Berlin, 1891). There is also an article in *Allgemeine Deutsche Biographie*, 1817–44 (Frankfurt, 1959). These should be supplemented with the letters and notes in Duncker, *Politischer Briefwechsel aus seinem Nachlaß* , ed. Johannes Schulze (Leipzig, 1923). It is at least amusing to see a devoted, fictional portrait of Duncker as a kid in the family novel by Dora Duncker, *Das Haus Duncker. Ein Buchhändlerroman aus der Biedermeierzeit* (Berlin, 1918). Haym told his own story, and told it well, in *Aus meinem Leben. Erinnerungen aus der Nachlaß herausgegeben* (Berlin, 1902). As in his account of Duncker's life, however, Haym treats the events of his life through the crisis of 1848 and 1849 as the conquest of naïveté by hard-won wisdom. There is also Hans Rosenberg's excellent *Habilitationschrift*, which he wrote in tandem with editing Haym's letters for publication and just before his departure from Nazi Germany, *Rudolf Haym und die Anfänge des klassischen Liberalismus* (Munich, 1933). Both Haym's and Duncker's work for the *Preußische Jahrbücher* are discussed in the old but still important group portrait by Otto Westphal, *Welt und Staatsauffassung des deutschen Liberalismus. Eine Untersuchung über die Preußischen Jahrbücher und den konstitutionellen Liberalismus in Deutschland von 1858 bis 1863* (Munich, 1919). Sybel's political philosophy is impressively and cogently analyzed by Hellmut Seier, *Die Staatsidee Heinrich von Sybels in den Wandlungen der Reichsgründungszeit* (Lübeck, 1961), an early and admirable example of German's postwar examinations of political presuppositions. For a hostile Marxist view, see Hans Schleier, *Sybel und Treitschke. Antidemo kratismus und Militarismus im historischen-politischen Denken großbourgeoiser Geschichtsideologen* (Berlin, 1965). Schleier's title succinctly restates his argument. Heinrich von Treitschke, whose historical career began after the period covered above, is analyzed from a very different perspective in Walter Bussmann, *Treitschke: Sein Welt und Geschichtsbild* (Göttingen, 1962). See, too, Andreas Dorpalen's biography *Heinrich von Treitschke* (New Haven, 1957). The one account of the largely like-minded but independent Ludwig Häusser is Annaliese Kaltenbach, *Orientation et définition du patriotisme allemand chez un historien de l'Allemagne du Sud: Le Palatin-Badois Ludwig Haeusser, 1818–1867* (Paris, 1965).

Historians in Nineteenth-century Germany

The more fully to place in context the historians of the Prussian School, it is necessary to read about major historians and historical thinkers (not always one and the same) who worked just before and during their careers. The best history of German historical writing in any language is Georg Iggers, *The German Conception of History* (Middletown, Conn., 1968). Iggers provides a cogent analytic narration of German historical ideas and provides his own very useful annotated bibliography. Also in English, well written, but inevitably dated, is G.P. Gooch's *History and Historians in the nineteenth Century* (London, 1914). Critical, Marxist analyses of German historians are available from the East German Joachim Streisand, ed., *Studien über die deutschen Geschichtswissenschaft*, 2 vols. (Berlin, 1963–65). Also useful is Heinrich Ritter von Srbik's misleadingly titled *Geist und Geschichte des deutschen Humanismus bis zur Gegenwart*, 2 vols. (Munich, 1950–51). Srbik sympathizes with the older, idealistic historiographic assumptions, though as an Austrian pan-German he did not approve of the politics of the Prussian School. His tone is curiously noncommittal, perhaps prudently, because he wrote while suspended from teaching on account of his earlier enthusiastic support of Hitler. Not in the least noncommittal is Georg von Below, *Die deutsche Geschichtsschreibung von den Befreiungskriegen bis zu unseren Tagen* (Berlin, 1916). An intellectual heir of the Prussian School, writing in the superheated patriotism of the First World War, he described these historians as they might have wished to be described. Somewhat similar in outlook is Eduard Fueter's very brief *Geschichte der neueren Historiographie*, 3d ed. (Munich, 1936).

The Prussian School's optimistic belief in historical purpose prevented its adherents from being historicists, but they shared many historicist assumptions. Indispensable for serious study, therefore, is Friedrich Meinecke's adoring but magisterial *Entstehung des Historismus*, available in a nicely readable English translation as *Historicism: The Rise of a New Historical Outlook* (London, 1972). Meinecke's *Weltbürgerthum and Nationalstaat*, also avaliable in English as *Cosmopolitanism and the National State* (Princeton, 1970), is also very useful for understanding the presuppositions of these historians. Also good on the subject of historicism is Carlo Antoni, *Lo Storicismo* (Rome, 1957), available in French as *L'historisme* (Geneva, 1963). *Historicism* is a slippery term. Helpful for definition is Dwight Lee and Robert Beck, "The Meaning of Historicism," in *American Historical Review* 59 (1953–54): 568–77. In searching for presuppositions, it is also revealing to study historians compositely in terms of their views on other nations. Heinz-Otto Sieburg, *Deutschland und Frankreich in der Geschichtsschreibung des 19. Jahrhundert,* 2 vols. (Wiesbaden, 1954–58) ably tells how Germans pictured the French and vice versa. Very useful, especially with respect to German misinterpretation of English constitutional history, is Charles McClelland, *The German Historians and England: A Study in Nineteenth-Century Views* (Cambridge, 1971). The much older work by Antoine Guilland, *L'Allemagne nouvelle et ses historiens. Niebuhr—Ranke—Mommsen—Sybel* (Paris, 1899), translated as *Modern Germany and her Historians* (London, 1915), gives a sense of how this looked from across the border. Michael Niemüller's *Liberalismus und Revolution. Das Problem der Revolution in der deutschen liberalen Geschichtsschreibung des 19. Jahrhunderts* (Düsseldorf, 1972) establishes convincingly the dominant Protestantism in these historians' outlook, and the instability of their idea of revolution. See also Andrew Lees, *Revolution and Reflection. Intellectual Change in Germany during the 1850's* (The Hague, 1974). Lees categorizes change and included many historians in his sample.

The historians of the Prussian School need to be contrasted with other practitioners with whom they did not agree. They differed from Ranke, with whom Duncker and Sybel studied, chiefly because he did not believe in progress; rather, every age was "immediate to God." See especially Carl Hinrichs, *Ranke und die Geschichtstheologie der Goethezeit* (Göttingen, 1954); Theodore von Laue, *Leopold von Ranke. The Formative Years* (Princeton, 1950); and Wilhelm Mommsen, *Stein, Ranke, Bismarck* (Munich, 1954). Mommsen is especially interesting because of his effort to recover a lost political-historical vocabulary. Hegel also belongs on this list, as a historical thinker, though not as a historian. Excellent for seeing what in Hegel attracted them is the Israeli scholar Shlomo Avineri's *Hegel's Theory of the Modern State* (Cambridge, 1972). Also useful is the older study by Hermann Heller, *Hegel und die nationale Staatsgedanke* (Leipzig and Berlin, 1921). Of course, what Hegel actually meant is less important than what his followers thought he meant. See Karl Löwith, *From Hegel to Nietzsche: The Revolution in Nineteenth Century Thought* (New York, 1964) and Herbert Marcuse, *Reason and Revolution: Hegel and the Rise of Social Theory* (New York, 1963). More recently, John Edward Toews does a first-rate job of tracing the history of hegelianism in *Hegelianism: The Path toward Dialectical Humanism 1805–1841* (Cambridge, 1980). Also see William J. Brazill, *The Young Hegelians* (New Haven, 1970). It is easy to study Droysen's teacher August Boeckh in *On Interpretation and Criticism,* ed. and trans. John Paul Pritchard (Norman, Okla., 1968). Their contemporary Theodor Mommsen, sometimes an ally and sometimes a critic, is ably discussed in Albert Wucher's suggestive *Theodor Mommsen. Geschichtsschreibung und Politik* (Göttingen, 1956). Wucher asks very important questions, and his notion of historical research as vicarious politics applies to these men at many points in their careers. Mommsen's life is exhaustively retold in Lothar Wickert's monumental *Theodor Mommsen. Eine Biographie,* 4 vols. (Frankfort, 1959–80). Both Droysen and Sybel personally were close to the older, more Whiggish Friedrich Christoph Dahlmann, discussed in Friedrich Heimpel, *Zwei Historiker. Friedrich Christoph Dahlmann. Jacob Burckhardt* (Göttingen, 1962). For a complete biography, see Anton Springer, *F. C. Dahlmann,* 2 vols. (Leipzig, 1870–71). See also Dahlmann's *Die Politik auf den Grund und das Mass der gegeben Zustände zurückgeführt,* ed. and intro. by Otto Westphal (Berlin, 1924).

History and Providence

For the purposes of this study, the following specimens of a very extensive literature are especially germane. Robert Nisbet, in the course of a sociological polemic, provides a vital distinction between development and progress in *Social Change and History: Aspects of the Western Theory of Development* (Oxford, 1969). A compact, reasoned overview of the history of providential history is Karl Löwith, *Meaning in History* (Chicago, 1949). J.G.A. Pocock provides a compelling history of the Augustinian basis of much prudential political thinking in his erudite *Machiavellian Moment: Florentine Political Thought and the Atlantic Republican Tradition* (Princeton, 1975). For some insights on philosophical historians' tastes, see Frank E. Manuel's "Leaps into Free Consciousness: Resonances from the German Academy," in *Shapes of Philosophical History* (Stanford, 1965). For an overwhelmingly sympathetic account of the consolations of Augustinian providentialism, read Charles Norris Cochrane, *Christianity and Classical Culture* (Oxford, 1940). For a more recent study, see R.A. Markus, *Saeculum: History and Society in the Theology of St. Augustine* (Cambridge, 1970).

German Academic Life

The historians of the Prussian School worked in a social as well as an intellectual context. Without pointing to the large and growing literature on the social history of nineteenth-century Germany, I want to recommend some important works in German academic history. Works that, in very different ways, deal critically with German universities in the Imperial Germany are Helmut Schelsky, *Einsamkeit und Freiheit: Idee und Gestalt der deutschen Universität und ihrer Reform* (Reinbek, 1963); Fritz Ringer, *The Decline of the German Mandarins. The German Academic Community, 1890–1933* (Cambridge, 1969); and Konrad H. Jarausch, *Students, Society and Politics in Imperial Germany. The Rise of Academic Illiberalism* (Princeton, 1982). For an explanation of the structure of German universities, the older work by Friedrich Paulsen, *Die deutschen Universitäten und das Universitätsstudium*, 2d ed. (Hildesheim, 1966) is very valuable. These historians were part of the "university reform" of the nineteenth century, nicely discussed by R. Steven Turner in "University Reformers and Professorial Research in Germany, 1760 to 1806" in *The University in Society*, ed. Lawrence Stone, (Princeton, 1974), 2:495–531. Suggestive in ways that include but go far beyond the academy is Hajo Holborn, "German Idealism in the Light of Social History," reprinted in Holborn, *Germany and Europe: Historical Essays* (New York, 1971), and, relatedly, Leonore O'Boyle, "Klassische Bildung und soziale Struktur in Deutschland zwischen 1800 und 1848," in *Historische Zeitschrift* 207 (1968): 584ff. Useful for watching the political effects of scholarly exchanges is R. Hinton Thomas, *Liberalism, Nationalism, and the German Intellectual, 1822–1847: An Analysis of the Academic and Scientific Conferences of the Period* (Cambridge, 1951).

German Liberalism

As I have tried to indicate in the text, the term *liberalism*—a nineteenth-century neologism always hard to define precisely—is problematic but necessary to describe Droysen and his colleagues. Their theology made them more radical and their

Prussianism and monarchism more conservative than their French and English counterparts. Nor did they speak for all German liberals, despite their eventual prestige and influence. In the aftermath of Hitler, the standard approach to German liberalism, understandably, was to seek the reasons for its failure. This literature is part of the *Sonderweg* argument (see below). The title of Friedrich Sell's book, *Die Tragödie des deutschen Liberalismus* (Stuttgart, 1953) is a case in point. Sell is right about tragedy, but I question the degree to which 1848 spoiled German liberalism. Its prerevolutionary character was also illiberal. The most impressive example of that thesis, and one whose viewpoint I share, is Leonard Krieger's *German Idea of Freedom* (Boston, 1957), which argues that Germans imagined individual mental freedom and collective freedom, but not freedom as pluralism. This argument is a distant descendant of Ernst Troeltsch's essay, written in the early Weimar Republic, "The Ideas of Natural Law and Humanity in World Politics," in *Natural Law and the Theory of Society 1500 to 1800*, ed. Otto Gierke (Boston, 1957), 201–22. Troeltsch claimed that Germany lost its natural law tradition after the eighteenth century. The more economic emphasis of the Rhenish liberals, such as Haym's patron David Hansemann, is well covered in Jacques Droz, *Le Libéralisme rhénan 1815–1848* (Paris, 1940). Liberal interest in economic practicalities thoroughly and cogently discussed in Theodore Hamerow, *The Social Foundations of German Unification 1858–71*, 2 vols. (Princeton, 1969–72). James J. Sheehan, *German Liberalism in the Nineteenth Century* (Chicago, 1978) is comprehensive, clearly written, and up-to-date. See also the provocative essays in Konrad H. Jarausch and Larry Eugene Jones, eds., *In Search of a Liberal Germany: Studies in the History of German Liberlism from 1789 to the Present* (New York, 1990). The history of German ideas on representative government is exhaustively but lucidly treated in Heinrich Heffter, *Die deutsche Selbstverwaltung im 19 Jahrhundert: Geschichte der Ideen und Institutionen* (Stuttgart, 1950).

Vormärz and 1848

Contemporary accounts of very great interest are: Karl Biedermann, *Erinnerungen aus der Paulskirche* (Leipzig, 1849); Johann Gustav Droysen, *Die Verhandlungen des Verfassungsausschusses der deutschen Nationalversammlung. Erster Theil* (Leipzig, 1849); Max Duncker, *Zur Geschichte der deutschen Reichsversammlung in Frankfurt* (Berlin, 1849); Rudolf Haym, *Die deutsche Nationversammlung. Ein Bericht aus der Partei des rechten Centrum*, 3 vols. (Frankfort, 1848–50); and Heinrich Laube, *Das erste deutsche Parlament* (Leipzig, 1849).

The standard German account is the liberal Veit Valentin's *Geschichte der deutschen Revolution von 1848–49*, 2 vols. (Berlin, 1931). Even better is Jacque Droz, *Les Révolutions allemandes de 1848* (Paris, 1957). Specifically on the situation in Frankfort is the fine narration by Frank Eyck, *The Frankfort Parliament, 1848–1849* (New York, 1968). An exciting critical perspective, also useful for the history of liberalism, is Wilhelm Mommsen, *Grösse und Versagen des deutschen Bürgerthums* (Stuttgart, 1949). Two further works to consult to put the revolution in social perspective are Rudolf Stadelmann, *Soziale und politische Geschichte der Revolution von 1848* (Munich, 1956), which is brief yet comprehensive, and Theodore Hamerow, *Restoration, Revolution, and Reaction. Economics and Politics in Germany, 1815–1871* (Princeton, 1958). Hamerow's chapters on the revolution go far to explain why it failed.

The Question of a German Sonderweg

That German political and historical thought was nationally distinctive is really beyond cavil, as some of the texts mentioned above under "Liberalism" nicely illustrate. That claim is conceptually distinct from the question of whether, socially and politically, Germany took a distinctive path into modernity. (The two questions become one, however, either if one presumes the social determination of all ideas or one assumes that true social history should ignore individual thinkers.) Two German exceptionalist accounts I have found useful for thinking about the Prussian School are Hellmut Plessner, *Die verspätete Nation* (Stuttgart, 1959) and Ralf Dahrendorf, *Society and Democracy in Germany* (New York, 1967). Plessner argues that Germany modernized very fast, very late. Dahrendorf provocatively and cogently explains the German problem in terms of social causes for a "constitution of authority" rather than a "constitution of freedom." Anyone interested in this sort of argument must read Barrington Moore, Jr., *Social Origins of Dictatorship and Democracy* (London, 1967). Though Marxists such as Eckhart Kehr in *Schlachtflottenbau und Parteipolitik 1894–1901* (Berlin, 1930) also argued about a special path, this notion has been usefully challenged from a Marxist perspective in David Blackbourn and Geoff Eley, *The Peculiarities of German History. Bourgeois Society and Politics in Nineteenth Century Germany* (Oxford, 1984). For a good, critical overview of the problem, see Richard J. Evans, "The Myth of Germany's Missing Revolution," in his *Rethinking German History. Nineteenth-Century Germany and the Origins of the Third Reich* (London, 1987), 93–122.

Index